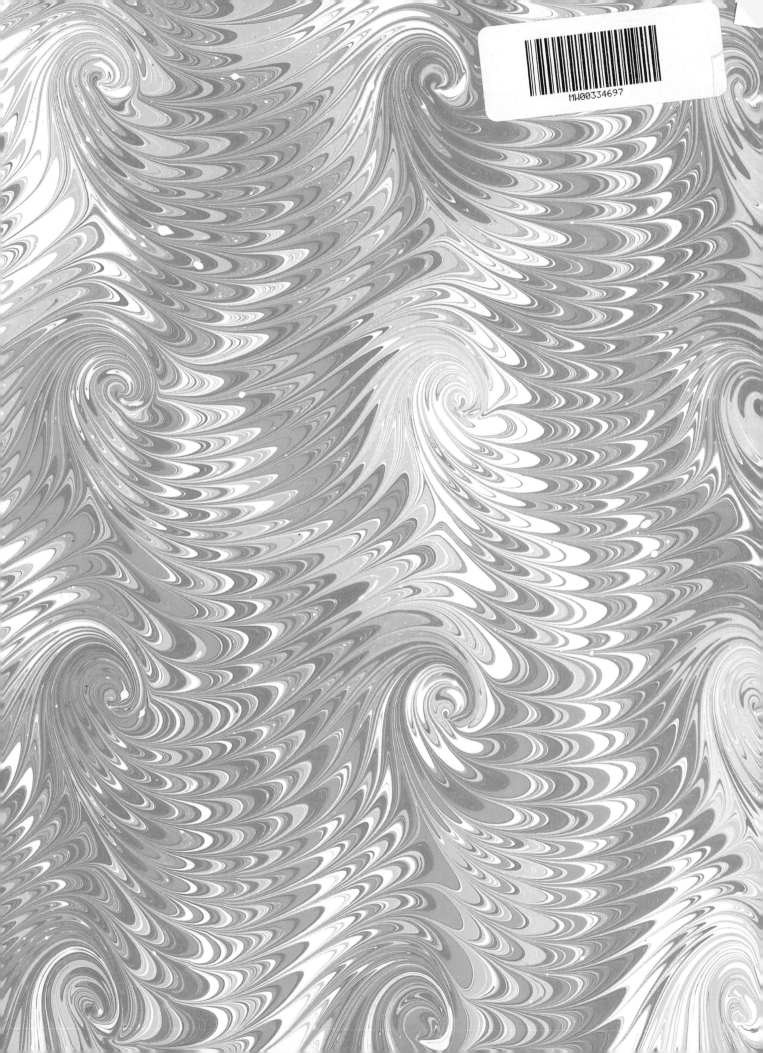

George Jones Ceramics

Robert Cluett
with Foreword by Geoffrey Godden

Schiffer Publishing Ltd

4880 Lower Valley Rd. Atglen, PA 19310 USA

Book design by Laurie A. Smucker

ISBN: 0-7643-0470-4
Printed in China
1 2 3 4

Front Cover: 'Mr Punch' bowl, ca. 1875. Registered design 13 September 1875. *Courtesy of Sotheby's, London.*

Published by Schiffer Publishing Ltd.
4880 Lower Valley Road
Atglen, PA 19310
Phone: (610) 593-1777; Fax: (610) 593-2002
E-mail: Schifferbk@aol.com
Please write for a free catalog.
This book may be purchased from the publisher.
Please include $3.95 for shipping.

Please try your bookstore first.

We are interested in hearing from authors
with book ideas on related subjects.

Dedications

To my wife, Thelma, whose enthusiasm and immense encouragement helped me to complete this book. I would also like to dedicate this book to my father, Tom, who was greatly interested in its progress, but sadly was never to see it completed.

Acknowledgements

Victoria Bergesen for her help and assistance in the early stages of my research.

Heather Burt for taking the time to read my unedited manuscript, and being 'over the moon' when she discovered that she was the proud owner of a piece of George Jones ware.

Peter and Margaret Crumpton for their enthusiasm.

Mike and Jenny Dunn for allowing me access to photograph their collection.

Geoffrey Godden for his help with the records of the *London Gazette,* and for being so encouraging as to write a foreword to the book.

A very special thank you to Rodney and Eileen Hampson for all their help, guidance and encouragement during the past seven years. Rodney has been a true mentor.

Sybil Hulme for all her valuable information.

Catherine Overton Jones for her help in researching her husband Edward Overton Jones.

Joan Jones for allowing me access to the Minton Archives.

David and Catriona Maisels for all their help in researching Horace Overton Jones.

Fred and Joyce Moseley for their enthusiasm and allowing me to photograph their collection.

Terry Pankhurst for his help in untangling the Pankhurst family.

Christopher Perkins for his artwork.

Martin Phillips for his help at the University of Keele.

Christopher Phillips for his enthusiastic assistance in researching the Benham family.

Kenneth and Ingrid Phillips for allowing me to photograph the bust of Henry Beecroft Jackson.

Gaye Blake Roberts and the Trustees of the Wedgwood Archives for allowing me access to the George Jones pattern books.

Betty Roper for allowing me access to family photographs and possessions.

David Schenck for all his information and valuable assistance in compiling the biography of his grandfather, Frederick Schenck.

Debbie Skinner and the staff of the Hanley Museum for all their assistance.

Staff of the Hanley Reference Library.

Staff of the Gladstone Museum for allowing me access to their extensive collection of *Pottery Gazettes.*

Staff of the Public Record Office during my research into the registered designs.

Staff of the Wedgwood Museum, especially Lynne Miller, for all their help.

A special mention must be made of the valuable assistance given by Ian and Rita Smythe in supplying the majority of the photographs for the majolica section and also for supplying all the information contained in Appendix 4.

Tony and Hazel Steven for allowing me access to important family papers.

Margaret Steven for information on the Twigg and Benham families.

Frank and Hazel Stevens for information on the family of Frederick Jones.

Robin and Leslie Swinton for allowing me access to the effects of Horace Overton Jones.

Marjorie Winters for allowing me to photograph her collection.

Derek and Shirley Weyman for all their enthusiastic help and for allowing me to photograph their collection.

I would also like to thank the very many people, too numerous to mention here, who have assisted me in my research.

Contents

Foreword

I am extremely pleased to write this Foreword to Robert Cluett's in-depth study of the life and products of George Jones.

Much has changed since in 1961. I wrote - tentatively, inadequately and in part inaccurately of this Stoke potter in my first book *Victorian Porcelain*. Now, more than thirty years later; and in the week that I received this typescript, I heard a leading Roadshow expert so rightly state, that George Jones colourful, well-modelled majolica glazed earthenwares were more attractive and amusing than Wedgwood's, or indeed than Minton's essays in the same, so popular style.

In this same week I have been asked - not unreasonably - a sum well in excess of a thousand pounds for another Crescent Pottery piece, not this time majolica. Such appreciation and high-prices are so different from the attitudes prevailing only twenty or so years ago.

What has also changed for the better is the very high standard of current research and of our interest in some of the hitherto neglected potters. This welcome advance is here well illustrated in Robert Cluett's splendid book. I have been amazed at his deep research. I know well how time consuming it is to wade through masses of old newspapers, trade journals, design registration files and a host of other source material, that our author has quite obviously sought out. The happy result must be the ultimate work on this Stoke firm.

It has surely been a labour of love, a lengthy courtship — that had such a mundane start — the purchase, by his wife, of a standard blue-printed "Abbey" pattern dish, because she liked it. The best of reasons. The undreamed of result is here for us all to enjoy. A success story — not only for Wedgwood's former commercial traveller — George Jones, but for the author and for all collectors of George Jones's varied products.

Enjoy the fruits of his research and, as a result, enjoy all the more the George Jones wares.

Geoffrey Godden
May 1997

Price Guide

The author does not accept any liability for the accuracy of the prices stated in this book. The prices quoted are the average for pieces in fine condition with the exception of majolica. This tends to be easily damaged and the prices quoted are the average for pieces in either good condition or professionally restored, although these days the condition of majolica does not seem to have any bearing on the prices paid at auctions.

Introduction

Go to any antique fair today and you will probably find on some of the ceramic stalls, pieces marked George Jones or 'Crescent' ware. Ask the dealer who George Jones was or what 'Crescent' ware is and the chances are that they will be able to tell you very little about either. From Jewitt's time in 1878, the firm has only been noted in general works: Geoffrey Godden on porcelain, Victoria Bergesen, Nicholas Dawes and Marilyn Karmason & Joan Stacke on majolica, and Bernard Bumpus on *pâte-sur-pâte*.

By 1900, George Jones & Sons Ltd. was the third largest pottery manufacturer in Stoke-upon-Trent, employing over a thousand people and exporting over 50% of its production to all parts of the world. Its ranking in the pottery industry in England was possibly sixth behind Minton, Wedgwood, Coalport, Derby and Copeland-Spode, yet very little is known about the company, the people who made it what it was, and the beautiful and very varied types of wares it produced.

Apart from some seventy pattern books that have survived, which are held in the Wedgwood Archives and a few derelict buildings in South Wolfe Street, Stoke-on-Trent, nothing else exists. No company records or documents are to be found. In researching this book I have had to go back to the very beginning and search through years of old newspapers, magazines, birth, marriage and death certificates, census records, directories, old records held in various University libraries and County Record Offices to try to piece together the history of this company.

After seven years of hard but interesting and rewarding work I hope that I have at least made some inroads into what is a fascinating story of a family-run company, dedicated to producing beautiful ceramics.

The book is split into two main sections; the first section dealing with the early life of George Jones, how he came to open his own manufactory and the history of that company — which spanned 90 years from 1861 to 1951. The second section deals with the types of wares produced by the company. These include the well known majolica wares that are so highly prized at the present time, especially by Americans. The *pâte-sur-pâte* decorated wares which, although not as highly regarded as the *pâte-sur-pâte* produced by Solon for Mintons, were still very popular with the Victorians and, due to the company's unique manufacturing method, enabled many more to own ornamental wares decorated in this style. The 'Abbey' blue and white underglaze transfer printed ware, which was produced for over forty years is today very popular among lovers of blue and white. Other types of wares manufactured by the company included art pottery, fine bone china, and earthenware made and decorated in styles to suit all tastes and purses.

Two more important sections in this book are Appendices 1 and 5. Appendix 1 contains the biographies of twenty-four men who played a major role in helping to make the company so successful. Some were members of the George Jones family and nearly all were employees of the company. Appendix 5 contains information on how to date the wares, especially from the earlier years.

My only regret and frustration, after all the painstaking research I have carried out, is that I have been unable to locate a picture of George Jones himself. So, if anyone who reads this book knows of the whereabouts of such a picture, I would be more than grateful to hear about it. Likewise, if any reader wishes to enquire or add to my knowledge of the George Jones company, they may do so by contacting me through the publisher.

I hope this book will add another chapter to the fascinating history of the 'Potteries' of Stoke-on-Trent, and that it is of value and interest to anyone who may care to read it.

Could this be George Jones? This photograph was found in an album which belonged to the family of Horace Overton Jones. The man is dressed in the style of the 1880s.

Four generations, from left to right, George Benham Benham, William Benham, Francis Ralph Benham and Frances Jones (George Jones widow). This photograph was taken ca. 1899.

GEORGE JONES FAMILY TREE

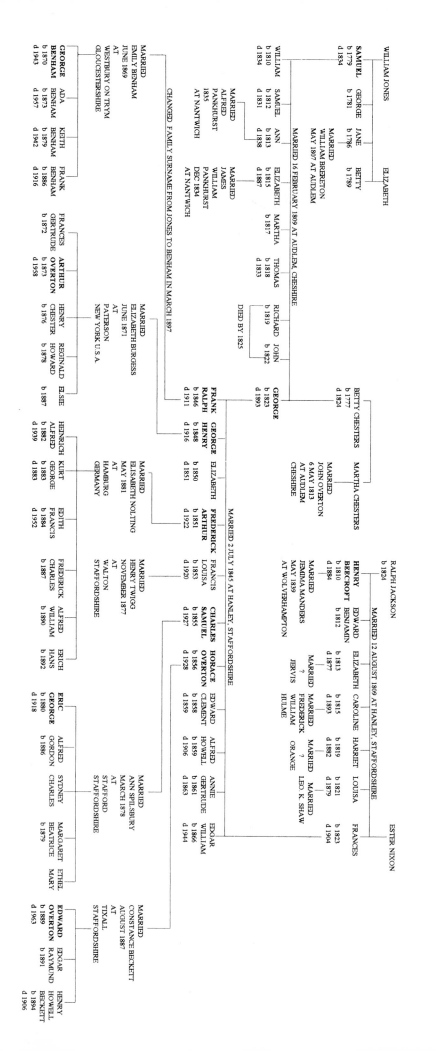

Chapter 1 George Jones – Merchant and Pottery Manufacturer

His early days 1823-1850

George Jones was born in Nantwich, Cheshire on 27 June 1823. He was the youngest of nine children. It is interesting to note that George's family had no connection with the pottery industry. His father, Samuel, was a maltster and his mother, Betty, came from a farming background.

George Jones's mother died when he was only fifteen months old and his father died in April 1834 when George was ten. The task of bringing George up fell upon the shoulders of his three sisters, Ann, Elizabeth and Martha, who were, by this time, the only remaining members of his family still alive. In December 1834, George's sister Elizabeth married James Pankhurst, a widower who lived at Hanley and was a commercial traveller for Charles Meigh of the Old Hall Pottery, there. In February 1835, another of George's sisters Ann, married James Pankhurst's brother Alfred, a draper from Wybunbury, Cheshire. They lived in Nantwich until they both died in 1838.

After the marriage of James and Elizabeth Pankhurst, the couple, together with George Jones and his sister Martha, went to live in Bucknell Road, Hanley. George Jones finished his formal education at the age of fourteen and immediately began a seven year pottery apprenticeship with Mintons at Stoke-upon-Trent, which he successfully completed in 1844. After his apprenticeship, he continued to work for Mintons for a few months, but on 24 August 1844, George signed a three year agreement between himself and the pottery manufacturers, Wedgwood & Boyle of Etruria. George Jones was to begin his employment with Wedgwood & Boyle on 1 October 1844 as a writing clerk; however, this agreement was cancelled and a further agreement was signed between himself and Francis Wedgwood to serve as a commercial traveller (travelling salesman), for a period of three years from the 1 October 1844. George's initial salary was £70 per annum to be increased to £100 per annum by the third year.[1]

From letters written by George Jones to Francis Wedgwood, it would appear that George had a good knowledge of the pottery industry, from both the business and technical aspects, as he makes many suggestions as to how shapes and patterns may be modified to assist sales. The letters,[2] (now held in the Wedgwood Archives) show that George travelled extensively. From February 1845 to February 1846, George had visited places as far afield as Exeter in the South of England to Aberdeen in the North of Scotland, in addition to Dublin in Ireland.

Being a commercial traveller meant that George was away from home for long periods, but he still found time to court a young Hanley girl. On 2 July 1845, he married Frances Jackson at Hanley Chapel. Frances was twenty one years old, a milliner who lived with her widowed mother Ester, in Parliament Row, Hanley. George and Frances's first home was in Mount Pleasant, Hanley.

On the 24 November 1845, after George Jones had completed only one year of his three year contract with Wedgwood, Francis Wedgwood gave George three months' notice of his intention to terminate his employment. George consequently left in February 1846.

After leaving Wedgwood, George continued as a commercial traveller, but by May 1848, he had changed his occupation to that of a clerk and was living in Liverpool Road, Stoke-upon-Trent. By this time George and Frances had two sons, Frank Ralph, born in May 1846 and George Henry born in April 1848. By early 1849, George and his family had moved from Liverpool Road in the centre of Stoke, to Brisley Hill, Penkhull, on the outskirts of Stoke, where he lived in a rented house with one eighth of an acre of garden. By the time George and France's third child, a daughter, Elizabeth, was born in March 1850, George had established his own business as a commission agent and earthenware broker, operating from premises in Liverpool Road, Stoke-upon-Trent. A commission agent is one who buys and sells on a percentage or commission, not a wholesaler who buys stock on spec. One of the first people to work for George Jones after he became a commission agent was William Candland, who was initially employed as a china salesman.

Merchant 1850-1862

George's business expanded rapidly and, by 1853, it had become necessary to move to larger premises. George Jones was now operating from Wharf Street, Stoke-upon-Trent, where he had more substantial warehousing facilities. George Jones's customers not only came from all parts of Britain; he also had clients in North and South America, Canada, the Caribbean, Australia, New Zealand, France and Germany. He was selling all types of wares bought from most of the major 'Potteries' manufacturers of the time including Mintons and Wedgwood.

As well as moving to new business premises in 1853, George also moved house. He went to live at 12 The Villas, Stoke-upon-Trent. This was one of the houses built as part of the development of twenty-four houses built by the Stokeville Building Society on land purchased from the Rev. Thomas Minton in 1850. The houses were occupied by many prominent people of Stoke and George Jones occupied the largest one on the site.

By the beginning of 1854, as well as operating very successfully as a commission agent, selling earthenware and china etc., George also became an insurance agent for the Legal & Commercial Fire & Life Office at his Wharf Street office. This agency was to continue for some thirteen years.

George Jones's merchandising business had become successful to such an extent that in late 1854, he opened additional premises at 1 Hatton Yard, London (the traditional pottery wholesaling area), where he operated as a wholesale china and earthenware dealer.[3]

Toward the end of 1855, George formed a partnership with his brother-in-law, Henry Beecroft Jackson. Henry Jackson was a successful and wealthy business man who owned Jackson, Brierly & Briggs of Cannon Street, Manchester, commission agents and merchants. The purpose of the partnership was for Henry Jackson to inject capital into George's business to enable him to open a new showroom and additional warehousing facilities in Glebe Street, Stoke-upon-Trent.

By August 1856, the new showrooms and warehouses were ready for occupation. An advertisement first appeared in *The Staffordshire Advertiser* of 23 August. It stated:

British and Foreign China, Glass and Earthenware Showroom near Railway Station, Stoke-upon-Trent.

George Jones has the pleasure to inform the nobility, gentry, clergy and the inhabitants generally of Staffordshire and the adjoining counties that his extensive and elegant showrooms and warehouses situated at Glebe Street, Stoke-upon-Trent are now finished and he respectfully invites a visit from all parties desirous of purchasing on the best terms, glass, china or earthenware whether of a useful or ornamental description. The showrooms are replete with a choice collection of French china, bronzes, moderator lamps and

German ornaments imported direct from the manufacturers. George Jones also calls attention to his stock of English Porcelain and earthenware consisting of dinner, tea, breakfast, toilet and dessert services of the best quality and most recent designs; parian statuettes, vases, Wedgwood ware and classical pottery, terracotta and Staffordshire ware of all kinds. The whole of the goods are marked in plain figures from which no abatement is made and the prices are such as cannot fail to give satisfaction.

By the end of 1856, George's family had increased with the birth of another three sons and one daughter. Two of the sons, Charles Samuel Jones (born April 1855) and Horace Overton Jones (born July 1856) were to become involved in the family business. A third son Frederick Arthur (born in December 1852) was, for a short period in the 1870s, involved with his father's business.

On 1 January 1858, the partnership between George Jones and Henry Jackson, that had run successfully since 1855, came to its end and George continued to run the business on his own account.[4] The next two years were to see George consolidating his position as a leading wholesaler and retail dealer of earthenware, china and glass, in both Stoke and London.

In 1860, George Jones appointed Henry J. Giller as his London representative and country traveller, an engagement which continued for many years. Henry Giller had been employed in this capacity for various firms for more than fourteen years. With the appointment of Henry Giller, George moved his London premises from Hatton Yard to 47, Mark Lane London. At the same time, the firm was renamed George Jones & Co.

In Stoke-upon-Trent, George Jones was still operating from Wharf Street and Glebe Street and was now acting for three insurance companies. At his Wharf Street office, he was agent for The Legal & Commercial Fire & Life Office and at his Glebe Street premises, he was agent for The Manchester Fire Assurance and The Victoria & Legal & Commercial Life Co.[5]

George's wholesaling business at Wharf Street continued until 1866 when he ceased to be a dealer in other manufacturers' wares and concentrated solely on selling his own manufactured pottery. He retained his showrooms at Glebe Street until around 1870.

Bridge Works 1862-1865

George began his pottery manufacturing business in early 1862. According to W. P. Jervis in his book *Rough Notes on Pottery*: 'In 1861 Messrs. J & G Meakins having more orders than they could execute, commissioned George Jones to make white granite ware for them'. Jervis also wrote in his *Dictionary of Pottery Terms* that the George Jones manufactory was: 'established by George Jones with the assistance of Henry Beecroft Jackson' at the Bridge Works, Stoke-upon-Trent.

The circumstances that led to George Jones establishing his pottery manufacturing business at the Bridge Works, Stoke, presented themselves around 1859-60. In 1859, J. & G. Meakins completed the construction of their new Eagle Pottery in Hanley. It was a manufactory of exceptional efficiency. According to Bernard Hollowood in his book *The Story of J & G Meakins*:

dinner and tea ware made of white granite of a strength eminently suitable for the export market of those days were their chief products. They soon won a wide popularity throughout North America and subsequently South America. So rapidly did demand increase, that extensions to the Eagle Pottery became necessary: even so, the brothers could not themselves satisfy all their customers and it became necessary during the "sixties" to commission work from other manufacturers...

At this time, George Jones's brother-in-law, James Pankhurst, had become a successful, established pottery manufacturer at Old Street, Hanley. James Pankhurst was in partnership with a James Meakin. It is reasonable to assume that George Jones may have obtained his manufacturing commission from J. & G. Meakin with the assistance of James Pankhurst.

At the beginning of 1860 the Bridge Works, which was owned by the Reverend George Horatio Davenport of Foxley, Herefordshire, was in the occupation of Messrs. William Adams, but in February 1860, the factory ceased production when the firm found it necessary to file a petition in the Birmingham District Court of Bankruptcy.[6] At the time it was hoped the factory would commence production again; however, it did not, and the factory laid idle for some time and began to fall into a state of disrepair.

On 8th & 9th April 1861, an auction was held at Stoke to sell the entire stock of china and earthenware manufactured by Messrs. Adams. On 10 April, a further auction was held to sell around 5 tons of copper plate engravings belonging to Messrs. Adams.[7] At this auction George Jones purchased many of the engraved patterns; one of the most well known being Adams' 'Abbey Wreath' pattern, which George Jones was later to produce and sell under his 'Abbey' backstamp.

On Saturday 19 October 1861 an advertisement appeared in *The Staffordshire Advertiser* stating:

To be let at Stoke-upon-Trent, earthenware manufactory called the Bridge Works now occupied by Messrs. Adams. Possession may be had at Martinmas' (Nov 11th).

The advertisement appeared for only one week. George Jones, who by this time had changed the name of his company to George Jones & Co., to enable Henry Jackson to help finance part of the venture, agreed to take over the Bridge Works from November 11, 1861. The lease for the factory was signed on the 21 March 1862.[8] It was a year-on-year lease running from 11 November 1861. The rent for the works was £220 per annum; however, in the first year, George Jones paid £165, presumably because he did not start production until February 1862. One of the clauses in the lease stated that no brown or coloured wares were to be produced, only wares made from white clay. The Bridge Works had three glost ovens and two biscuit ovens.

Although George Jones was very much pre-occupied with establishing his new pottery manufacturing business, he also became involved with public life. In early 1862, he became an Improvement Commissioner, today's equivalent of a town councillor, initially on the Rates Committee for Stoke-upon-Trent.

When George Jones started production in February 1862, he probably employed much of the labour force that had been made available when Messrs. Adams closed. He initially produced wares for J. & G. Meakin, but very soon began to design and produce wares sold under his own name. On the 14 May 1862, George Jones registered his first two designs at the Patent Office in London. These were patent numbers 151672 and 151673 and were for engraved border and centre patterns for dinner and tea ware. His next design was registered on the 18 December 1862, patent number 158498 and was for an engraved border pattern.

An International Exhibition was held in London in 1862. In the early 1880s, George Jones & Sons advertised their company in *The Pottery Gazette*. In their advertisement they stated that medals and/or awards were presented to the company at this exhibition. A search of the official catalogue and also the published list of awards and medals makes no mention of George Jones either having been an exhibitor at this exhibition, or winning any awards. Quite why the company advertised differently is unclear, possibly a London dealer may have exhibited some of George Jones's wares and gained a medal. An original blank invoice, held at the Wedgwood Museum and produced after 1873, states that prize medals were won at the Universal Exhibition held in Paris in 1867 but makes no mention of the 1862 London exhibition.

For the first two years, George Jones concentrated on establishing his manufacturing business, although he still continued to run his wholesaling business. By the end of 1863, George had been successful to such an extent that he decided to build his own factory.

On the 6 May 1864, George Jones purchased from Colin Minton Campbell, owner of the Minton factory, three pieces or parcels of land very close to the Bridge Works. Two pieces were known as 'Canal Meadows' and were of 2 acres and 1 acre 3 roods 17 perches. They were situated on the eastern side of the Newcastle-under-Lyme canal. The third piece was the eastern portion of a plot of land of 2 acres 2 roods 20 perches, that also adjoined the eastern bank of the Newcastle-under-Lyme canal.[9] Having purchased this land, George Jones then commissioned Charles Lynam, a local architect who had designed the Stokeville housing development, to design and supervise the erection of his new manufactory.

The years 1864 - 65 were monumental for George Jones. As well as having his new manufactory built, he was, in June 1864, elected to be Chief Bailiff of Stoke — it must have been a great honour for him.

By October 1865, the new works were ready for occupation and the Bridge Works were vacated for re-letting. An advertisement in *The Staffordshire Advertiser* on 14 October 1865 read: 'To be let and entered at Martinmas next, all that commodious earthenware manufactory situated at Stoke-upon-Trent adjoining the Newcastle-under-Lyme branch canal and to the turnpike road from Newcastle to Uttoxeter at present in the occupation of Mr. George Jones.'

The Trent Potteries 1865-1873

A reporter from *The Staffordshire Advertiser* was invited to visit George Jones's new manufactory and a report of the visit published on the 25th November 1865 read:

Mr G. Jones's New Manufactory. We have had this week an opportunity of inspecting Mr. George Jones's new manufactory at Stoke, and find that it contains several points worthy of public notice, especially in this particular, that the various workshops and warehouses have been much more methodically arranged than is the case in most of the old works, the consecutive order of the several processes being considered in the distribution of the various parts of the building, thereby ensuring economy of time and labour. The clay is prepared by the new hydraulic process, so clean and wholesome when contrasted with the old-fashioned but still prevalent slipkilns, and the machinery for this department together with that necessary for grinding colour and glazes, and turning 26 steam jiggers, is set in motion by an 18 horse power engine. Adjoining the slip-house is a large room in which the steam jiggers are to be erected, and under this is a spacious clay cellar. These buildings are at present detached from the main body, but they will probably be connected when the new works (which at present are being carried on in connection with Mr. Jones's old factory) are in full operation. Taking into account the productive capacity of the establishment, it probably occupies less ground than any other in the district. Speaking generally the main body lies in two squares, one of which is composed of buildings appropriated to the arrangement and disposal of the finished ware. A visitor would be struck in every part of the works with the ample space provided for the workmen, and the general air of neatness and comfort prevailing throughout the place. We noticed that in the pressers' rooms the old form of stove, with some slight modifications, is retained, being preferred by the workmen, by whom it is considered to have advantages - for pressers' purposes - over any new model yet produced. On the other hand, the platemakers' room, in which seven men will be accommodated, is fitted with a stove on the same principle as that first introduced at Messrs. Wedgwood's works, with the exception that the interior of the chamber is heated by means of flues instead of

an iron stove. The stove used by the dish and hand-basin makers, again, is in the main on the old principle, but the proprietor has introduced slate instead of plaster of Paris slabs, the former being more durable and ensuring a truer plane at the upper edge of the ware. The greenhouses and the placers' benches are close to the biscuit ovens, and the biscuit warehouse is over the greenhouse. This is only one illustration of the care which has been taken to bring the various related departments into close connection. The principal staircases are of stone and are unusually broad, and these and most of the workshops are lighted with gas. The convenience of the workpeople, and orderly and decent conduct of the establishment, and requirements of the Factory Act have evidently been present in a lively manner to the mind of the proprietor and his architect (Mr. Lynam), and the result is a manufactory which, for completeness, compactness, and comfort, is not excelled by any in the district.

The new factory was named the Trent Potteries and the rateable value was set at £300.[10] However, no sooner had the new works been completed than additional workshops were required and on the 1st November 1865, plans were submitted to the Improvement Commissioners for approval.

Fire was always a problem in the potteries and on the night of December 7, 1865, a serious fire broke out in the new factory. The fire was discovered around 9 pm by a man who lived nearby. The fire began in one of the flat pressers' rooms, which was situated in the centre of the factory. It took nearly an hour for the fire to be brought under control and four hours to extinguish the flames. The whole of the material and fittings in the room, which was 60 feet long by 40 feet wide, were destroyed. An extract from the report of the fire in *The Staffordshire Sentinel* stated:

The fire made its way through the flooring of the warehouse above, doing great damage. The pressers' room was fitted with patent stoves having revolving racks. These were totally destroyed. The doors of the adjoining rooms were burned but the flames did not penetrate beyond the room named. Damage was done to the extent of between £600 - £700. The building was insured.

On the 9th December, George Jones published a 'thank-you' to all who helped assist in putting out: 'this most damaging fire'.

Although the damage caused by the fire was still creating production problems, 1866 began on a jovial and optimistic note for the employees of the Trent Potteries as can be seen by the report from *The Staffordshire Advertiser* of the 1st January :

The employees of Mr. George Jones to the number of about three hundred assembled in the large decorating shops of his new manufactory, which had been adorned with evergreens etc., for the occasion and partook of a substantial tea which had been provided for them by the liberality of their employer. After tea a number of songs were sung and a band being in attendance, dancing and other amusements were kept up until a late hour. Early in the evening Mr. John Bourne, in the name of the work people, presented to Mr. Jones an address of thanks and of congratulations on the completion of his new works. Mr. Jones in reply said that it had always been his desire to give his work people constant employment and good wages, and in building this manufactory to give them plenty of fresh air and to make them as comfortable as possible. All that he hoped was that in return they would strive to do their work well, and advance his interests. The past four years had been trying times to all parties, many had had great difficulty in paying their way, owing to the slackness of the trade consequent on the war in America, but now he was happy to say that the war was over and that the people of the United States were now demanding large quantities of earthenware so that it would be their own fault if they did not reap an abundant harvest.

He did not intend to trust to that market alone but to open connections with other markets of the globe.

The address presented to George Jones by John Bourne was as follows:

Sir,

We deem it our duty to convey to you our hearty thanks for the bountiful repast you have so generously provided for us on this occasion. We take this opportunity respectfully of congratulating you on the completion of your new and beautiful works, and we sincerely hope that the undertaking may receive the award it so eminently deserves.

When we remember (as too many of us do) the unhealthy dens in which the generality of potters follow their employment and the waste of health and life consequent thereon, we feel that you have no ordinary claim upon our gratitude, and we thankfully acknowledge the liberal and enlightened spirit in which you have provided for the comfort and health of your workpeople.

We also desire to express our deep sense of the kindness we invariably receive from you and of the anxiety you display to act justly and honourably towards us in all our business relations, and we earnestly trust the good feeling that at present exists between us, may always be maintained.

We heartily wish you and your amiable family "A happy new year" hoping it may prove a year of prosperity and happiness to you and that each recurring year may bring you increase of both, is the heartfelt wish of your workpeople.

Signed. Jno. Bourne,

On behalf of the Committee

In August 1866, another destructive fire occurred at the factory. This time it began in twenty tons of straw stored in the packing shop. The shop was gutted, the roof and floors were destroyed and one end of the warehouse was damaged. The damage to the building and to the stock was estimated to be between £300 - £400.

It was around 1866 that George Jones's eldest son, Frank Ralph Jones, joined the firm after an initial training period at the Royal Porcelain Factory, Sévres, France. Frank was a talented artist who, with the assistance of John Bourne, a potter who had been in the industry for more than 40 years, contributed a great deal to the early success of the factory.

With the opening of his new manufactory, George Jones was no longer restricted in the types of wares he was able to produce and it was in 1866 that he commenced the manufacture of majolica.

At about the same time as Frank Jones joined the firm, George Jones's second son, George Henry Jones, joined. He was to be trained in the financial and commercial side of the business, probably by William Candland, who by this time was a manager at the factory in the finance department.

As 1866 came to a close, the manager of the factory, Mr. Nicholson, left and two hundred of the work people gave him a tea party at the Stoke Town Hall. They presented him with a handsome inkstand and a portrait of himself painted by Mr. Henshall of Hanley.

By the middle of 1867, George Jones was no longer operating an insurance agency for the Manchester Fire Office and had closed down his Wharf Street warehouse, although he still retained his showrooms in Glebe Street, Stoke. In the annual review of the trade in the district of Stoke in late 1869, it was noted by *The Staffordshire Advertiser* that some of the leading houses, including those of Mintons, Brown Westhead & Co., Bodley, George Jones & Co., and others had been compelled to increase their production by enlarging their respective works. At this particular time George Jones & Co. were producing wares in earthenware, stone china and majolica.

In 1870 George Jones moved his London premises to 19, Bartlett's Buildings, Holborn Hill, but by 1871 he had moved them again to 21, Bartlett's Buildings[11] where he opened his new London showrooms with Henry Giller continuing as the manager. At about the same time

as he opened his new London showrooms, George Jones closed down his showrooms and offices in Glebe Street, Stoke.

By April 1871, three of George Jones's sons were employed in the business. They were Frank Ralph Jones, George Henry Jones and Frederick Arthur Jones, the last named working for a short time as a potter's manager. A fourth son, Charles Samuel Jones, joined the business in June 1871 at the age of 15 years as an apprentice. At this time the number of employees at George Jones & Co. had risen from 300 in 1866 to 590.

In late August 1871, a strike by crate makers at George Jones & Co. caused considerable problems for the company and threatened to halt production. Charges were made by George Jones against eleven crate makers, for absenteeism from the works, thus breaching their contracts with him and £2 damages was claimed from each man. The resultant court case was heard at the local police court at Fenton. The strike was part of a move by the unions to secure better wages. A report of the court case, in *The Staffordshire Advertiser*, stated that the union concerned did more harm than good and that the strikers were acting under pressure put on them by outsiders. After considerable discussion during which the men stated they had struck for better wages in accordance with the wishes of the majority in the trade of the district, the defendants yielded to the advice of their barrister and agreed to return to work. George Jones offered that if they did return to work and behaved properly, he would not press for costs. After two weeks, the strike was resolved and production returned to normal.

As well as being involved with his factory and public life, George, in his private life, was keenly interested in horticulture and had had stovehouses (hothouses) and greenhouses erected at his home. He was a frequent exhibitor at the local annual floral and horticultural society shows where he was awarded many prizes for his exhibits.

The family partnership 1873-1894

In June 1873, George Jones was 50 years old. His manufacturing business was firmly established and was becoming one of the leading pottery manufacturing companies in the Stoke area. His two eldest sons, Frank Ralph and George Henry Jones, had become well versed in the day-to-day running of the company, so it was at this time that George Jones decided to become less involved and take a 'backseat' in the running of the company. By late 1873, a partnership had been formed, with George Jones as the senior partner and his two sons, Frank Ralph Jones and George Henry Jones, as partners. The company was re-named George Jones & Sons. At the same time, the name 'Crescent' was registered as the trade mark for the new company.

As well as deciding to hand over the day-to-day running of the company to his sons, George also decided to move his family away from Stoke-upon-Trent to the cleaner air of rural Staffordshire. By September 1873 they had moved from The Villas, where their home had been for the past twenty years, to Milford House, Milford, near Stafford, to a property with adjoining land that George Jones rented from the executors of John Twigg, a local land owner who had lived at Weeping Cross, Stafford, until his death in early 1873. At the same time George bought a small residence in James Street, Stoke, which he used on his frequent visits to Stoke on company and other business.

Although George Jones had moved to Milford, he was still involved in the public life of Stoke. At the beginning of 1874, he was appointed returning officer for the first elections for the new Borough of Stoke-upon-Trent which were held on the 3 March 1874.[12]

Up to 1875 the company's production consisted of earthenware, stone-china and majolica; but in 1875, plans were made to increase the range of wares produced to include the manufacture of bone china. This was a market which was greatly expanding, and many established earthenware manufacturers were preparing themselves for the production of bone china, with new factories being built specifically for the production of these fine wares.

During 1876, to make way for production of bone china at the Trent Pottery, the company leased an old Thomas Wolfe factory in Welch Street, Stoke,[13] opposite the Trent Pottery site. This factory was leased for the production of earthenware until 1881, by which time additional buildings had been erected at the Trent Pottery to enable all the company's production to be concentrated on the one site. From the rateable values of the two factories (Trent works £903 and the Wolfe Works £124-10s) it would appear that the leased Wolfe factory was approximately 1/7th the size of the Trent works. The rent on the Wolfe factory was £61-14s per half year and was paid to the executors of the late Thomas Wolfe.[14]

In April 1876, John Bourne, a pottery manager at the Trent Pottery, died and his position was filled by Henry Brunt. Henry was a former apprentice of George Jones who had been working for Mintons.

By mid-1877 Charles James Birbeck had joined the company as an apprentice ceramic artist. Charles was the grandson of William Birbeck, a well-known ceramic artist who had worked for many of the Stoke Potteries, including Copelands and Mintons.

In the period 1877-79, the average weekly wage bill for the company was £500 and George Jones himself was paid £150 per month.[15] At this time, the company was producing earthenware, majolica, bone china and *pâte-sur-pâte*, the production of which had been introduced about 1878. Joan Jones, in her book, *Minton--The First Two Hundred Years of Design and Production*, describes *pâte-sur-pâte as*: "a decorative technique by which low-relief decoration is obtained through the application of successive layers of liquid clay onto a tinted clay body." The majority of *pâte-sur-pâte* produced by George Jones was designed by Frederick Schenck, who was almost certainly working on a freelance basis, designing and making moulds for the *pâte-sur-pâte* pieces.

At this time George Jones & Sons were exporting over 50% of their output. In America their agent was W. B. Maddock, 48 and 50 Park Place, New York and in Australia their agents were Messrs. Bright Bros., & Co. of Sydney and Melbourne.

The last of George Jones's sons to join the family business was Horace Overton Jones. He commenced his employment at the Trent Pottery toward the end of 1880. Horace Jones by then was 24 years old and had spent some considerable time studying at the National Art Training School, South Kensington. Horace was initially employed as an artist/designer.

A young man of fourteen years had joined the company as a ceramic painter by March 1881; he was William Albert Ernest Birbeck, half brother of Charles Birbeck, who had been working for George Jones in a similar capacity since 1877.

Another young man to join the company about the same time as William Birbeck was Thomas Hammersley. Thomas Hammersley, (whose father Thomas, was also employed by George Jones as a potters clerk), was initially employed as a clerk in the commercial department, but went on to become managing director in 1915.

In 1883 Charles Samuel Jones, who had joined the company as an apprentice in 1871, was made a partner in George Jones & Sons joining his two brothers, Frank and George Henry, and their father George, who was still the senior partner in the company. Charles Jones was involved in the practical side of the potting business.

In June 1884, George Jones moved home from Milford to Newport House, Newport Road, Stafford. This was a large house, situated just outside the then town boundary, which George had bought for £1620 in 1876 from its builders, Messrs. Joseph & William Cooke. For a time it had been occupied by his son Frederick Arthur Jones.

The company at this time was trading extensively, not only at home, but also in the United States, South America and South Africa. 'Crescent', the registered trade mark of George Jones & Sons,

was becoming recognised throughout the trade as representing a quality product.

The four partners in George Jones & Sons all received a salary, plus one quarter share of the profits. For the year ending December 1885, they each received £1000 as their share of the profits,[16] and that was in a year when the state of the trade had been so bad that the pottery manufacturers had applied for, and had been granted, a reduction in the price of potters' materials.

Under the heading 'treat for workpeople' *The Staffordshire Advertiser* published, on Saturday, 9 October 1886, a report of a visit to London by employees of George Jones & Sons. The article read:

> Through the kindness of Messrs. George Jones & Sons of Stoke-upon-Trent about 400 of their workpeople were last Saturday enabled to visit The Indian & Colonial Exhibition. Special arrangements having been made with the railway companies. The party left Stoke at 2 am arriving at Euston at 6.30 am. The people spread themselves in parties varying from half a dozen to fifty people throughout the Metropolis, Covent Garden market falling in for a good share of the visitors. Westminster Abbey, St. Paul's, The Tower, The Crystal Palace and other places of interest were inspected by most, while sooner or later all reached the exhibition at South Kensington. The weather being exceptionally fine, a most enjoyable day was spent. The return journey to Stoke was very comfortably performed. The train left Euston at 12.30 am and reached Stoke at 5.30 on the Sunday morning.

In the 1880s, George Jones & Sons had a good trade with Hamburg, Germany, from which port a lot of the company's exports to various parts of the world were shipped. Their agents in Hamburg were H. C. Nolting, a commission agency in which Frederick Arthur Jones, one of George Jones's sons, was a partner, having joined the company in 1879.

By the beginning of 1889, Horace Overton Jones, who by then had been appointed art director of the company, had been made the fifth partner in George Jones & Sons, joining his three older brothers and father, who was still the senior partner. On the 23 June 1890, an agreement was made for the partnership of George Jones & Sons to be extended for a further four years.[17]

At this time, the factory was still mortgaged to The Manchester and Liverpool Bank, but on November 4, 1890, the last payment of £7672-13s-4d was made on this mortgage and, on the following day, the deeds of the factory were handed over by the bank to the company[7]. Commenting on the state of the company at this time, the manager of the Stoke branch of the Manchester and Liverpool District Bank wrote on 19 November 1890, in the branch 'Information Book', that:

> They hold a large stock do an immense business which is well distributed at home, with the U.S.A., South America and the Cape etc. and is very lucrative. The partners, all of whom are excellent business men are steadily becoming well to do — for every £1 they owe they have £4 owing to them.

At a meeting of the partners on the 15 August 1891[19], it was agreed that 'at the expiration of the extended terms of the present partnership, a limited liability company under the style of George Jones & Sons Ltd, was to be formed'. Sadly George Jones was never to see this happen, as on 3 December 1893 he died at his home, Newport House, Stafford. He was seventy years old.

$\mathcal{L}$imited company 1894-1929

On 7 April 1894, the limited liability company was registered. The capital was £48,000, made up of £23,000 in 6% preference shares and £25,000 in ordinary shares. There was also £25,000 in debenture bonds at 5% on the security of the Trent Potteries which had cost £50,000 to build. The objective of the new company was to acquire and carry on the business of manufacturers and dealers in china, porcelain, earthenware and stoneware etc., belonging to George Jones & Sons of Trent Potteries. The first directors of the new limited company were Frank Ralph Jones, George Henry Jones and Charles Samuel Jones. The position of chairman was held by the eldest brother, Frank Ralph Jones. All the bonds and shares in the company were owned by the Jones family.[20]

Horace Overton Jones, who was art director and had been one of the five partners, was not appointed a director of the new company. Quite why this was is not known, but in early 1895 he relinquished his position as full time art director to devote more time to his love of painting. W. P. Jervis, in his book *A Pottery Primer*, said of Horace Jones: 'he was a clever artist who was responsible for much of the decoration'. His position as art director was eventually filled by Charles Birbeck, who had joined the company in 1877 as a ceramic painter and who was one of the company's leading designers.

Henry Giller, the manager of the London showrooms, died in December 1896. Henry had held this position since the showrooms were opened in 1870. His obituary in *The Pottery Gazette* included: 'Mr Giller contributed in no small degree to raising the well-known firm he represented to its present high position in the trade'. The vacant position of manager of the London showrooms was filled by Arthur Overton Jones, the 23 year old son of George Henry Jones, who had recently completed his apprenticeship with the company.

On 4 March 1897, Frank Ralph Jones, chairman of the company, changed his surname by deed poll to Benham.[21] It is now known that he was influenced in this by his wife, whose maiden name was Benham.

With Arthur Overton Jones's appointment, a more open policy was adopted with regard to publicising the company's products. The first of many articles commenting on the current products of George Jones & Sons Ltd. on show in the London showrooms was published in *The Pottery Gazette* in October 1897. The article described the range of art pottery on display including ' Melrose' and 'Crescentine' ware. Art pottery had become popular in the late 1880s, after majolica had lost its public appeal.

Toward the end of 1898, work had begun to increase the manufacturing capability of the factory. New ovens, kilns and warehouses were erected specifically to produce 'Anglo French China' (A-F China) which was becoming very popular and was forming a major part of the company's production. The extension cost over £6,000[22] and was completed and in operation by 1900.

In April 1900, a wage dispute developed in the Potteries involving the printers, transferrers, ovenmen and clay potters. Most of the North Staffordshire pottery manufacturers were involved, including George Jones & Sons Ltd. A strike ensued which lasted for eight weeks. At one point, the manufacturers involved served all their employees with four weeks' notice to terminate their employment. By June, the strike had been settled and normal production resumed.

Whenever a pottery manufactory closed, other manufacturers were always keen to buy its shapes and patterns. The company of George Jones & Sons Ltd. was no exception. In 1900, the firm of Brownfield's Pottery Ltd. closed down and at an auction of copper plate engravings, held in October 1900, George Jones & Sons Ltd. bought the engravings for four patterns, 'Bismark', 'Linda', 'Pompeii' and 'Rhine'.[23] In 1902, the Old Hall Pottery closed and at a similar auction the company bought two lots of engravings; one named 'Campanula' was for dinner ware and jugs, the other named 'Farm', a blue and white pattern, was for dinner, tea and toilet ware.[24] In another auction held in July 1904, after the firm of Messrs. J. Dimmock & Co., Albion Works, Hanley closed, George Jones & Sons Ltd. bought the moulds for 3 shapes: 'Anemone' (toilet ware), Delhi (dinner and tea ware) and 'Diaper Sheet' (dinner and jugs).[25]

By the end of 1902, William Candland had retired from the company and his position as cashier had been taken by Frank Benham's eldest son, George Benham Benham. William Candland

had been with the company since George Jones commenced on his own in 1850.

In 1905 *The Pottery Gazette* commented on the type of wares being produced by the company at that time:

They are extensive manufacturers of dinner and toilet earthenware and of china, tea, dinner, toilet, and dessert ware. They make a wide range in these goods, from neat but inexpensive sets up to the most elaborately ornamented. Their "Crescent" trade mark is well known in the trade. Dealers have long recognised it as sufficient guarantee of quality and the public are now doing the same...

In 1907, the Trent Potteries was renamed Crescent Potteries. Quite why this was is not known, but possibly it was to reflect the registered Crescent trade mark of the company.

For the past thirteen years the company had made good profits. The dividend, paid to shareholders, averaged 10% over the period 1895 to 1907.[26]

On 31 October 1911, Frank Ralph Benham died. He had been chairman of the company since it became limited in 1894. With the death of Frank Benham at the age of 65, the company had lost one of the original partners whose artistic and business talents helped, in only a short period of time, to create a very successful company. He was a well respected man, not only at the Crescent Potteries, but also in the pottery industry as a whole. W. P. Jervis said in his book *A Pottery Primer* that: 'Frank Benham was an expert potter and much of the success that had attended their efforts was due to his skills'. The position of chairman of the company was taken by George Henry Jones.

The year 1911 was to end with another fire at the factory. *The Staffordshire Advertiser* of 9 December reported :

Early on Wednesday morning an alarm of fire at the pottery of Messrs. George Jones & Sons Ltd. in Boothen Old Road, Stoke. The damage was chiefly confined to the kiln place and receiving room. The general work of the factory was not affected by the fire.

By the beginning of 1912, Edward Overton Jones had joined the company as an artist/designer. He was the eldest son of Horace Overton Jones. Edward Overton Jones was to stay for only a relatively short period. At the outbreak of the First World War, he left to join the Artists' Rifles. In June 1919, Edward Overton Jones was demobilised from the army and rejoined the company as an artist/designer.

In 1913, the company employed between 800 and 900 people and the factory covered an area of more than four acres. The directors of the company were George Henry Jones - chairman, Charles Samuel Jones, Arthur Overton Jones, George Benham Benham and Eric George Jones (Charles Jones's eldest son). Eric Jones had joined the company in 1898 and was, like his father, involved with the practical side of the business. Unfortunately, he died in October 1918, at the age of thirty-eight, whilst still a director of the company.

Around 1914-15, the company's fortune began to fail and Keith Benham (son of Frank Benham) was invited to join the company, but he decided to take up an offer with The Universal Grinding Wheel Co., Stafford, although he remained a major shareholder in the company. He was later to take a seat on the board as a part-time director. It was at this point in time that the first non-family member to be given a seat on the board of directors was appointed and Thomas Hammersley became managing director in May 1915. For the previous 20 years, Thomas Hammersley had been a commercial traveller, representing the company in many parts of the country. At about this time, following a family dispute, one of the directors, George Benham, was asked to leave the company .

The chairman of the company, George Henry Jones, died in October 1916 and his position was taken by Charles Samuel Jones (the last of George Jones's sons still serving the company). With the death of George H. Jones, at the age of 68, the company lost the last of the original three partners. It was with the help of George's financial expertise that the company had become a successful and profitable business.

During the First World War, labour was in very short supply. This was highlighted by a prosecution in November 1917 of a mother and child who were accused of theft from the factory. Mr. Hammersley intimated that, as a result of continued thefts from the works, no employees would be allowed to purchase wares through the factory. He stated that due to shortage of labour, the company was hard pressed to complete orders and that in some instances, only enough pieces were manufactured to complete a specific order and pilfering was causing great problems.

Since the appointment of Thomas Hammersley as managing director in 1915, the company had become less conservative in its attitudes, not only in the way the company was run, but also in the publicity given to the company's wares. This became apparent from the increased advertising which appeared in *The Pottery Gazette*. With the ending of the war in 1918, the company took full advantage of the increase in trade that peace brought about.

One of the steps taken was the opening in March 1919 of new London showrooms at 47, Holborn Viaduct. The new showrooms were on two floors and were much larger than those in Bartlett's Buildings, which they superseded. These new showrooms were more suitable for showing to the trade the infinite variety of wares produced by the company. Photographs of the exterior and interior of the showrooms are shown in Figures 6 to 8.The manager of the new showrooms was still Arthur Overton Jones, who by this time had also become deputy chairman of the company.

On 7 January 1920, the company also opened new showrooms in St. James Building, Broadway and 26th Street, New York. These were managed by Percy Leyland, the company's American agent.

The following month, the directors of the company held their first annual dinner for staff and management. The directors at that time were Charles Jones (chairman), Thomas Hammersley (managing director), Arthur Overton Jones (deputy chairman), Charles J. Birbeck (art director) and Keith Benham. At the dinner, Arthur Overton Jones referred to the fact that the pottery trade as a whole was suffering from under-production due to the shortage of labour, and he hoped all would do their level best to increase production and so assure the prosperity of the company. Charles Jones stated that in June 1921, he would have been associated with the company for fifty years. From the tone of the report, which appeared in *The Pottery Gazette and Glass Trade Review*,[27] it would appear that George Jones & Sons Ltd. was a happy company to work for and the well-being of all employees was always paramount in the directors' minds. The works manager at this time was Mr. A. Cartlidge, who was referred to by Thomas Hammersley as 'the right man in the right place'.

How things changed! At the following annual dinner held in February 1921, which was again reported in *The Pottery Gazette and Glass Trade Review*,[28] Thomas Hammersley hinted that there were troubled times ahead 'since there was hardly a market on the face of the globe which was at present able to purchase and pay for English pottery', although he believed the company would pull through and come out on top. At the same dinner, mention was made of Charles Birbeck, the company art director, 'although not a cubist, a futurist, or a post-impressionist, he has the faculty for turning art to practical commercial use'. Thomas Hammersley continued, 'that at this time Charles Birbeck is probably the finest commercial artist in the pottery trade'.

The third annual dinner was held at the North Stafford Hotel, Stoke, on the 1 March 1922, and in a report of the dinner appeared in *The Pottery Gazette and Glass Trade Review*. It stated:

> Mr. A. R. L. Saul (company accountant) referred to the fact that, although the past year had been a troublesome one in the pottery trade, the cohesion between the various mem-

bers of the "Crescent"' staff had never been greater. There was an obvious determination amongst the workers to pull strongly together in order to maintain in good repute the name which "Crescent Ware" had built for itself in a long and honourable career. Mr. A. Overton Jones responded for the principals, remarking that, so far as he could remember, the heads and the workers of the firm had always been a happy family. His uncle (Frank Benham) and his father (George Henry Jones) had always seemed to be able to pull together, just as their successors were now doing... Mr. Tom Hammersley, the managing director stated that, ever since the new directorate was formed (in 1915), they had tried to follow in the footsteps of those who had preceded them in endeavouring to make the workers happy and contented. He continued...it is impossible for any one man — managing director though he might be — to know everything that was connected with the making, the firing, the milling, the decoration and everything that was entailed in the production of pottery in its evolution from the mill to the warehouse. No factory which produced such a tremendous variety of wares, as did the Crescent Pottery, could be carried on without the fullest measure of co-operation and the technical advice and suggestions of the various heads of departments, who each knew the requirements of their respective departments very thoroughly.

To emphasise how bad trade had been, he mentioned that 1921 was only the third year, in his forty years' experience with Crescent Potteries, when he had encountered such a spell of poor trade, as he had always found that the reputation which the firm held for good work, in all its various departments, had secured a fair share of the trade that was at any time being done. At this time short-time working was being enforced and many workers were paid for just being at work. Thomas Hammersley concluded that he was:

> particularly grateful for the support which had been rendered to myself by the staff during the anxious times through which they had recently been passing and hoped better trade conditions would return soon.

As if trade conditions were not bad enough, 1922 was to end on a very serious note. In December, a disastrous fire broke out and considerable damage was done to the factory. A graphic description of the fire was given in the *Evening Sentinel*, including:

> The section of the building in which the fire originated was three stories high. On the ground floor was the greenhouse, over it was the earthenware biscuit warehouse and the top floor was the ground laying shop and lithographic shop. The fire brigade concentrated upon each end of the line of flames to save the adjoining glost printing shops, gilding shops and other lithographic departments. For some time after the brigade had obtained mastery, there continued loud crashes as the beams gave way and thousands of pieces of ware were dashed to the ground in the biscuit warehouse and decorating room. There was a large stock and a great proportion of it was destroyed.

Although the fire caused considerable damage, and at one stage it was feared that it would envelop the whole works, the company was able to reassure the trade that normal production and deliveries would only be slightly affected. A notice to this effect was placed in *The Pottery Gazette and Glass Trades Review* of January 1923 as follows :

> Our many readers who are customers of the Crescent Potteries of the well-known firm of George Jones & Sons Ltd., will be consoled to hear that despite a serious fire which occurred at the works on December 12th, whereby it was first feared that a considerable number of employees would be temporarily rendered idle, arrangements have been made by management to accommodate practically the whole of

the operatives affected, with the result that the firm's high class china trade will not be affected at all, whilst the earthenware department will only be incommoded to a limited extent. It is not every factory that would have been able to manage this and it is only because the Crescent Potteries are so large and so many sided in their activities that a fire of such serious dimensions has not caused the ranks of the unemployed to be considerably swelled.

At the fourth annual dinner held on the 24 January 1923, mention was made of the popularity of Crescent china. Comment was made on how bad trade had been in 1922 and that the company believed that 1923 would see an upturn in home business, but that foreign trade would not improve until a real peace was restored in Europe and the money markets were brought back to something like stability.

In October 1923, the company found it necessary to make mention in *The Pottery Gazette and Glass Trades Review* of the fact that they had been somewhat concerned at the unauthorised use of the word 'Crescent' in other quarters of the pottery industry. The article continued:

> George Jones & Sons Ltd. are naturally very jealous of their own proprietary trade mark, which was registered over 50 years ago and now signifies at once in pottery trade circles a special brand of ware rather than a mere shape or pattern.

The company hoped that it was only necessary to call attention to the matter for any further use of the word 'Crescent' by other pottery-producing houses to cease, otherwise further action was planned. This obviously had the desired effect as no further mention was made of the problem.

Two of the most important export markets for the company were America and Canada. In July 1924, Thomas Hammersley sailed to America to make a six week tour of the States and Canada, to acquaint himself with the conditions on the spot.[29] At this time, Emerson Nicholls of London, Ontario, was appointed the company's resident Canadian agent. The company was now operating agencies in North and South America, Canada and Australia.

By April 1925 trade was increasing and a comment in *The Pottery Gazette and Glass Trades Review* stated:

> We are glad to learn that the 'Crescent' Potteries are doing a steadily increasing trade in both china and earthenware with the United States and Canada, and we know from observations that they are holding their own amongst the best dealers in the home trade.

Two years later the pottery industry had shaken off the effects of the recession of the early 1920s and George Jones & Sons Ltd. in particular was receiving orders at a faster rate than could be executed.

The year 1927 was to be a bad one for the company in so far as loss of management was concerned. In the early part of the year, Thomas Hammersley, the managing director, was forced to retire early due to ill health and in October, Charles Jones, the chairman died at the age of seventy-three. Charles Jones had, for some years, been unable to take an active role in the running of the company due to his loss of sight, but he always attended the board meetings. These two losses were a great blow to the company. Another loss in December was that of Arthur Tatton, who was crate makers' manager at the works. He was in his seventy-fourth year and had spent his whole working life at George Jones'. He had started at the age of eight working under the supervision of his father, Daniel Tatton, who at that time was in charge of the crate making and packing department when the company was still at the Bridge Works.

The company was now being run by the deputy chairman, Arthur Overton Jones, until a successor to Thomas Hammersley could be found. Arthur was the last family member remaining in the company. In May 1928, Walter Bakewell joined the board of directors as managing director. He had been associated with the pottery industry for over 40 years.

On the 28th of December 1928, the family agreed to sell the land and buildings occupied by the company, to George Jones & Sons Ltd. The sale price was £25,000.[30] Up to that time, the property had been held in trust, the trustees being Arthur Overton Jones, his mother Elizabeth Walmsley Jones and his brother Henry Chester Jones, since the death of George Jones in 1893, and the company had paid rent to the trust for its use.

New owners 1929

When the company announced their financial results for 1928, they showed a loss of £6,000. The bank was starting to ask questions about what the directors intended to do to rectify the situation, when, in April 1929 Walter Bakewell, the managing director, approached the shareholders of George Jones & Sons Ltd., who were all members of the Jones family, and offered to buy the company. The offer was:

> £100 for every £125 debentures
> £25 for every £100 cumulative preference share
> £5 for every £100 ordinary share
> £100 - 4 1/4% debentures to be paid in full.

The majority of the shareholders thought Walter Bakewell's offer was fair and accepted. In mid-1929, Bakewell took financial control of the company, thus ending the George Jones family connection, which had lasted for over 67 years. The only family member still working for the company was Arthur Overton Jones, who continued as a director of the firm and manager of the London showrooms, a position he had held since 1896.

After Walter Bakewell took control of the company in 1929, he began formulating new policies. One of these was to concentrate production by producing patterns which were regarded as open stock patterns that could be obtained in every item for the table. At this time, the company was amongst the largest and best known manufacturers of china and earthenware, employing over 800 people. The factory was well-kept and had around twenty bottle kilns. According to former employees, it was a happy place to work and was well run. The company employed many paintresses and had a vast output of high quality earthenware and china. Over 50% of the factory's output was being exported. The company was able to supply the pottery markets of the world with goods of a brand which entitled them to rank amongst the most reputable makers whilst being, in the case of china, rather lower in price than wares of those firms which were included in what was known as the 'Fine China Group' (Wedgwood, Worcester, Derby, Mintons and Spode).

A reporter from *The Pottery Gazette and Glass Trades Review* visited the factory in June 1930. He commented that the factory was one of the best laid-out factories in the old Stoke township and the buildings struck a note of distinctiveness with regard to the architecture. At the entrance to the works, a round tower of the French turret type had been erected as part of the original works when it was built in 1864-65. This, according to the reporter, gave the works an air of superiority.

The wares produced at this time ranged from hotel and hospital ware, underglaze printed earthenware, multicoloured patterns in earthenware — both on and underglaze — middle priced china and sumptuously-decorated lines in china services, such as were called for by the wealthiest stores in England, and the most exclusive markets abroad.

In lithographed patterns, the firm was at a decided advantage to many of its rivals in exclusive designs, due to the company having its own litho-printing department, a plant which had been set up in the 1880s. Often the designs were a combination of litho and hand painting. Cyril Shingler, who later worked for Royal Worcester and also became curator of the Dyson Perrins Museum, designed many of these patterns.

The only remaining ceramic artist employed by the Crescent Potteries in the late 1920s and early 1930s was William Birbeck, who had been with the company since 1881.

Charles Birbeck, the art director, was forced to retire in September 1931 due to ill health. He had served the company for fifty four years and for about thirty six years had been responsible for the design of the majority of the wares produced. His position as art director was taken by Leon Grice, who had been employed as a designer when Cyril Shingler left the company. Under Walter Bakewell's leadership, the company retained its good name and production increased with the new types of wares being produced.

Amalgamations and closure 1933-1951

The next few years were to see several changes of ownership and amalgamations. In January 1933, the company announced that, due to ill-health, Walter Bakewell had been compelled to retire and that his place as managing director was to be taken by Mr. E. F. Ecclestone.[31] At the same time, the long-established company of Bishop & Stonier (which had only just been sold to Ridgways (Bedford Works) Ltd. of Shelton had been acquired by George Jones & Sons Ltd., and was subsequently moved to the Crescent Potteries.

The majority of the shares of George Jones & Sons Ltd. were now owned by Harrison & Son (Hanley) Ltd. who had bought them from Walter Bakewell. Harrison & Son were not potters, but their family business, which went back to 1810, was concerned with the manufacture of colours and other materials used in the manufacturing of pottery.

Following the retirement of Walter Bakewell, the company employed Harold T. Robinson as sales organiser for the combined businesses.[32] He had owned Bishop & Stonier, Cauldon and Coalport until he filed for bankruptcy in May 1932. When Harold Robinson came to the company, he brought with him his two sons, Eric and Philip Robinson. Philip Robinson was an artist who, in later life, was to become chairman of Royal Crown Derby. By this time, Arthur Overton Jones had relinquished his position as manager of the London showrooms and was no longer involved with the company. With Arthur's retirement, the company lost the last of the descendants of George Jones associated with it.

At the beginning of 1933, the wares produced at the Crescent Potteries bore the backstamps of George Jones, Bishop & Stonier, Goss and Allertons. The latter two companies had also been bought by Harrison & Son (Hanley) Ltd. and moved to the Crescent Potteries. When all the new companies moved to the site, the number of employees still remained around 900.

In October 1935, the following announcement appeared in *The Pottery Gazette and Glass Trades Review*:

> George Jones & Sons Ltd., Crescent Potteries, Stoke, announce that an amalgamation has been effected between the company and The Coalport China Co. (John Rose & Co.), Cauldon Place Works, Stoke. The latter business will shortly be moved to Crescent Potteries.

Coalport, (which included Cauldon) was also owned by Harrison & Son (Hanley) Ltd. who had decided, for economic reasons, not to retain two large works on widely separate sites. To enable the move to go ahead, Sydney Harrison, chairman of Harrison & Son (Hanley) Ltd. and owner of the Crescent Potteries, purchased part of the old Minton tile works from Messrs. Mintons in August 1935 for £1100. This property of 1780 sq. yards adjoined the western edge of the Crescent Potteries. After the move this property was sold by Sydney Harrison to George Jones & Sons Ltd. in December 1936 for £1450.[33]

The moving of Coalport and Cauldon to the Crescent Potteries' site was overseen by Harold Robinson, but the task took its toll on him and in late 1936, he severed his connections with the combined companies, due to ill-health.[34] Stanley Harrison, Sydney Harrison's son, was then appointed chairman and managing director of the amalgamated companies.

Edward Liveing wrote in his book The Story of Royal Cauldon:

> it is not without interest that an industry ancillary to potting came to take control of a group containing some of the most distinguished pottery businesses of the day. Sifting and pruning had to be applied to the ramifications of what was a considerable combination of interests in 1936.

In about 1937, the Crescent Potteries installed a gas fired kiln. They were one of the first pottery manufacturers in the area to install such a kiln. Eventually gas or electric fired kilns were to cause the demise of the bottle kiln, being a much cleaner and environmentally friendly way of firing pottery.

In June 1938, George Jones & Sons Ltd. opened a new showroom in Queens Street, Glasgow. The manager was Mr. J. E. Brunt.

When the Second World War broke out in 1939, the Harrison company was still engaged in disentangling their interests at the Crescent Potteries. The war-time restrictions curtailed the production of coloured wares and most fine bone china for the home market, although it was still produced for export, to earn much-needed foreign currency to pay for the war effort.

At this time George Jones & Sons Ltd. had agents in various countries around the world. They were:

Canada:	Miller Bros. 32 Front St. West Toronto.
Australia:	Russell Cowan Pty Ltd. 352 Kent St Sydney.
South Africa:	Edmund C. Matson Capetown.
India:	Dewan Chand & Sons 315 Thakurdwar Bombay.
U.S.A.:	M. & D. Miller Inc. 129 Fifth Ave New York.

A former employee, who began as an apprentice gilder at the Crescent Potteries in March 1941, aged 16 years, had to finish in February 1943 to join the army. She recalls that the head gilder was Miss Florrie Mollart who had been with George Jones & Sons Ltd. for many years. Her cousin, Miss Annie Mollart, was in charge of the main gilding shop. Annie Mollart had lived in America at Trentham, New Jersey, for many years, her parents having emigrated there. She recalls the Mollarts were old-fashioned ladies who wore long dresses and lace-up boots. She also remembers William Birbeck painting beautiful roses. There were two designers working at the factory in the early 1940s: Mr. D. Simmill, who was decorating manager for the combined group, and Peter Price, who later worked for Coalport at Fenton. She also remembers one shop at the factory, producing hand painted china dolls heads.

In September 1942, George Jones & Sons Ltd. was licensed under the *Domestic Pottery (Manufacturers & Supply) Order*, to produce undecorated domestic earthenware (utility) Group II, marked 'B.'[35] This was after the factory had complied with the Government's concentration arrangements. At this time, the firms registered as belonging to the George Jones Group and producing wares at the Crescent Potteries were:[36]

Charles Allerton & Sons
Bakewell Bros.
Bishop & Stonier Ltd.
Cauldon Potteries Ltd.
Coalport China Co. Ltd.
Goss China Co. Ltd.
George Jones & Sons Ltd.
Swansea China Co. Ltd.

By 1943, only a few hundred people were employed on the whole site, compared with over 1100 before the outbreak of the war. The

17

rest of the employees had had to leave to either work at the munitions factory at Swinnerton, or to join the armed forces.

Although the work force had been considerably reduced, the directors of the combined companys decided to convert an old warehouse on the site into a new canteen. This was encouraged by the government, who allowed food for works canteens, which of course supplemented domestic rations. The canteen was finished in June 1943, only after numerous difficulties had been overcome by the company, including the inability to get permits from the various government controls for the materials required. In consequence, the directors invited the company's art department to combine in undertaking the decorating of the canteen. Murals were painted on the plaster walls and nine plaques were hung between the murals; the plaques represented three of the outstanding designs of each of the group's principal firms: George Jones & Sons Ltd., Coalport China Co., and Cauldon Potteries. A view of the canteen is shown in Figure 742.

Another former employee remembers returning to the factory in August 1943 and 'unofficially' looking inside what had been the main gilding shop. It was full of young women operating sewing machines — possibly making uniforms for the armed forces.

After the war had ended in 1945, the pottery manufacturers still remained restricted with regard to the types of wares they could produce for the home market. In October 1945, a new government order was issued and under that order George Jones & Sons Ltd. was allowed to produce undecorated domestic pottery.[37] The wares produced were marked with the letter 'B' under the glaze.

In 1947, the Harrison company, which had wholly owned George Jones & Sons Ltd. since 1936, became disassociated from the George Jones group of companies. Sydney Harrison and his son, Stanley, took over the proprietorship of the George Jones Group, Stanley Harrison retaining his position as chairman and managing director.

The Crescent works were largely reorganised in 1949 and its facilities were modernised with the installation of the latest type of plant and machinery. All the old and familiar bottle kilns were demolished and replaced with electric kilns.

In 1951, the trade name of George Jones & Sons Ltd. ceased to be used.[38] However, the Crescent Potteries continued to produce mainly Coalport and Cauldon wares until 1959, when Coalport was bought by E. Brain & Co. Ltd. The Crescent works were then closed for good and partially demolished. E. Brain & Co. Ltd. was subsequently bought by Josiah Wedgwood & Sons Ltd., who also acquired the George Jones pattern books, now held at the Wedgwood Museum, Barlaston.

The last directors of George Jones & Sons Ltd. were:

Stanley Harrison	Chairman and Managing Director
F. E. Ridgway	Sales Manager
E. Boulton	Commercial Director
P. Simpson	Decorating Manager
D. Eardley	Director and Works Manager
J. Dutton	Director and Secretary

This ends the story of the history of a company which ran for one hundred years. A former employee visited the site in 1992. She wrote: 'it was a desolate experience, no laughter, no singing in chorus, no talking, no happy experiences around the corners'. She continued: 'the sense of pride in work well done, praise from superiors, the beautiful wares, wonderful pottery and shapes decorated with best gold, no liquid gold, all replaced by empty shops and waste ground'.

[1] Wedgwood Archives, Ref. Hiring Book 1837-92
[2] Wedgwood Archives, Ref. W/M1644, 14985-15 to 15038-15
[3] P.O. Directory, London 1855
[4] London Gazette, 25 January 1858, 451
[5] Kellys P.O. Directory of Birmingham, Warwickshire, Worcestershire & Staffordshire 1860
[6] The Staffordshire Advertiser, February 25, 1860
[7] The Staffordshire Advertiser, April 6, 1861
[8] Staffordshire County Record Office, Ref. D3272/1/4/3/104
[9] Staffordshire County Record Office, Ref. D3272/1/13/3
[10] Stoke-upon-Trent Commissioners Minute book 1865-74
[11] P.O. Directory, London 1871
[12] Stoke-upon-Trent Council Minute book 1874-81
[13] Borough of Stoke-upon-Trent Rating Book
[14] National Westminster Bank Archives, Current Account Ledger, Ref. B11138
[15] National Westminster Bank Archives, Current Account Ledger, Ref. B11138
[16] National Westminster Bank Archives, Information Book, Ref. B11139
[17] The Probate Registry, George Jones Will proved 9 February 1894
[18] National Westminster Bank Archives, Information Book Ref. B11139
[19] The Probate Registry, George Jones Will proved 9 February 1894
[20] National Westminster Bank Archives, Information Book, Ref. B11139
[21] National Westminster Bank Archives, Letter Book, District Bank, Stafford,
[22] National Westminster Bank Archives, Information Book, Ref. B11139
[23] The Pottery Gazette, March 1902, 293
[24] The Pottery Gazette, August 1902, 798
[25] The Pottery Gazette Diary, 1905

Figure 1. A print from an old engraving showing the Bridge Works, Church Street, Stoke-upon-Trent.

Where the "Old English Abbey" was made in 1790.

[26] National Westminster Bank Archives, Information Book, Ref. B11139
[27] The Pottery Gazette & Glass Trades Review, March 1921, 466
[28] The Pottery Gazette & Glass Trades Review, April 1922, 607
[29] The Pottery Gazette & Glass Trades Review, August 1924, 1375
[30] Royal Doulton (UK) Ltd, Title Deeds & Land Records - Minton Site
[31] The Pottery Gazette & Glass Trades Review, January 1933, 93
[32] The Pottery Gazette & Glass Trades Review, January 1933, 93
[33] Royal Doulton(UK) Ltd, Title Deeds & Land Records - Minton Site
[34] The Pottery Gazette & Glass Trades Review, February 1937, 282
[35] The Pottery Gazette & Glass Trades Review, September 1942, 511
[36] The Pottery Gazette & Glass Trades Review, November 1941, xii
[37] The Pottery Gazette & Glass Trades Review, October 1945, 590
[38] The Pottery Gazette & Glass Trades Review, Reference Book 1952

Figure 2. Map showing the layout and boundary of the Trent Potteries and Bridge Works in 1878. Reproduced from the 1878 Ordnance Survey map.

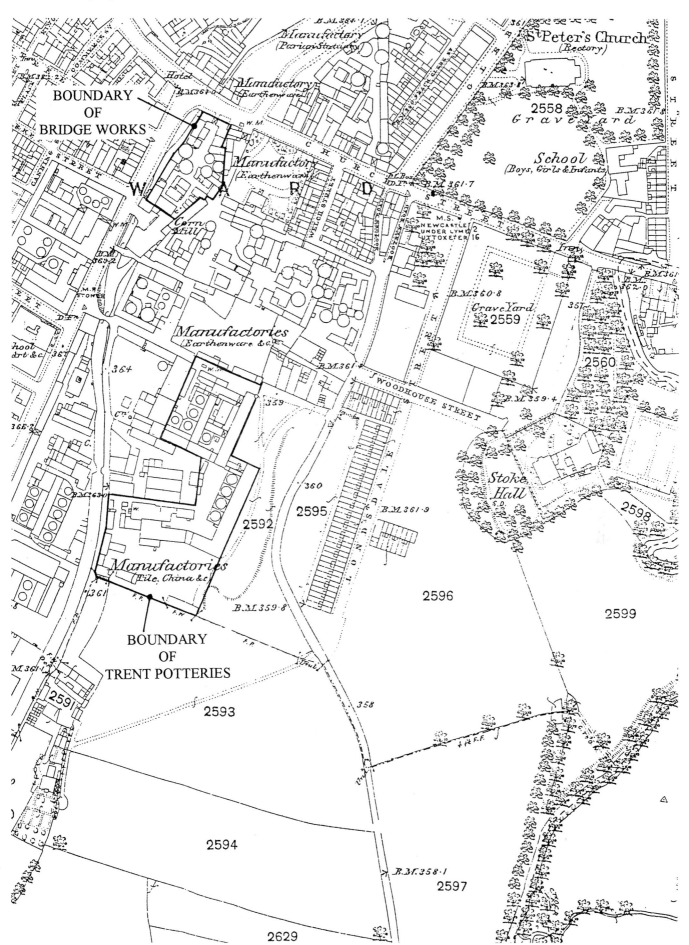

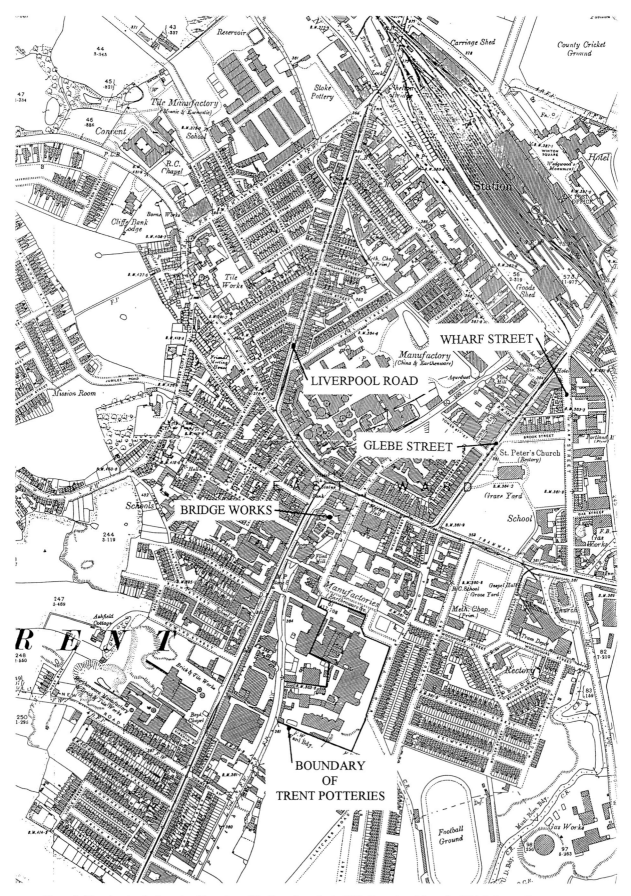

Figure 3. Map showing the layout and boundary of the Trent Potteries in 1900. Reproduced from the 1900 Ordnance Survey map.

Figure 4. Henry Giller.

Figure 6. Exterior of new showrooms opened in 1919 at 47 Holborn Viaduct, London. *Courtesy of Tableware International.*

Figure 5. Eric George Jones.

Figure 7. Ground floor of new showrooms. *Courtesy of Tableware International.*

Figure 8. Basement of new showrooms, note 'Abbey' pattern pedestal and pot on the right hand side. *Courtesy of Tableware International.*

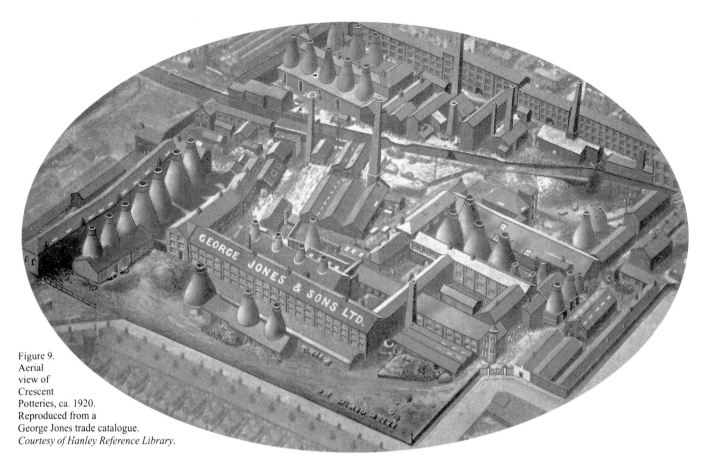

Figure 9.
Aerial
view of
Crescent
Potteries, ca. 1920.
Reproduced from a
George Jones trade catalogue.
Courtesy of Hanley Reference Library.

Figure 10. Aerial view of the Crescent Potteries (centre of photograph) in September 1948. *Courtesy of Aerofilms*. Photograph reference no. R10058.

Figure 11. Map showing layout and boundary of the Crescent Potteries in 1937. Reproduced from the 1937 Ordnance Survey map.

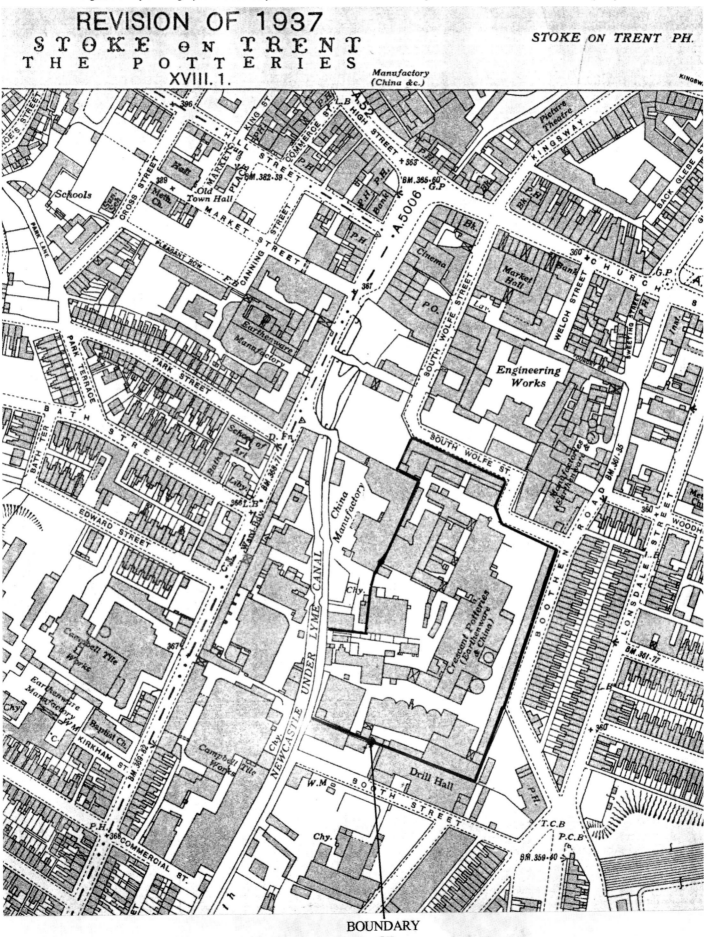

George Jones opened his original pottery manufacturing company, George Jones & Co., at the Bridge Works, Stoke-upon-Trent, in February 1862 to produce white granite ware (also known as ironstone china or stone china) for the American market. Initially the wares were produced for J. & G. Meakin of Hanley, who, having more orders than they could cope with, had commissioned George Jones to manufacture wares on their behalf.

As well as producing wares for Meakins, George Jones very soon started to manufacture white granite ware under his own name. A clause in the lease, which George Jones signed for the Bridge Works, stated that no brown or coloured wares were to be produced, only wares made from white clay.

Whether George Jones marked his early wares is not known, as very few examples of wares that can be attributed to his early manufacturing days have survived. To find out what sort of wares he was producing, and the types of decoration he was using, we have to look at the designs he was submitting to the Patent Office in London for registration. George Jones submitted his first two designs in May 1862. These were the border and centre patterns illustrated in Figures 12 and 13 and were registered on 14 May 1862, patent no's. 151672 and 151673. They were probably for the ornamentation of breakfast, dinner and tea wares.

On 18 December 1862, his third design was registered. Patent no. 158498 was given to the border pattern illustrated in Figure 14. This pattern could possibly have been used in conjunction with an engraved landscape centre, or, on wares with plain centres.

It was to be ten months before George Jones registered more designs. On 28 October 1863, patent no. 167715 was given to another design for a border and centre pattern. This pattern was named 'Country Wreath' and is shown in Figure 15. Two more border and centre patterns, shown in Figures 16 and 17, were registered on 6 November 1863, patent no's. 168234 and 168235.

A border pattern registered on 15 April 1864, patent no. 173659, was again registered on 10 May 1864, but this time George Jones named the pattern 'Stratford', and it was given patent no. 174457. Quite why this was so is not known, as the only difference between the two designs is that patent no. 173659 is a green print and patent no. 174457 is a brown print.

At the same time as the pattern named 'Stratford' was registered, three more border and centre patterns were also registered. Patent no. 174455 was a pattern named 'Ionia', patent no. 174456 was not named on the illustration held at the Public Record Office, Kew, but patent no. 174458 was a pattern named 'Persian'. All four designs are illustrated in Figures 18 to 21. A compote decorated in the 'Persian' pattern is shown in Figures 22 and 23.

The first design which George Jones submitted for a shape was registered on 20 August 1864, patent no. 177912. It was for the de-

sign of a tureen for a dinner service and is illustrated in Figure 24. The shape was named 'Laurel', and was to be manufactured in five sizes: 8", 9", 10", 11" and 12".

On 4 October 1864 another border pattern was registered, this was named 'Coburg Chain' and was given patent no. 179445. Coburg was a word associated with Queen Victoria's husband, Prince Albert of Saxe-Coburg-Gotha. In the 19th century various items had the word 'Coburg' incorporated into their names. One such item was a rounded loaf of bread with a cross cut on the top, the loaf was called a 'Coburg loaf'. As can be seen from the pattern, illustrated in Figure 25, the chain-like design running around the border also has a cross incorporated into it.

Some of these early border patterns could have been designed by Christopher Dresser for George Jones, or the designer of these patterns could have been influenced by the designs which Christopher Dresser was producing for neighbouring Mintons, during the same period.

The first design for an embossed border pattern to be submitted by George Jones to the Patent Office was named 'York' and was registered on 10 November 1864, patent no. 181286. This embossed border pattern, shown in Figure 26, was to be used to decorate dinner, tea, breakfast and toilet services.

The last design to be submitted by George Jones for registration in 1864 was registered on 31 December, and was given patent no. 182699. This was another border pattern, named 'Laurel', (a name already used for a shape) and was possibly to be used in conjunction with other patterns. The pattern consisted of two narrow bands within which were groups of laurel leaves, each group was made up of three green leaves. Variations of this border pattern were to appear incorporated into other George Jones patterns, and were later copied by other manufacturers.

Although George Jones initially produced white granite ware, by the beginning of 1865 he had also commenced the manufacture of earthenware — a body fired at a lower temperature than white granite. The first design to be submitted for registration, specifically stating to be manufactured in earthenware, was registered on 14 January 1865 and was given patent no. 183331. Written on the design, held at the Public Record Office, Kew, is 'An embossed decoration for cake tray, cheese tray, butter tub and stand, potting tub and stand for earthenware'. This design is shown in Figure 27. Incidentally, the handwriting is that of George Jones himself.

It was to be 18 months (July 1866) before the next design was submitted to the Patent Office for registration, by which time George Jones had moved his manufacturing business from the Bridge Works, Stoke-upon-Trent, to his new, purpose built Trent Potteries, also in

Stoke-upon-Trent. Patent no. 199295 was given to this design which was registered on 25 July 1866. This design was for a tureen for a table service and is shown in Figure 28.

One year later, on 12 July 1867, another design was submitted for a table service to be manufactured in earthenware. This design, patent no. 209530, was for a tureen shape to be used for soup tureens, sauce tureens, and vegetable dishes and is shown in Figure 29. The tureens were to be manufactured in 7", 8", 9" and 10" sizes.

Another design for a tureen was registered on 1 January 1869 and was given patent no. 226051. This shape, named 'Grecian', is shown in Figure 30. It was to be manufactured in earthenware and china (stone china). This name was to be used again when on 11 February 1869 a pattern for ornamenting dinner, tea and toilet services, to be manufactured in earthenware, was registered and given patent no. 227277. This later design, shown in Figure 31, also included a backstamp which incorporated the pattern name.

On 9 March 1869 a pattern named 'Crete' was registered, patent no. 227744. This was a border pattern to be used on dinner, tea, dessert and toilet services. This pattern, which had a border similar to the 'Grecian' pattern, is shown in Figure 32.

On 1 December 1869 a border and centre pattern named 'Lotus' was registered, patent no. 236756. It was to be used for decorating earthenware. This pattern, shown in Figure 33, was again very similar to ones being designed by Christopher Dresser for Mintons.

Though utilising a large proportion of his production capacity for the output of majolica decorated wares, George Jones also continued to produce large quantities of tableware and toilet ware, manufactured in either earthenware or stone china and decorated in white glaze or white glaze and gold. Sometimes services were also decorated with underglaze printed patterns. Other types of wares being manufactured at this time ranged from dog troughs to spittoons, and sardine dishes to slop pails, together with heated covered dishes for bacon, chops and steak.

The first design to be submitted by George Jones for embossed dinner ware was registered on 3 January 1870 and was given patent no. 237742. This design, named 'Erica', was featured on a tureen and for use on earthenware. The embossed design was made up of small sprays of cowslips with leaves, and was on both the lid and body of the tureen.

Patent no. 239474 was given to a design for a 'rope handle for ewer with basin & chamber set' which was registered on 10 March 1870. This design of handle and variations of it were to be used on many different designs of ewers and jugs over a long period of time. A large vase produced in the 1890s has two such handles.

Another design for a dinner service tureen, to be manufactured in both earthenware and china (stone-china) was registered on 30 May 1870 and was given patent no. 242077. An example of this design is shown in Figure 34. This particular piece, marked with the impressed date letter 'X', was manufactured in 1872 and has the early impressed George Jones mark incorporating the words 'STONE CHINA' and 'STOKE on TRENT' and is decorated with pattern no. 2350.

A design registered on 22 November 1870 and given patent no. 247944, was described as a 'Fruit shape dinner service' for manufacturing in earthenware and china. The design shows a tureen, the lid of which has a knob in the shape of an apple. This design of knob was still being used on tureens as late as 1924.

On 10 January 1873 a design was registered for a dinner service and was given patent no. 269585. The design shows a wavy edged dinner plate with an unusual embossed border, made up of a waist belt complete with a fastened buckle, and opposite the buckle, the belt passed through a loop.

Two months later, on 26 March 1873, another design was registered for a dinner service tureen and was given patent no. 271561.

On 13 October 1873 two patterns were registered. Patent no. 277148 was given to a pattern named 'Cuba'. This engraved pattern was to be used extensively on all types of wares. Figures 320, 346

and 385 show three different examples of tableware decorated in this underglaze transfer printed pattern. The second pattern registered was given patent no. 277149 and was a border pattern named 'Stafford'.

Two of the next three designs to be registered, by the now renamed company George Jones & Sons, reflected the Victorian's fascination for the grotesque and are featured on the ewer shown in Figure 401. The first design, patent no. 280609, registered on 19 February 1874, was for a lizard handle jug. The second design, registered on 21 April 1874, patent no. 281899, was for a pattern named 'Adansi'. The engraved pattern, which was for decorating dinner and bedroom services, included bats, tortoises, weird looking insects, a sting-ray and a bird carrying a fish in its beak, together with an array of ferns and broad leafed tropical foliage. Parts of this pattern are shown on the ewer. Note the bat moulded into the lip of the ewer. Figure 402 shows a chamber pot with the same lizard handle, and this chamber pot is also decorated in the 'Adansi' underglaze transfer printed pattern.

On 3 March 1874 an engraved pattern named 'Kent' was registered and was given patent no. 280907. An example of this pattern is shown on a dinner service tureen in Figure 321.

A design for a ewer was registered on 25 April 1874 and was given patent no. 281984. This ewer was of a similar shape to the lizard handled ewer but the lizard handle had been replaced with a geometrically shaped handle.

It had been nearly two years since the last design for a tureen had been submitted for registering by George Jones & Sons, when the next design for a tureen was registered on 21 January 1875 and was given patent no. 288682. This design stated it was also for 'sauces on stand large and small', suggesting that the shape could be used for vegetable tureens and sauce tureens.

During this period, as well as producing table and toilet wares, George Jones also produced ornamental wares. The design for one such piece was registered on 1 December 1871 and was given patent no. 258095. This design for an ornamental tray was to be manufactured in earthenware or china. The design incorporated two birds' nests complete with birds, possibly blackbirds, sitting on the nests. This piece could have been produced in majolica.

On 23 May 1874 a design for a 'flowers bracket' was registered and was given patent no. 282568. This design for a wall bracket features a humming bird entering a flower with flower stems and leaves, all moulded in high relief. Examples of this piece have been seen with a celadon ground body, white glazed leaves and stems and the humming bird and flower coloured from nature.

The first design for a 'napkin and menu holder' was registered on 21 October 1874, patent no. 286424. This design consisted of three 'lily of the valley' leaves mounted on a base. The first leaf was mounted upright and had 'lily of the valley' flowers embossed on it, the second leaf was mounted to form a slot with the first leaf, for holding the menu. This leaf had its top bent over to meet the third leaf, which was curved, thus forming an irregularly shaped hole in which could be placed a napkin.

On 26 June 1875 four separate designs were registered. Two designs were for pieces to be decorated in majolica and two were for pieces that *might* have been decorated in majolica. The first of these possible majolica designs was given patent no. 292368 and was for a 'leaf shaped dessert service' complete with a leaf shaped compote. Three different leaf shapes are shown on the design now held at the Public Record Office, Kew. The second design was given patent no. 292369 and was for a 'Wilopose' flower holder. This flower holder comprised of a slightly inclined, curved horn-shaped vase held up by a curved support. The vase had an embossed flower near the top and grasses at the bottom.

Up until 1870, the majority of the production coming from firstly the Bridge Works and then the Trent Potteries was made up of tableware and toilet ware produced in either earthenware or stone china; but, by the end of the year 1870, George Jones was becoming well-known for his majolica decorated wares. During the next decade this type of ware was to form an important and profitable part of the company's output.

Majolica

The word majolica is an Anglicisation of the Italian word maiolica. It has been said that the name was first given by fifteenth century Italians to wares imported from Spain via Majorca, then called Maiolica. Later the name maiolica was the generic term given to all Italian earthenware painted over a ground of white tin glaze.

Majolica was virtually unknown in England until 1849, when Leon Arnoux, the art director and chief chemist at Mintons, perfected the appropriate lead glazes for Mintons. Majolica was officially introduced by Herbert Minton at the Great Exhibition of 1851 held at the Crystal Palace in London. Minton majolica was made from a cane coloured earthenware body, either moulded or pressed into high relief, with sharp clear details, dipped into white tin enamel and fired. The majolica colours were then thickly applied and the piece fired again. The cane coloured body tinted the white glaze so that when the majolica colours were applied and the piece fired, the majolica colours became enriched. The colours used for majolica decoration included red, pink, blue, green ,brown, yellow, and turquoise.

Following the Great Exhibition, the popularity of majolica soared and many other English pottery manufacturers began to produce it in subsequent years including Wedgwood and George Jones.

Although George Jones started his pottery manufacturing business in early 1862, it was not until he moved into his new Trent Potteries around 1866 that he commenced the production of majolica. By this time his son, Frank Jones, had returned from a period of training at the Royal Porcelain Factory at Sèvres in France. Frank Jones's artistic talents were put to good use and it was he who helped his father to design and produce the beautiful and often humorous majolica pieces. The other important person involved with the design and production of majolica, was John Bourne, a potter of some forty years experience and an influential member of the Potteries Mechanics Institute in Stoke.

In 1884, a book was published which contained a collection of ceramic receipts (recipes) used by John Bourne during his lifetime's work as a potter. The recipes were for earthenware bodies, i.e. clays etc., fluxes for enamel colours, printing colours and oils, underglaze colours, glazes, lustres and majolica colours. One of the majolica colours mentioned was 'Snake'. The receipt for this was 8 pounds soft glaze, 4 pounds yellow, 4 pounds brown, 8 pounds number 13 green. These colours were loosely mixed together and produced the distinctive glaze used by George Jones on the underside of many of his pieces of majolica. Sometimes it is referred to as tortoiseshell, but, in fact, it was meant to represent snake skin.

By 1867, majolica was beginning to form a substantial part of the production of the factory. Many of the early pieces were available in white glaze, white and gold, or majolica. A report in *The Staffordshire Advertiser* of the 2 March 1867 stated:

An extensive collection of tasteful wares ordinarily produced at the works has been forwarded to Paris by Messrs. George Jones & Co. There are a number of articles such as garden seats and card baskets designed upon the Palissy models and similar objects have also been produced in Majolica.

Although George Jones was awarded a medal for his exhibits at the Paris Universal Exhibition held in June 1867, a special correspondent, writing for the *Standard* newspaper, commented on the unfair way the exhibits were judged by the French jurors, giving favouritism to the French wares in place of what the correspondent described as far superior products from the English factories of Wedgwood, Minton, Copeland and of the other firms less world wide in their reputation, such as Messrs. Jones of Stoke etc.

The first mention of a registered design for manufacture in majolica was patent no. 227746. This design was registered on 9 March 1869 and was for a tray to be manufactured in earthenware, china or majolica. It consisted of an oval shaped tray with a fox hanging on one side by its feet with its head looking into the tray, see Figure 38.

Before this design, only three other designs registered by George Jones were used for majolica decorated pieces. The first was patent no. 183331 registered on 14 January 1865 and was for an embossed decoration for a 'cake tray, cheese tray, butter tub and stand and a potting pot and stand'. This design is shown in Figure 27. The second design was registered on 14 October 1868, patent no. 222736. This design was for 'toilet ware ornamentation'. The representation of the design held at the Public Record Office, Kew, shows a ewer embossed with large leaves and small flowers on stems. An example is shown in Figure 35. The third design that was used for majolica decorated wares was patent no. 227743, registered on 9 March 1869 (at the same time as the tray with the fox head). This registered design, shown in Figure 36, was for decorating dessert wares and was named 'Lotus'. An example of a plate to this design is shown in Figure 37.

After these four designs, the majority of the designs registered by George Jones up to 1883 were for pieces to be produced in majolica. In October 1869 two designs were registered, one on the 15th was given patent no. 234486 and was for a 'mince pie and cake dish' to be made in earthenware or majolica and the second, registered on the 23rd and given patent no. 235012, was for a 'cigar ash tray'. This design showed a frog on a rock, sheltering beneath a cupped leaf, with the leaf attached to the rock by its stem.

On 22 December 1869 a design was registered for a 'nut tray with squirrel', and this design was given patent no. 237500. An example of this design is shown in Figure 39.

Two more designs for trays were registered on 8 March 1870. One was given patent no. 239424 and was described as a 'bird trinket tray'. This design shows a leaf lying on a foot formed from a branch with a handle formed from the leaf stem. On the handle is perched a bird with open wings. An example of this design is shown in Figure 40. The second design for a tray was given patent no. 239425 and was described as a 'leaf on expanded wings trinket tray'. This design shows a bird with open wings having a large leaf resting on top of its wings with the stem of the leaf in the bird's beak. It looks as if the leaf has just fallen from a tree onto the bird's back and the bird has the stem in its beak, trying to pull the leaf off. This is one of the more humorous pieces that George Jones became noted for. As well as these two trays, a 'bird strawberry set' was also registered on the same day and was given patent no. 239426. An example of this design is shown in Figure 41 without the jug and sugar basin which should be sitting in the nests.

The first design for a majolica tea pot to be registered by George Jones, was given patent no. 242715, and was registered on 27 June 1870. This design shows a tea pot in the shape of a pineapple. Our illustration Figure 72 (top left), taken from an early George Jones catalogue, shows a tea kettle with the same shaped body and spout as the tea pot.

One of the first pieces to include figures was registered on 23 August 1870 and was given patent no. 244173. It was described as a 'cupid grape tray' to be manufactured in majolica, earthenware and china. This design shows a long narrow dish which is embossed inside with grape vines, and has a cupid attached to each end with their faces looking into the dish.

Many of George Jones's early majolica pieces incorporated birds into their designs. On 19 October 1870 two designs were registered. The first design was given patent no. 245985 and was for a triple tray with two birds nestled between the tray sections. An example is shown in Figure 50. The second was given patent no. 245986 and was described as a 'bird biscuit box'. An illustration of this design shown in Figure 71 (no. 2587) is taken from an early George Jones catalogue. An example of this design is shown in Figure 51.

A rather amusing piece was registered on 10 January 1871, patent no. 249439. It shows a small dog, possibly a Yorkshire Terrier, sitting on a cushion, and was described as a 'box' for making in earthenware, majolica and china.

By the time the International Exhibition was held in London in 1871, George Jones had become one of the leading manufacturers of English majolica. The following report appeared in the *Art Journal Catalogue* produced at the time of the exhibition:

Mr George Jones of Stoke-upon-Trent contributes largely to the exhibition. His works are of the class known as majolica, a style that has been very 'fashionable' of late years. His exhibits are generally of a 'domestic' character, often very graceful and frequently good examples of art. Many of them are trifles for the boudoir or the drawing room table - pretty and pleasant flower holders and so forth. His productions, however are very varied and for the most part of a sound and good order, well modelled, carefully coloured and displaying much taste in treatment and harmonious arrangement of subjects.

The illustrations, Figure 52, show examples of some of the majolica pieces exhibited by George Jones at this exhibition and it should be noted that none of the pieces shown in this engraved picture were registered designs. George Jones was obviously producing a wide variety of designs for various types of articles but only certain designs warranted the protection of the British patent system.

In early 1871, the company's design department must have been very busy preparing the exhibits for this exhibition, because, the next design to be registered was not until 29 August 1871. This design was for a fish basket and cover and was given patent no. 255274. The cover, that has a whole salmon lying upon it, looks so life-like that you feel that you could cook it!

On 23 December 1871, patent no. 258956 was given to the first of many compote designs to be registered. This design was described as a 'fruit centre piece' and shows a deer standing by a tree trunk. An example of this design is shown in Figures 53 and 54. On the same day a 'camel fruit and flower holder' for manufacture in majolica, earthenware or china was also registered and given patent no. 258957. An example of this design is shown in Figure 55.

Two more designs for compotes were registered in early 1872. The first of these designs was registered on 20 January was given patent no. 259854. It was very similar in design to patent no. 258956, but in place of the deer there was a fox lying around the base of the tree trunk. An example of this design is shown in Figure 56. The second compote design was registered on 3 February and was given patent no 260255. It was described as a 'camel fruit centre piece' and was similar in design to the previous compotes but the bowl was formed of palm leaves and the trunk was a palm tree. There were two camels moulded on to the base, one standing and one sitting by the trunk.

The design for a piece that was subsequently to be exhibited by George Jones at the International Exhibition in Vienna in 1873, was registered on 3 February 1872 and was given patent no. 260256. It was described as a flower stand and was given the shape name 'Louise'. The stand, shown in the engraved illustration Figure 67 (top centre), was for manufacture in either earthenware, majolica or china.

Strawberry dishes and strawberry sets were very popular with the Victorians and George Jones produced some beautiful designs. One such design registered on 16 February 1872 was given patent no. 260504 and is shown in Figure 371. This example was manufactured in 1885, when cream glazed earthenware had become more popular than majolica glazed wares. At the same time as this design was registered, two more designs were registered. The first of these

was for a fruit centre piece with the shape name 'Africa' and was given patent no. 260505, and the second design was for an elevated fruit stand which was given patent no. 260506. The fruit centre piece 'Africa' was a compote similar in design to the previous ones but at the base of the tree trunk were two lions, one standing and one sitting. The elevated fruit stand comprised a long wicker type basket sitting on legs made up of crossed branches. A drawing of this design, taken from the George Jones majolica pattern book, is shown in Figure 57.

Another piece, that was to be exhibited by George Jones at the 1873 International Exhibition in Vienna, was registered on 4 March 1872 and given patent no. 260868 It was described as an 'elephant vase' for manufacture in earthenware, majolica or china. The vase, shown in Figure 67 (middle left), was so described because the container was held aloft by three legs moulded in the shape of elephant trunks.

Figure 58 shows a 'beer or covered claret jug'. This design was registered on 27 May 1872 and was given patent no. 262951. The jug was produced in two sizes, and although the example shown in Figure 58 has a pewter lid, the one that George Jones exhibited in Vienna, shown on the engraved picture Figure 67 (bottom middle), has what appears to be a fox moulded on a ceramic lid.

A novel design was registered on 29 May 1872 and was given patent no. 262990. It was described as a 'matchbox' and was in the shape of 'Noah's Ark'.

George Jones designed vases in all sorts of shapes and sizes. A design called a 'bamboo flower holder' was registered on 20 July 1872 and was given patent no. 264306. The main body of the vase was in the shape of a large diameter piece of bamboo with a small bamboo support to one side, both fixed to a base. The small support was attached to the main piece by bamboo leaves. On the same day as the bamboo flower holder was registered, a design called a 'lily leaf tray' was also registered. This design was given patent no. 264307. The tray was formed from a single lily leaf with a flower at one end, the stem of the leaf was bent under to form the foot of the tray.

On October 18, 1872, three designs were registered. The first design was given patent no. 267317 and was for the jug shown in Figure 73 (no. 3256). The second design was for a basket with moulded 'bamboo' handles and was given patent no. 267318. Examples of this design are shown in Figures 63 and 64. The third design was given patent no. 267319 and was for a piece that could be used as a butter pot, honey pot or a stilton cheese stand. An example of this was exhibited in Vienna and is shown in the engraved illustration, Figure 67 (middle left). Examples of this design are shown in Figures 65 and 66.

One of the first designs to be registered featuring the apple blossom moulded pattern, that George Jones is so well known for, was described as a 'wicker and apple blossom jug' and was registered on 25 February 1873. This design was given patent no. 270700, and is shown in Figure 73 (no. 3303). This illustration is taken from an early George Jones catalogue.

A very pretty design for a dessert service to be manufactured in either majolica or china was registered on 26 March 1873 and was given patent no. 271562. Figure 343 shows four china plates together with a compote; when it was produced in majolica the leaf was a single colour and examples painted in deep green have been seen.

The Vienna International Exhibition opened on May 1st 1873, but much preparation had to be done by the exhibitors well before the opening date. A report in *The Staffordshire Advertiser* dated 8 March 1873 stated :

Mr. George Jones of Trent Potteries, Stoke-upon-Trent is preparing a considerable number of articles in majolica and earthenware. His efforts have in a great degree been devoted to the former.

Many of the pieces they exhibited were for everyday use, such as flower pots, Stilton cheese dishes, butter dishes, dessert pieces and jugs. They also exhibited some unusual pieces such as a conservatory or hall elbow chair of a novel shape and jardinières with a dark blue ground and decorations of humming birds and Stephanotis. A pair of vases of circular form had paintings of tropical birds and foliage, the effect of the painting was enhanced by the contrast of two African supporters. The engraved illustrations shown in Figure 67 are taken from an article published in the *Art Journal* in 1873, which featured some of the wares exhibited by George Jones. The article accompanying these illustrations stated:

They are of much excellent in design, graceful accessories of the drawing room, the boudoir, and the conservatory; those we select are chiefly for the latter; but the better known works of the firm are elegant utilities for fruit and flowers.

On 21 June 1873 a report in *The Staffordshire Advertiser* quoted a somewhat romantic description from *The Times* newspaper correspondent:

Jones of Stoke-upon-Trent exhibits some exquisite painting which take one as much as any: especially one Eastern scene, with love birds fluttering about among the boughs in the foreground, reeds, palm trees and dreamy pelicans with blue water and white water lilies sleeping in dim shadows in the middle distance. The whole work and some others of this kind display wonderful breadth and softness.

George Jones was awarded a medal at the exhibition.

Although the company had been busy preparing the exhibits for this exhibition, the work of the design department continued. Majolica was very popular at this time and new designs were always needed to increase the range of items available for sale to an eager public.

On 29 April 1873, two designs were registered. The first design was given patent no. 272384 and was for a strawberry set complete with three ladles. An example of this design is shown in Figure 70. The second design was given patent no. 272385 and was for an 'apple blossom tea and breakfast set'. This set was made up of a butter dish, honey pot, sugar box, milk jug, coffee pot, tea pot and tray. The whole of the set is shown in the illustration, Figure 72 (no. 3304), and is taken from a George Jones registered design book held at the Wedgwood Museum, only part of which still exists.

All types of wares were produced by the pottery manufacturers to satisfy public demand. An item that thankfully is not in use today, but was common in Victorian and later times, was the spittoon. George Jones registered a design for such an item on 25 August 1873, patent no. 275514. It was made in the shape of a tortoise with the shell hollowed out to form a bowl. Various designs for spittoons were produced, but this was the only one to be patented.

An unusually shaped Stilton cheese dish was registered on 25 August 1873 and was given patent no. 275515. Called a 'Tower' Stilton dish, the dome was in the shape of a castle with a castellated rampart and creeping ivy up the wall.

The next four registered designs all featured pieces incorporating birds. Three of the designs were registered on 3 November 1873. Patent no. 277845 was given to a design for an oval tray with a bird at one end, see Figures 75 and 76. Patent no 277846 was given to a design for a tray with a bird at both ends, see Figures 77 and 78. Patent no. 277847 was given to design for a 'jam pot' with a bird on the lid. The bird, a blue tit, is similar to the birds on Figure 111. The fourth design to feature a bird was registered on 10 December 1873 and was given patent no. 279180, consisting of a tray moulded in the shape of a large leaf with a kingfisher perched at one end. Examples of this design are shown in Figures 79 and 80. George Jones majolica is renowned for its fine modelling, and this is shown to good effect in a piece that was registered on 27 December 1873 and given patent no. 279437. The design was for a game pie dish of oval form with branch handles. The body of the dish was moulded with rabbits

sitting among ferns and beneath ivy and oak foliage and the cover has a bird with seven chicks applied to it. As can be seen from Figure 81, the whole piece is stunningly beautiful. Variations of this pie dish were produced, one has a hare on the lid and another has a fox on the lid.

A design for a cruet set named 'Bird Carlton Set' was registered on 25 February 1874 and was given patent no. 280786. An illustration of this design is shown in Figure 72 (3377), and comes from a George Jones book of registered designs.

Sardine boxes were very popular and were produced with all types of moulded designs. The first design for a sardine box was registered on 28 March 1874, by George Jones, and was given patent no. 281429. This box had a duck finial on the cover and moulded fish on the side of the box, whilst the feet were moulded in the form of seaweed. An example of this design is shown in Figure 84. At the same time as this sardine box design was registered, patent no. 281430 was given to a design for a 'flower and card holder'. This flower holder was in the shape of a conical birds' nest with a bird on the side. The greetings or calling card was placed between the bird and the nest.

A design registered on 9 May 1874, and given patent no. 282218, was described as a 'flower stand'. This design was made up of four hollow pine cones held aloft on three curved legs.

In 1867, George Jones was reported as having made garden seats, but it was not until 9 May 1874 that he registered his first design. This design was given patent no. 282219 and was called a 'garden seat or pedestal'. Two examples of this design are shown in Figures 85 and 86.

A design for another 'flower stand' was registered on 23 May 1874 and was given patent no. 282567. It was formed from rolled leaves with a central trumpet like vase and four small vases splayed out from the base and was to be manufactured in either china or majolica.

The Victorians loved to fill their houses with large exotic plants and consequently flower pots or jardinières were needed to hide the ugly terracotta plant pots, thus making the arrangements more attractive. On 28 August 1874, George Jones had registered the design for such a flower pot which was given patent no. 284699. The body of the pot was shaped like a cauldron and the feet made to represent bent branches. The body was embossed with flowers and leaves and dotted about were insects moulded in high relief. The rim of the pot was moulded in the shape of a branch.

Also on 28 August 1874, patent no. 284700 was given to a design for a small tray with a butterfly, wings opened, moulded in full relief at one end. An example of this design is shown in Figure 87.

George Jones produced many different designs for oyster plates, but only one design was to be registered. This design was given patent no. 285281 and was registered on the 15 September 1874. This design incorporated an oyster shell in high relief in the centre and seaweed moulded in low relief from the centre to the edges of the plate.

As well as exotic plants the Victorians also liked to have cut flowers around their homes. Many different designs for vases were produced by George Jones. On 10 November 1874 a design was submitted for one such vase and was given patent no. 286794. The body was cylindrical in shape with a moulded basket weave effect and was fixed to a mounded base. To one side of the vase was a flower on a stem with leaves moulded in high relief. The flower reached halfway up the side of the vase.

Figure 88 shows a jug, the design of which was registered on 8 December 1874 and was given patent no. 287699.

George Jones produced many different designs for covered Stilton cheese stands. On 12 December 1874, patent no. 287776 was given to a design for the one shown in Figure 89. Variations of this design were produced with the bird knob replaced by a budding lily flower, as shown in Figure 90.

On 18 December 1874, patent no. 287982 was given to a design for an 'eight piece toilet set'. The theme of the set was butterflies and it consisted of a large tray, chamber sticks, candle sticks, small box with lid, a large and small vase, and a small tray with opened winged butterflies at each end. An example of the large tray from this set is shown in Figure 91.

On 9 February 1875 George Jones registered a design for a strawberry set which was given patent no. 289173. The set named 'Marie' is shown in Figure 111. Note the very attractive and well modelled blue tits — these birds were to feature on later pieces. When the strawberry set is complete, it should have three ladles.

A design for a 'spill case' was registered on 23 February 1875 and was given patent no. 289504. The body was cylindrical in shape with a butterfly moulded in high relief on the side and leafed branches trailing up the side in low relief.

Three designs were registered on 12 March 1875. The first design, which was given patent no. 289874, was for a jug with a pebble effect body and a handle moulded to form a flattened stem, the body had large leaves and flowers moulded in low relief. An example of this design is shown in Figure 92. The second design was for a 'sardine box and stand' and was given patent no. 289875. The cover of this sardine box had a pelican in high relief mounted on the top and flying pelicans in low relief on the sides. The box had fishes in low relief on the sides together with vertical pieces in the form of bamboo at each of its eight corner. An example of this design is shown in Figure 93. The third design was for another jug and was given patent no. 289876. This jug also had a pebble effect body but with a blue tit forming the handle. An example of this design is shown in Figure 94. The bird was similar to the ones on the strawberry set, Figure 111.

A 'jewel or trinket stand' design was registered on 7 May 1875, and was given patent no. 291109. The bowl was in the form of an open lily flower mounted on a stem with three lily pad feet and small lily flowers attached to each pad.

Another design for a flower pot complete with stand was registered on 31 May 1875 and was given patent no. 291568. This flower pot had a bark effect embossed body of cylindrical form with dog rose leaves and flowers in low relief and rose buds in high relief.

Four designs were submitted for registration on 26 June 1875 but only two were probably manufactured in majolica. The first design was given patent no. 292367 and was for a 'monkey tea and jug service'. This set was made up of a tea pot, a large jug and a small jug. The bodies of all three pieces were the same shape, with vertical sides and curved ends. The vertical sides were embossed with leaves, flowers and flower buds in low relief. The handles were formed in the shape of a monkey and the knob on the tea pot lid was a flower bud in high relief. The base of each piece was not flat, as is usual, but curved in form. Two examples of this design are shown in Figures 95 and 96. The second design was a jug, shape name 'Park', and was given patent no. 292370. This jug had a cylindrical body which splayed out at the base. The handle was in the form of a leaf stem with the leaves, in low relief moulded to the side of the jug at the top. It also had flowers in low relief on the main part of the body. An example of this design is shown in Figure 97.

The design for one of the most well known and loved pieces of majolica produced by George Jones was registered on the 13 September 1875 and was given patent no. 294434. This design was for a 'Mr Punch' bowl. An example illustrated in Figure 111, shows Mr. Punch lying on his back holding a bowl moulded in the shape of half an orange, with holly leaves and berries in low relief. Mr. Punch is dressed in his usual colourful attire. The piece was produced with the bowl in four different colours, cobalt blue, turquoise as in Figure 111, orange and yellow. Definitely a piece to be coveted.

On the same day as the design for the 'Mr Punch' bowl was registered, a design for another jug was registered and given patent no. 294435. This jug had tapered sides leading into a curved base on a small upstand (a small raised base or plinth). The handle was curved and the body embossed with flowers on stems in low relief.

Two designs were registered on 18 September 1875. The first design was given patent no. 294571 and was for a 'flower holder'. This vase was formed from an open crocus flower held up by the stem. The stem ran into a mounded base and a crocus bud attached to the stem formed an aperture between the stem and the bud to hold a card. The second design, which was given patent no. 294572, was for a 'flower stand'. This design consisted of three conical shaped vases with basket weave effect embossed bodies, one of the vases being held aloft by two curved branches. The bottom of the branches were held apart by a tray. The two remaining vases were mounted at the bottom of these branches.

On 5 November 1875 three designs were registered. Patent no. 295551 was given to a design for an 'Orange tray'. This design consisted of an irregular shaped tray with an orange shaped pot fixed in the centre. The orange was split in two with the top half forming the lid. The stalk of the orange was moulded to form the knob of the lid. An example of this design is shown in Figure 113. The second design (for a tray of circular form) was given patent no. 295552 and the third design (for a bread tray of rectangular form) was given patent no. 295553. An example of this design is shown in Figure 114. The embossed design on both these trays was the same — the raised outer edges being of basket weave effect and the centres having ears of wheat and leaves, together with various butterflies all in low relief.

A design for a 'flower vase' was registered on 12 November 1875 and was given patent no. 295908. The base of the vase was modelled in the shape of a tree trunk lying on its side, and the vase was in the shape of a crocus bud with iris type flowers embossed in low relief on its side.

The design for a piece described as a 'fruit tray' that was registered on 3 December 1875 and given patent no. 296531, incorporated parts of two other registered designs. The 'fruit tray' was made up of an irregularly shaped tray with an orange at one end, similar to patent no. 295551. The handle that joined the tray to the orange was in the shape of a monkey, like the one in patent no. 292367. A small ladle was included in the orange pot.

Three designs were registered on 22 January 1876, but only two were for manufacture in majolica. The first design, which was given patent no. 297809, was for an 'ash tray' with a dog moulded in high relief on one side and the second design, patent no. 297810, was for a similar ash tray but with a cat replacing the dog.

Another design for a strawberry dish was registered on 19 February 1876 and was given patent no. 298458. When it was manufactured it came with three ladles, but as can be seen from Figures 115 and 116, they did not always survive.

A design for a beautiful flower pot was registered by George Jones on 30 March 1876 and was given patent no. 299497. As can be seen from Figures 117 and 118, the modelling on this piece was superb.

A design for a very unusual tea pot was also registered on the same day, patent no. 299498. The main body of the tea pot was in the shape of a Chinese junk. The design showed the hull of the boat with a small wheelhouse in the centre. The spout was the raised bow and the handle was a similarly shaped stern. The lid was on top of the wheelhouse and the knob on the lid was in the shape of the top half of a man. I cannot imagine that it was too successful as a tea pot, but quite an amusing piece to have on display. An example of this design is shown in Figure 119.

On 10 May 1876 an 'ash tray or trinket tray' was registered and was given patent no. 300463. The tray was oval in shape with a bird with open wings perched at one end.

George Jones & Sons' sole agent in New York was W. B. Maddock. Under the heading 'Majolica', a reporter from the *Crockery & Glass Journal* of New York, made a visit to Mr. Maddock's showrooms, at 48-50 Park Place, New York: 'to inspect the new goods in the shape of Staffordshire fancy ware' which he had recently received in readiness for the fall (autumn) trade. A report of his visit appeared in the 31 August 1876 edition and stated :

George Jones & Sons - The display in this line is marked for the richness and variety of shape and decoration. The leading articles can be only mentioned. The first of these is a "centre" with two side pieces. The bowl of the main piece is in turquoise colour and is elaborately ornamented with leaves and scallop shells in bas relief. This rests on a base of bronze dolphins. From the midst of the bowl rises the main shaft, above the lower part of which, a short space above the bowl, are three scalloped shell receivers, between which are seated cupids. Above these, the shaft is in imitation of white spray coral. This supports a large bowl of shell pattern, from the midst of which springs a cupid holding a boquetier. The two side pieces are similar in design. This is a superb set. A diamond shaped jardinière is a gem also. The body of this is in Mazarine blue. The corners are banded with strips of bamboo and the sides decorated with cranes, flowers and plants. A snowy crane crowns the top. It is a quaint and beautiful piece of goods. There is also a host of vases, tea sets, plates, brackets, fruit stands and centre pieces of different designs. We noticed one tea set particularly. This is in cottage style and in turquoise decorated with raised basket work and sprays of roses. A superb pair of vases towering above the other specimens of majolica, made us break the "tenth commandment:" we coveted them. These were in the peculiar blue for which this factory is so noted, and modelled after the Palissy goods. Their sides were rich with ferns, shells and leaves, and nothing can be imagined more graceful than their whole appearance. Beside these there were any amount of bread-plates richly adorned with birds, butterflies and flowers. The garden seats decorated in the same manner were equally beautiful. The birds, etc. on these were in many instances of life size and life-like.

The Nankinese ware is similar in shape and design to the majolica. The body of this is white, however, while the ornaments, raised work, roses, vines, leaves, and flowers, are in mazarine blue shaded with white. The effect is novel and pleasing. This ware is very popular in England, and bids fair to become so in our own country.

The next two designs, for pieces to be manufactured in majolica, were registered on 12 September 1876. Patent no's. 303522 and 303523 were given to two versions of 'covered dish on stand'. The body of the dishes had an embossed basket weave effect. On the first design the cover had a fish knob and on the second design the cover had a lobster knob. An example of the second design is shown in Figure 122.

Another design to incorporate the basket weave effect was patent no. 304149. This design, for a sardine box and stand, was registered on 9 October 1876. The knob on the lid was made up of fishes moulded in high relief and the body of the box had a basket weave effect embossed design.

By the end of 1876, the number of designs being registered for wares to be produced in majolica, was beginning to diminish. The next design to be registered was on 25 January 1877 and was given patent no. 307239. This design was for a tea service in which all the pieces were drum shaped. The tea pot had a twin drumstick spout and all the handles on the pieces were in the form of buckled straps.

On 10 March 1877 a design for a 'strawberry and fruit basket', patent no. 308357, was registered. An example of this design is shown in Figure 123. This example is unusual in that it normally has strawberries at the base of the handle in place of the nut pods. This design was also produced with cup shape pieces either side of the handle to house a cream jug and sugar basin. A ladle completed the set. The

jug had a plaited rope-type handle, similar to patent no. 239474. An example of this design manufactured in bone china is shown in Figure 369.

The next design to be registered, for a piece to be produced in majolica, was for a 'caviar set'. This design was registered on 2 May 1877 and was given patent no. 309818. The 'caviar set' comprised of an oval tray incorporating seven moulded racks for biscuits or toast. Placed on the tray was a large barrel shaped pot with 'caviar' written on its side, together with two small bowls and a small pepper pot.

It was toward the end of 1877 when the next designs for majolica decorated pieces were submitted for registration. On 15 October 1877 two designs for 'flower pots' were registered. Patent no. 315271 was given to a large cauldron shaped pot with lilies in low relief on the main body and standing on four pad-type feet. Two examples of this design are shown in Figure 124. The second design, patent no. 315272, was for a flower pot of cylindrical form with a slightly bulbous base, the rim of the pot having angled faces that overhung the main body. The low relief pattern, on the main body of the pot, was of swans swimming among water lilies.

On 31 October 1877 another flower pot design was registered. Patent no. 315765 was given to a design for what was described in the George Jones pattern book as a 'ribbon jardiniere'. Our illustration, Figure 427, shows an example produced with *pâte-sur-pâte* panels but the jardiniere was also produced without the *pâte-sur-pâte* and in majolica colours. This jardiniere was also manufactured in bone china.

Another 'flower pot' design was registered on 1 February 1878 and was given patent no. 318239. This too was cauldron shaped, similar to patent no. 315271, but the four feet on this pot were moulded in the form of flower bulbs with flowers on stems rising out of the bulbs up the side of the pot in high relief. The rim was turned out and had leaves in low relief around it.

In November 1878, the company exhibited at the New Borough Hall, Stafford. A report in *The Pottery Gazette & Glass Trade Review* stated :

Messrs. George Jones & Sons of Stoke-upon-Trent, make a remarkably good display of majolica, which is scattered about the hall in several very effective groups of vases, tazzas, pedestals, wine coolers, dishes—in fact, things for use and ornament in the house, the garden, and the conservatory— in great variety. A pair of dishes in this ware painted by A. Gravier are very good.

Another report on the same exhibition, this time from *The Staffordshire Advertiser* of the 9 November 1878 stated:

we now have to speak of their majolica, of which there is a large collection. At the end of the room, under the gallery, is a pyramid of large works in the body composed of pedestals, tripods, vases and jardinieres. Two large pedestals with vases occupy recesses in another part of the room, and there is also a collection of centre pieces, painted slabs, and other objects, all marked by excellence of design, and rich and brilliant glaze on which, for its due effect, ware of this class so much depends.

In 1878, commenting on the types of wares produced by George Jones & Sons, Llewellynn Jewitt wrote in his book *Ceramic Art of Great Britain:*

The firm also makes a large and striking variety of articles in majolica, in which they successfully vie with most houses in the trade. In this they make both useful and ornamental articles, most of which are of a high order of art, being well modelled, carefully finished, and of a quality that will bear comparison with most others. Some of the productions exhibited at Paris in 1867 (when they obtained a medal), at London in 1871, and at Vienna in 1873, are shown [illustrated]. The imitation Palissy ware is highly successful. In vases, candelabra, centre and side pieces, flower shells, and numberless other articles, Messrs. Jones have produced many striking and good designs. Some of these are shown on the engravings; others, especially an aquatic centre-piece of four heights, in Cupids, shells, dolphins, and coral; a flower-pot, in which the magnolia forms the basis of ornamentation; and an ewer abundantly decorated with lizards, snakes, etc., are bold, good, and highly effective in design...

Another international exhibition was organised in 1879. This time it was held in Sydney, Australia. George Jones & Sons were well represented at this exhibition, where their stand was made up of porcelain and majolica wares. The majolica on display included vases on stands and majolica tiles. Comment was made in the judges' report that:

The large majolica vase and stand, and the other vases and stands, are of very high artistic design, fine colours and shades...
The majolica tiles are very good.

The company was awarded a 'First degree of Merit' for the vases and stands and a 'First degree of Merit Special' for its porcelain and majolica ware.

Between 1878 and 1882, only one design was registered by George Jones & Sons for a piece to be manufactured in majolica. This was on 8 June 1880, when a design for a moulded jug was registered and was given patent no. 350477.

On 11 April 1882 patent no. 379434 was given to a design for a strawberry dish for manufacture in china, majolica and ivory ware. An example of this design is shown in Figure 134, and an example with an ivory glaze is shown in Figure 370. This was the last design to be registered by George Jones & Sons for pieces to be manufactured in majolica. Majolica remained very popular, especially with the Americans, until the early 1880s when, due to over exposure in the market of poor quality products and crazy designs, the manufacturers were forced to produce more functional and sober designs. One of the major problems with majolica was glaze cracking due mainly to the low temperatures used to fire the majolica colours.

In the mid-1880s, a depression sent pottery sales plummeting and majolica was never to regain its popularity. Many of the majolica designs produced by George Jones & Sons were used again in the 1880s for the manufacturer of pieces with ivory coloured bodies and also in bone china. Toward the end of the 1880s many manufacturers, including George Jones & Sons, turned some of their manufacturing capacity, once used for the production of majolica, to the production of art pottery.

Figure 12. Design of border pattern registered on the 14 May 1862, patent no. 151672. *Courtesy of the Public Record Office*. Reference no.BT43/67.

Figure 13. Design of pattern registered on the 14 May 1862, patent no. 151673. *Courtesy of the Public Record Office*. Reference no.BT43/67.

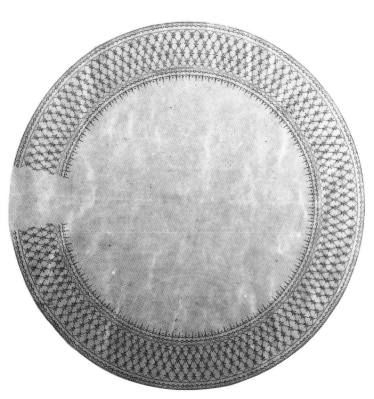

Figure 14. Design of border pattern registered on the 18 December 1862, patent no. 158498. *Courtesy of the Public Record Office*. Reference no. BT43/67.

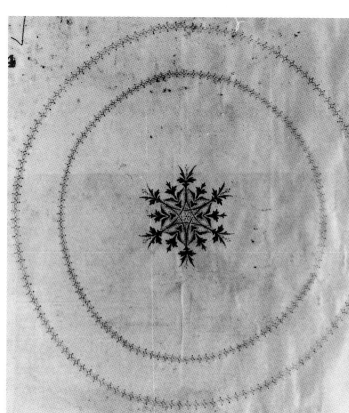

Figure 16. Design of pattern registered on the 6 November 1863, patent no. 168234. *Courtesy of the Public Record Office*. Reference no. BT43/67.

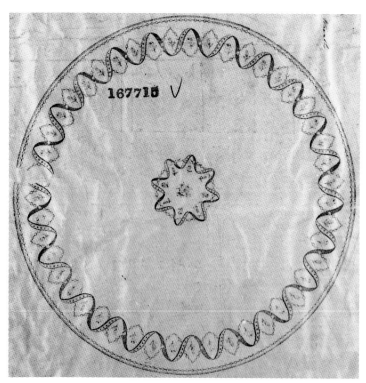

Figure 15. Design of pattern, name 'Country Wreath', registered on the 28 October 1863, patent no. 167715. *Courtesy of the Public Record Office*. Reference no. BT43/67.

Figure 17. Design of pattern registered on the 6 November 1863, patent no. 168235. *Courtesy of the Public Record Office*. Reference no. BT43/67.

Figure 18. Design of pattern, name 'Ionia', registered on the 10 May 1864, patent no. 174455. *Courtesy of the Public Record Office*. Reference no. BT43/67.

Figure 19. Design of pattern registered on the 10 May 1864, patent no. 174456. *Courtesy of the Public Record Office*. Reference no. BT43/67.

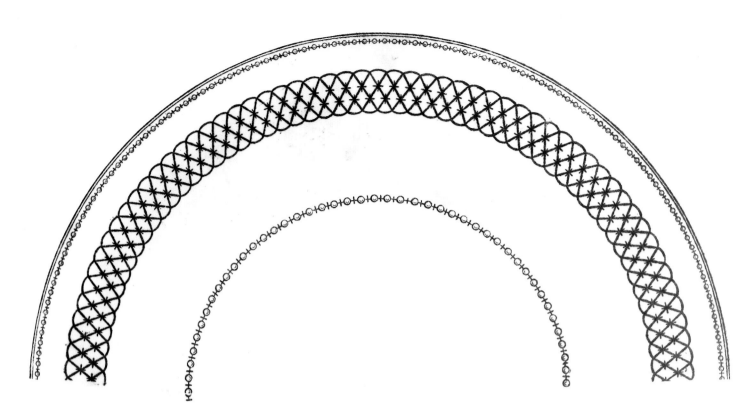

Figure 20. Design of pattern, name 'Stratford', registered on the 10 May 1864, patent no. 174457. *Courtesy of the Public Record Office*. Reference no. BT43/67.

Figure 21. Design of pattern, name 'Persian', registered on the 10 May 1864, patent no. 174458. *Courtesy of the Public Record Office*. Reference no. BT43/67.

Figure 22. An early comport, ca. 1864. Pattern registered design 10 May 1864, pattern name 'Persian', pattern no. 934, height 5". *Courtesy of Mike and Jenny Dunn.* £100-120; $165-200.

Figure 23. 'Persian' pattern on comport figure 22. *Courtesy of Mike and Jenny Dunn.*

Figure 24. Design of tureen, shape name 'Laurel', registered on the 20 August 1864, patent no. 177912. *Courtesy of the Public Record Office.* Reference no. BT43/67.

Figure 25. Design of pattern, name 'Coburg Chain', registered on the 4 October 1864, patent no. 179445. *Courtesy of the Public Record Office*. Reference no. BT43/67

Figure 26. Design of embossed pattern, name 'York', registered on the 10 November 1864, patent no. 181286. *Courtesy of the Public Record Office*. *Reference* no. BT43/68.

Figure 27. Design of embossed decoration registered on the 14 January 1865, patent no. 183331. *Courtesy of the Public Record Office*. Reference no. BT43/68.

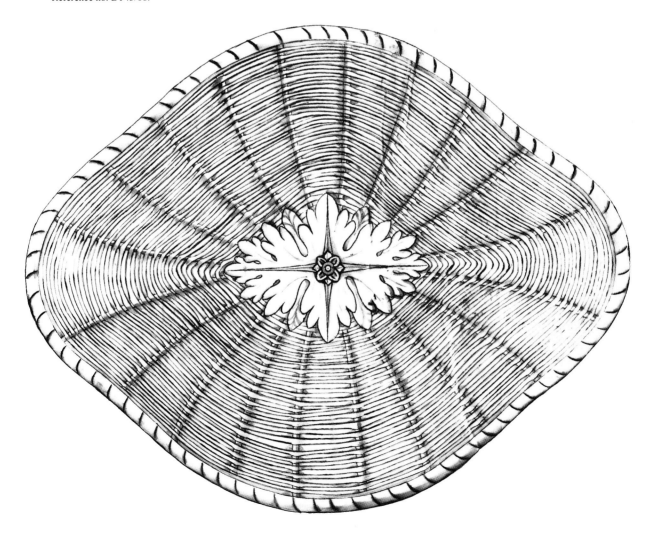

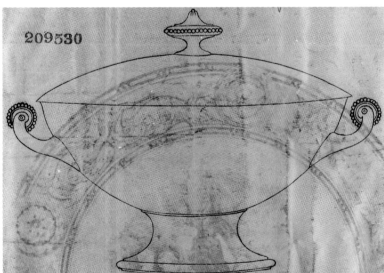

Figure 28. Design of tureen registered on the 25 July 1866, patent no. 199295. *Courtesy of the Public Record Office.* Reference no. BT43/68.

Figure 29. Design of tureen registered on the 12 July 1867, patent no. 209530. *Courtesy of the Public Record Office.* Reference no. BT43/68.

Figure 30. Design of tureen, shape name 'Grecian', registered on the 1 January 1869, patent no. 226051. *Courtesy of the Public Record Office.* Reference no. BT43/68.

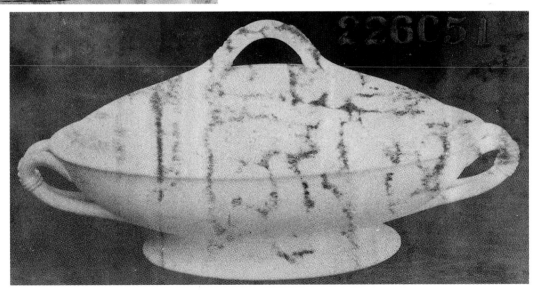

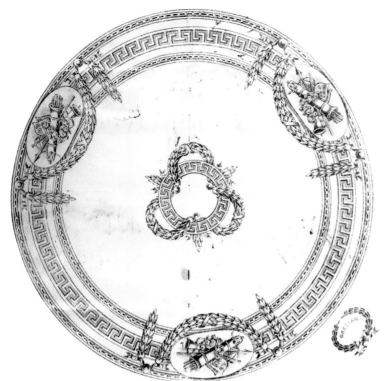

Figure 31. Design of pattern, name 'Grecian', registered on the 11 February 1869, patent no. 227277. *Courtesy of the Public Record Office.* Reference no. BT43/68.

Figure 33. Design of pattern, name 'Lotus', registered on the 1 December 1869, patent no. 236756. *Courtesy of the Public Record Office.* Reference no. BT43/68.

Figure 32. Design of pattern, name 'Crete', registered on the 9 March 1869, patent no. 227744. *Courtesy of the Public Record Office*, Reference no. BT43/68.

Figure 34. Earthenware sauce tureen and stand, ca. 1872. Registered design 30 May 1870, pattern no. 2350, length 9". £50-75; $80-120.

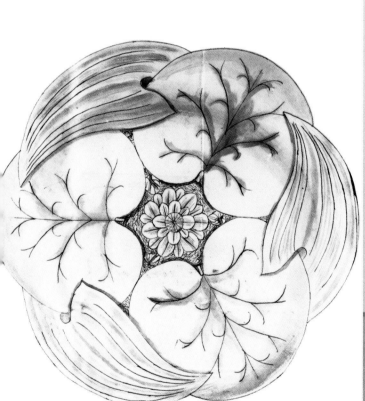

Figure 36. Design of dessert ware, shape name 'Lotus', registered on the 9 March 1869, patent no. 227743. *Courtesy of the Public Record Office.* Reference no. BT43/68.

Figure 35. Ewer, ca. 1869. Registered design 14 October 1868. *Courtesy of Britannia, Grays Antique Market, London.* £1600-1800; $2640-2970.

Figure 37. Dessert plate, ca. 1869. Registered design 9 March 1869, shape name 'Lotus'. *Courtesy of Britannia, Grays Antique Market, London.* £250-300; $415-495.

Figure 38. Tray, ca. 1869. Registered design 9 March 1869, diameter 4". *Courtesy of Britannia, Grays Antique Market, London.* £700-1000; $1155-1650.

Figure 39. Nut tray, ca. 1870. Registered design 22 December 1869, pattern no. 2513, length 10.5". *Courtesy of Britannia, Grays Antique Market, London.* £700-900; $1155-1485.

Figure 40. Bird trinket tray, ca. 1870.
Registered design 8 March 1870. *Courtesy of Britannia, Grays Antique Market, London.* £900-1100; $1485-1815.

Figure 41. Bird strawberry set, ca. 1870.
Registered design 8 March 1870, length 10.25". *Courtesy of Britannia, Grays Antique Market, London.* £2200-2400; $3630-3960.

Figure 42. Potted meat dish, cover and stand, ca. 1870. Length 7.5". *Courtesy of Britannia, Grays Antique Market, London.* £1600-1800; $2640-2970.

Figure 43. Game pie dish, ca. 1870. Pattern no. 1986, length 11.5". *Courtesy of Britannia, Grays Antique Market, London.* £1000-1200; $1650-1980.

Figure 44. Game pie dish, ca. 1870. Pattern no. 2716. *Courtesy of Britannia, Grays Antique Market, London.* £2500-2800; $4125-4620.

Figure 45. Jug, ca. 1870. Pattern no. 1806. *Courtesy of Britannia, Grays Antique Market, London.* £1000-1200; $1650-1980.

Figure 46. Part dessert service, ca. 1870. Pattern no. 2993, diameter 9".
Courtesy of Sotheby's, Sussex. £300-400; $495-600 each plate.

Figure 47. Potting pot with stand, ca. 1870.
Pattern no. 1473, length 7.5". £200-250;
$330-415.

Figure 48. Dessert plate, ca. 1870. Diameter 8.5". *Courtesy of Derek and
Shirley Weyman.* £175-225; $290-370.

Figure 49. Dessert plate, ca. 1870. Centre painted in the style of Antonin Boullemier, diameter 9.5". *Courtesy of Hanley Museum.* £600-800; $990-1320.

Figure 50. Bird tray, ca. 1871. Registered design 19 October 1870. *Courtesy of Britannia, Grays Antique Market, London.* £1300-1500; $2145-2475.

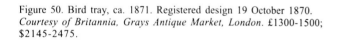

Figure 51. Bird biscuit box, ca. 1870. Registered design 19 October 1870, pattern no. 2544, height 7.5". *Courtesy of Britannia, Grays Antique Market, London.* £1600-1800; $2640-2970.

Figure 52. Print taken from an engraving showing George Jones majolica wares exhibited at the International Exhibition, London, 1871. Print taken from the *Art Journal Catalogue of the International Exhibition of 1871*.

Figure 53. Fruit centre piece, ca. 1872. Registered design 23 December 1871. *Courtesy of Britannia, Grays Antique Market, London.* £3100-3300; $5115-5445.

Figure 55. Camel fruit and flower holder, ca. 1872. Registered design 23 December 1871, height 9.25". *Courtesy of Britannia, Grays Antique Market, London.* £3100-3400; $5115-5610.

Figure 54. Enlargement showing the deer moulded around the stem of Figure 53.

Figure 56. Fruit compote, ca. 1872. Registered design 20 January 1872, pattern no. 3205, height 5.75". *Courtesy of Britannia, Grays Antique Market, London.* £2800-3100; $4620-5115.

Figure 57. Drawing of an elevated fruit stand, ca. 1872. Registered design 16 February 1872, pattern no. 3216, length 9.5". Illustration from the George Jones majolica pattern book. *Courtesy of Trustees of the Wedgwood Museum, Barlaston.* £3000-3200; $4950-5280.

Figure 59. Game pie dish, ca. 1872. Pattern no. 2296, length 10.5". *Courtesy of Britannia, Grays Antique Market, London.* £2700-3100; $4455-5115.

Figure 58. Covered claret or beer jug, ca. 1872. Registered design 27 May 1872, pattern no. 3228, height 10". £2500-2700; $4125-4455.

Figure 60. Dessert plate, ca. 1872. Diameter 9.5". *Courtesy of Britannia, Grays Antique Market, London.* £400-500; $660-825.

Figure 61. Fruit compote, ca. 1872. Height 10". *Courtesy of Britannia, Grays Antique Market, London.* £2800-3100; $4620-5115.

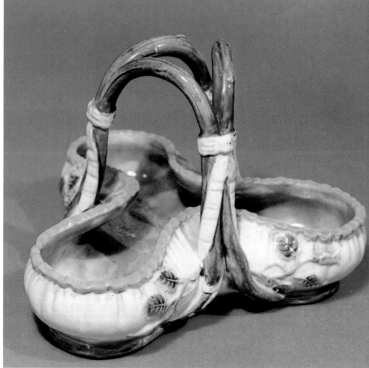

Figure 63. Rose basket, ca. 1872. Registered design 18 October 1872, height 6.75". *Courtesy of Britannia, Grays Antique Market, London.* £600-800; $990-1320.

Figure 62. Fruit compote, ca. 1872. *Courtesy of Britannia, Grays Antique Market, London.* £3100-3300; $5115-5445.

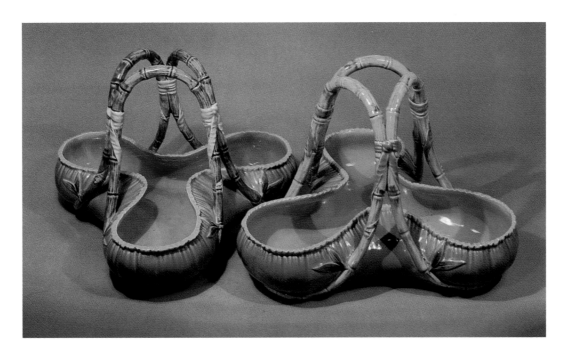

Figure 64. Pair of rose baskets, ca. 1872. Registered design 18 October 1872, height 6.75". Courtesy *of Britannia, Grays Antique Market, London.* £600-800; $990-1320 each.

Figure 66. Four butter pots, honey pots or Stilton cheese stands and covers, ca. 1872. Registered design 18 October 1872, large yellow pot pattern no. 3249, height 13.5", small white pot pattern no. 3277, height 7.5". *Courtesy of Sotheby's, Inc., New York.* Large pots £3300-3800; $5445-6270, small pots £2500-2800; $4125-4620.

Figure 65. Butter pots, honey pots or Stilton cheese stand and cover, ca. 1872. Registered design 18 October 1872, height 13.5". Courtesy *of Britannia, Grays Antique Market, London.* £3300-3800; $5445-6270.

Figure 67. Prints taken from engravings showing George Jones wares exhibited at the International Exhibition, Vienna, 1873. From the *Art Journal*, September 1873.

Figure 68. Jardinière, ca. 1873. Height 10". *Courtesy of Britannia, Grays Antique Market, London.* £1700-2200; $2805-3630.

Figure 70. Strawberry set, ca. 1873. Registered design 29 April 1873, pattern no. 3300, length 14.625". *Courtesy of Hanley Museum.* £2500-2700; $4125-4455.

Figure 69. Dog bowl, ca. 1873. Pattern no. 1842, diameter 10". *Courtesy of Britannia, Grays Antique Market, London.* £400-500; $660-825.

Figure 71. Illustrations from George Jones trade catalogue, ca. 1873. *Courtesy of Trustees of the Wedgwood Museum, Barlaston.*

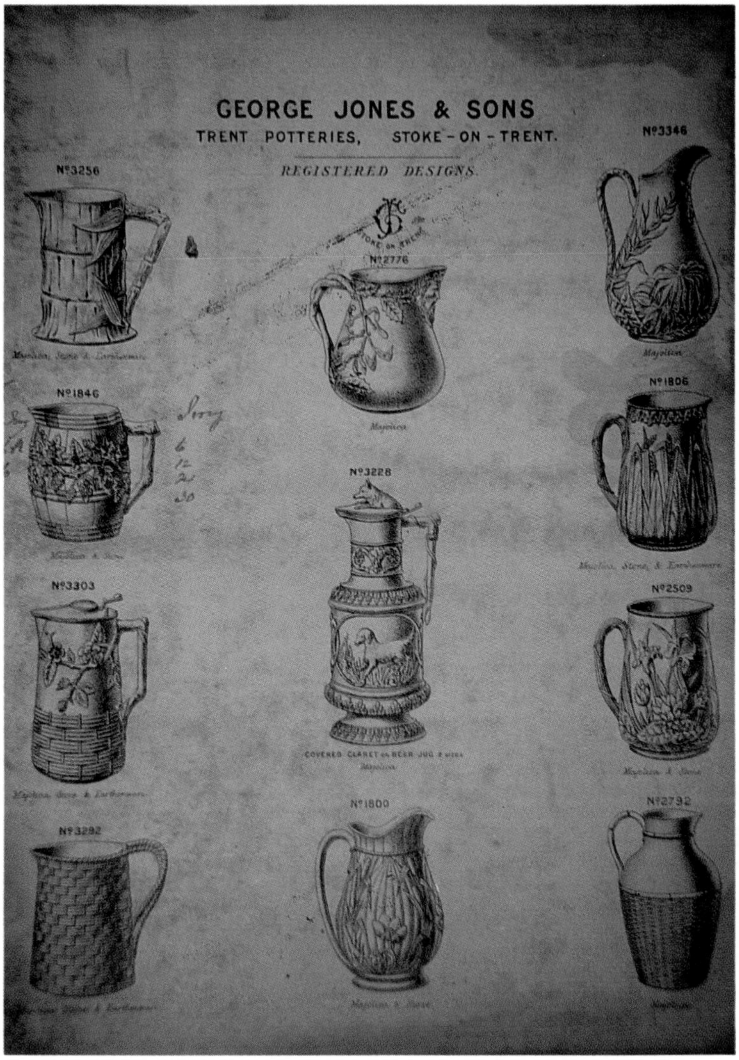

Figure 73. Illustrations from George Jones trade catalogue, ca. 1873. *Courtesy of Trustees of the Wedgwood Museum, Barlaston.*

Figure 72. Illustrations from George Jones trade catalogue, ca. 1873. *Courtesy of Trustees of the Wedgwood Museum, Barlaston.*

Figure 74. Strawberry dish, ca. 1873. Length 14.5". *Courtesy of Britannia, Grays Antique Market, London.* £1300-1500; $2145-2475.

Figure 75. Tray with blackbird, ca. 1874. Registered design 3 November 1873, length 10". *Courtesy of Britannia, Grays Antique Market, London.* £900-1100; $1485-1815.

Figure 76. Tray with thrush, ca. 1874. Registered design 3 November 1873, pattern no. 2556, diameter 10". *Courtesy of Derek and Shirley Weyman.* £900-1100; $1485-1815.

Figure 77. Tray, ca. 1873. Registered design 3 November 1873, pattern no. 3349, length 15.5". *Courtesy of Britannia, Grays Antique Market, London.* £1800-2000; $2970-3300.

Figure 78. Enlargement of bird on Figure 77.

Figure 79. Tray with kingfisher, ca. 1874. Registered design 10 December 1873, length 12". *Courtesy of Britannia, Grays Antique Market, London.* £2700-3100; $4455-5115.

Figure 80. Enlargement of kingfisher in Figure 79.

Figure 81. Game pie dish, ca. 1874. Registered design 27 December 1873, pattern no. 3371, length 14.25". *Courtesy of Sotheby's Inc., New York.* £5000-7000; $8250-11,545.

Figure 82. Game pie dish, ca. 1874. Registered design 27 December 1873, length 14.25". *Courtesy of Britannia, Grays Antique Market, London.* £3300-3800; $5445-6270.

Figure 83. Game pie dish, ca. 1874. Registered design 27 December 1873, length 14.25". *Courtesy of Britannia, Grays Antique Market, London.* £3300-3800; $5445-6270.

Figure 84. Sardine dish, ca. 1874. Registered design 28 March 1874, pattern no. 3383, length 6". *Courtesy of Britannia, Grays Antique Market, London.* £900-1100; $1485-1815.

Figure 85. Garden seat, ca. 1874. Registered design 9 May 1874, height 17.5". *Courtesy of Sotheby's, Sussex.* £3300-3800; $5445-6270.

Figure 86. Garden seat or pedestal, ca. 1874. Registered design 9 May 1874, height 19". *Courtesy of Britannia, Grays Antique Market, London.* £3300-3800; $5445-6270.

Figure 88. Stork jug, ca. 1875. Registered design 8 December 1874, pattern no. 3409, height 8". £2200-2500; $3630-4125.

Figure 87. Tray, ca. 1874. Registered design 28 August 1874. *Courtesy of Britannia, Grays Antique Market, London.* £3100-3300; $5115-5445.

Figure 89. Stilton cheese bell, ca. 1875, note the rare kingfisher knob. Registered design 12 December 1874. *Courtesy of Britannia, Grays Antique Market, London.* £4200-4400; $6930-7260.

Figure 90. Two Stilton cheese bells, ca. 1874. Registered design 12 December 1874, height 11.75". *Courtesy of Britannia, Grays Antique Market, London.* £4000-4200; $6600-6930.

Figure 91. Oval dressing table tray, ca. 1875. Part of an eight piece toilet set, registered design 18 December 1874, length 11.25". *Courtesy of Britannia, Grays Antique Market, London.* £1600-2000; $2640-3300.

Figure 92. Jug with pewter lid, ca. 1875. Registered design 12 March 1875, height 5.5". *Courtesy of Britannia, Grays Antique Market, London.* £1100-1300; $1815-2145.

Figure 93. Sardine box with stand, ca. 1875. Registered design 12 March 1875, length 5.5". *Courtesy of Britannia, Grays Antique Market, London.* £1800-2000; $2970-3300.

Figure 95. Jug and basin from 'Monkey' tea service, ca. 1875. Registered design 26 June 1875. *Courtesy of Britannia, Grays Antique Market, London.* £400-500; $660-825.

Figure 94. Jug, ca. 1875. Registered design 12 March 1875. *Courtesy of Britannia, Grays Antique Market, London.* £500-700; $825-1155.

Figure 96. 'Monkey' tea set with tray, ca. 1875. Registered design 26 June 1875, tea pot pattern no. 3450, tea set pattern no. 3465, tray length 18.25". *Courtesy of Sotheby's Inc., New York.* £5000-7000; $8250-11,545.

Figure 97. Jug, ca. 1875. Registered design 26 June 1875, shape name 'Park'. *Courtesy of Britannia, Grays Antique Market, London.* £700-900; $1155-1485.

Figure 99. Underside of compote Figure 98.

Figure 98. Compote, ca. 1875. Pattern no. 3263. *Courtesy of Britannia, Grays Antique Market, London.* £400-600; $660-990.

Figure 100. 'Neptune with shell' centre piece, ca. 1875. Height 15.875". *Courtesy of Britannia, Grays Antique Market, London.* £2800-3100; $4620-5115.

Figure 102. Compote, ca. 1875. Pattern no. 3403, height 3.25". £400-500; $660-825.

Figure 101. Enlargement of Neptune on Figure 100.

Figure 103. Cat ash tray, ca. 1875. *Courtesy of Britannia, Grays Antique Market, London.* £400-600; $660-990.

Figure 104. Compote, ca. 1875. *Courtesy of Britannia, Grays Antique Market, London.* £2400-2700; $3960-4455.

Figure 105. Compote, ca. 1875. *Courtesy of Britannia, Grays Antique Market, London.* £2400-2700; $3960-4455.

Figure 107. Sardine dish and cover, ca. 1875. *Courtesy of Britannia, Grays Antique Market, London.* £700-900; $1155-1485.

Figure 106. Pâté pot, ca. 1875. *Courtesy of Britannia, Grays Antique Market, London.* £1300-1500; $2145-2475.

Figure 108. Coffee cup and saucer, ca. 1875. Pattern no. 3519, saucer diameter 5". *Courtesy of Britannia, Grays Antique Market, London.* £150-200; $250-330.

Figure 109. Selection of sardine boxes, ca. 1875. *Courtesy of Sotheby's Inc., New York.* £2000-2500; $3300-4125 each.

Figure 110. A selection of majolica ware, including a covered bowl with stand on the top right, a registered design dating to 3 November 1873. The Registered design was for the bird on the lid. *Courtesy of Sotheby's Inc., New York.* £1500-1800; $2475-2970.

Figure 112. Fruit centre piece, ca. 1875. *Courtesy of Britannia, Grays Antique Market, London.* £3000-3300; $4950-5445.

Figure 111. Strawberry set, ca. 1875. Registered design 9 February 1875, shape name 'Marie', pattern no. 3423, length 15". 'Mr Punch' bowl, ca. 1875. Registered design 13 September 1875, pattern no. 3468, diameter 11". *Courtesy of Phillips of Knowle.* Strawberry set £3500-3800, 'Mr Punch' bowl £4500-4800; $7420-7920.

Figure 113. Orange tray, ca. 1876. Registered design 5 November 1875. *Courtesy of Britannia, Grays Antique Market, London.* £2200-2600; $3630-4290.

Figure 114. Bread tray, ca. 1875. Registered design 5 November 1875, pattern no. 3470, length 13". *Courtesy of Britannia, Grays Antique Market, London.* £800-1000; $1320-1650.

Figure 116. Strawberry dish, ca. 1876. Registered design 19 February 1876, length 10.5". *Courtesy of Britannia, Grays Antique Market, London.* £1100-1300; $1815-2145.

Figure 115. Strawberry dish, ca. 1876. Registered design 19 February 1876, length 10.5". *Courtesy of Britannia, Grays Antique Market, London.* £1100-1300; $1815-2145.

Figure 117. Jardinière, ca. 1876. Registered design 30 March 1876. *Courtesy of Britannia, Grays Antique Market, London.* £2500-3000; $4125-4950.

Figure 119. Tea pot, ca. 1876. Registered design 30 March 1876. *Courtesy of Britannia, Grays Antique Market, London.* £4200-4400; $6930-7260.

Figure 118. Jardinière, ca. 1876. Registered design 30 March 1876. *Courtesy of Britannia, Grays Antique Market, London.* £2500-3000; $4125-4950.

Figure 120. Selection of George Jones majolica. Jug, ca. 1873, registered design 25 February 1873. Cheese stand and cover, ca. 1872. Game pie dish, ca. 1874, registered design 27 December 1873. Strawberry dish, ca. 1876, registered design 19 February 1876. Jardinière, ca. 1876. Vase, ca. 1876. Dish, ca. 1875. *Courtesy of Britannia, Grays Antique Market, London.*

Figure 122. Sardine dish, ca. 1876. Registered design 12 September 1876, pattern no. 3547, length 9.25". *Courtesy of Britannia, Grays Antique Market, London.* £1400-1600; $2310-2640.

Figure 121. Vase, ca. 1876. *Courtesy of Britannia, Grays Antique Market, London.* £2500-2800; $4125-4620.

Figure 123. Strawberry and fruit basket, ca. 1877. Registered design 10 March 1877, length 14.25". This piece is unusual in that it has hazel nut pods at the base of the handle instead of the usual strawberries. £1500-1700; $2475-2805.

Figure 124. A pair of jardinières, ca. 1877. Registered design 15 October 1877. *Courtesy of Britannia, Grays Antique Market, London.* £2500-2800; $4125-4620 each.

Figure 125. From left to right, Calla lily garden seat, ca. 1880, height 17.75". Jardinière, ca. 1875, pattern no. 3568, height 15". Garden seat, ca. 1875, height 17.875". *Courtesy of Sotheby's Inc., New York.* Garden seats £3300-3800; $5445-6270 each, jardinière £2000-2500; $3300-4125.

Figure 126. Drawing of a jug from the George Jones majolica pattern book. Registered design 30 January 1878, pattern no. 3576, height 7.5". *Courtesy Trustees of the Wedgwood Museum, Barlaston.*

Figure 127. Jug, ca. 1880. Height 7.125". *Courtesy of Britannia, Grays Antique Market, London.* £700-1000; $1155-1650.

Figure 129. Cheese bell, ca. 1880. Pattern no. 5253, diameter 10.25". *Courtesy of Britannia, Grays Antique Market, London.* £2700-3100; $4455-5115.

Figure 128. Cheese bell, ca. 1880. Height 10". *Courtesy of Britannia, Grays Antique Market, London.* £2000-2200; $3300-3630.

Figure 131. Jardinière, ca. 1880. Height 9.125". *Courtesy of Britannia, Grays Antique Market, London.* £2000-2200; $3300-3630.

Figure 132. Conservatory centrepiece (incomplete), ca. 1880. Pattern no. 5202, height 45". When complete, it had jardinière Figure 130 on each side of the base. *Courtesy of Britannia, Grays Antique Market, London.* £2400-2700; $3960-4455.

Figure 130. Jardinière, ca. 1880. *Courtesy of Britannia, Grays Antique Market, London.* £1600-1800; $2640-2970.

Figure 133. Majolica plaque, ca. 1880. Initialled F.R.J. (Francis Ralph Jones). A family piece, reputed to have been displayed at the Chicago exhibition of 1893. *Courtesy of Betty Roper.*

Figure 135. Jardinière, ca. 1884. Pattern no. 5281, height 12.75". *Courtesy of Britannia, Grays Antique Market, London.* £2500-2800; $4125-4620.

Figure 134. Strawberry dish, ca. 1882. Registered design 11 April 1882, length 13". *Courtesy of Britannia, Grays Antique Market, London.* £2700-3100; $4455-5115.

Chapter 3 Underglaze blue and white transfer-printed ware 1862-1930s

Underglaze blue and white transfer printed wares were first produced by the English porcelain manufacturers in the mid eighteenth century, but it was not until toward the end of the eighteenth century that this type of decoration appeared on earthenware. Josiah Spode of Stoke is acknowledged as having perfected the process whereby blue and white transfer patterns could be applied to earthenware bodies. The early wares had all-over deep blue printed patterns, but by 1830, lighter colours with more open designs were becoming popular.

By the time George Jones began his pottery manufacturing business in 1862, the popularity of blue and white printed wares had declined. The first blue and white pieces produced by the company were from old William Adams copper plate engravings. These were purchased by George Jones himself at an auction of William Adams copper plate engravings when this factory became bankrupt in 1861. The auction took place on the 10 April 1861, before George Jones had found a vacant factory in which to open his pottery business. At this auction (held at the auction rooms of Mr. W. Walton of Stoke), almost five tons of copper plate engravings belonging to Messrs. William Adams of Bridge Works, Stoke, were sold. A list of some of the more popular patterns were named in the advertisement that appeared in *The Staffordshire Advertiser* of the 6 April 1861. They were:

Balmoral, Tonquin, Casino, Oriental, Jeddo, Damascus, Abbey Wreath, Birds Eye, Seaweed, Net, Berlin Flowers, Windsor, Persian, Serene (sic - Cyrene), Geneva, Milan, Athens, Lasso, Clermont, Berlin Groups, Chusan, Cabbage, Spanish Festival, Pekin, Columbia, Florence, Spanish Borders, Willow, etc.

From this list, it is known that George Jones purchased Serene (Cyrene), Casino, Damascus, Spanish Festivities and Abbey Wreath. He also purchased the engravings of other patterns, namely Palestine, Genoa, Woodlands and possibly Willow.

Examples of some of George Jones's early blue and white pieces are illustrated. The small tea plate and large meat plate, Figures 137 and 138, are decorated with the 'Cyrene' pattern, and the dinner plate, Figure 136, is decorated with the 'Casino' pattern. These examples are impressed 'GJ, Stone China, Stoke-on-Trent'. These two patterns were originally produced by William Adams in the period 1830-40, when this type of design first became popular. Another pattern, shown in Figure 139, was used by George Jones in the late 1860s, this has a back stamp with the name 'Sistova' incorporated within it. Whether this was an old William Adams pattern is not known.

George Jones produced this type of decorated ware on earthenware bodies until the late 1860s. It was to be another twenty-five years (the mid-1890s) before the factory recommenced the manufacture of underglaze blue and white wares, although an example is shown in Figure 316 of a willow-type pattern produced on a bone china dinner plate in 1880.

An example of a pattern named 'Medici' is shown on a plate, Figure 140, produced by George Jones & Sons Ltd. in 1895. This pattern was originally produced by Mellor, Venables & Co. of Burslem, and was from a design registered by them at the Patent Office, London, on the 5 July 1847. It is not known how George Jones came to be in possession of this pattern, as Mellor, Venables & Co. ceased production in 1851. The backstamp used by George Jones & Sons Ltd. is the original backstamp but with G.J. replacing the M.V. & Co.

In the late 1890s, there was a resurgence in the popularity of underglaze blue and white patterns produced on earthenware, similar to those manufactured a hundred years earlier, and many Staffordshire pottery manufacturers, including George Jones & Sons Ltd., recommenced production.

In 1898, the company produced the plate shown in Figure 141. The pattern is named 'Pastoral' and, interestingly, the backstamp bears the number 1790 beneath the pattern name which is similar to the 'Abbey' backstamp. It is uncertain whether this too was an old William Adams pattern.

Without a doubt, the most popular blue and white pattern produced by George Jones & Sons Ltd. was the 'Abbey' pattern. It is assumed that the first 'Abbey' printed wares were produced in 1901, as the example shown in Figure 210 of a rectangular planter has the words 'reprinted 1901' printed beneath the 'Abbey' backstamp. The purchase of the 'Abbey' copper plate engravings by George Jones is confirmed in an article published in the October 1923 edition of *The Pottery Gazette & Glass Trade Review*. The article states :

It is a wonderful old pattern, and it has quite a history. It dates back, as a matter of fact, to the first few years of the nineteenth century, and the engravings were bought, somewhere about 65 years ago, by Mr. George Jones, the founder of the Crescent Potteries, from the firm of Adams, who at that time had a factory in Church St., Stoke.

The 'Abbey' pattern, when produced by William Adams, was originally called 'Abbey Wreath'. If one looks at the border, it appears to portray a series of abbey ruins enclosed within a wreath like surround. The article continues:

It is almost unnecessary to remind our readers what wonderfully fine engravings in rustic and pastoral designs were being produced about the time of which we write. It was extremely fortunate, therefore, for the proprietors of the Crescent Potteries that when the craze commenced some fifteen years or more ago for reproductions of old-fashioned pottery to suit the severer type of furnishings now in full swing, they were able to go to their own engraving store and put their hands upon a whole series of copper plates of this particular "Abbey" pattern, and make use of them for a full suite of general earthenware. Executed in a rich cobalt blue, the 'Abbey' pattern is a sure seller everywhere.

Although George Jones's 'Abbey' pattern was first produced in 1901, it was not until June 1915 that any mention was made in *The Pottery Gazette* regarding its production. An article describing the exhibits at the Board of Trade Exhibition held in London in March 1915 stated:

A feature of their stand was a full range of an antique all-over cobalt printed decoration, known as the 'Old English Abbey'. The engravings from which this pattern is supplied date back to 1790, but they have been revived to wonderfully good effect in the present age of antiques.

There is an article describing the new London showrooms of George Jones & Sons Ltd. in the September 1919 edition of *The Pottery Gazette & Glass Trade Review*. Accompanying this article is a photograph showing part of the showrooms. In the photograph, Figure 8, on the left, is a display of 'Abbey' ware, including a pedestal with pot, similar to the one shown in Figure 205.

The first advertisement placed in *The Pottery Gazette & Glass Trade Review* by George Jones & Sons Ltd. for 'Abbey' was in December 1923 when items of tea ware were featured. Later advertisements state that the 'Abbey' pattern was produced on dinner, tea, toilet and miscellaneous goods.

In the mid-1920s 'Abbey' plates were produced to be given as gifts. One such plate, shown in Figures 208 and 209, was made in 1926 for the wine and spirit merchant James Norris Ltd. of Burslem & Hanley for Christmas of that year. An advertisement placed in the *Sentinel* newspaper by James Norris (Burslem) Ltd., on Monday 20 December 1926 stated :

> This is a Specimen of our Christmas Presentation Plate, which will be given to every Customer Purchasing a Bottle of Wine or Spirits (Half bottle excepted), on Monday, Tuesday, Wednesday, Thursday & Friday, December 20th, 21st, 22nd, 23rd & 24th...

Two of the most well known pieces of 'Abbey' produced were the single and double 'Shredded Wheat Dishes'. These were manufactured from the early 1930s to around 1940. Coupons from Shredded Wheat breakfast cereal packets were collected and exchanged for the dishes. Other promotions, on packets of tea and cigarette packets, also invited the purchaser to collect coupons to be exchanged for pieces of 'Abbey' tea ware and dinner ware. It was possible, if enough coupons were collected, to build up complete tea and dinner services.

Some pieces were produced with an 'Abbey' border but with different pictures in the centre. A bread and butter plate is known to exist that has an 'Abbey' border and a centre print of Alnwick Castle, Northumberland. A vase has been seen with the large 'Abbey' print replaced by a small print of The Crescent, Filey. Other pieces were produced with centres showing a coach and horses outside an old blacksmith's shop. The two examples, shown in Figure 216, 217 and 218, are an octagonal tea plate, produced in 1936, with the coach and horse scene in the centre, and a combined ash tray, match box holder and cigarette box, the lid of which has the coach and horse picture on it. The inscription below the picture states:

> King William IV's Coach
> was used by Queen Adelaide an Aunt of
> Queen Victoria later as the state coach of the
> Judges of Assizes at Carlisle 75 years ago

As well as being produced in cobalt blue, pieces of 'Abbey' were also produced in underglaze red and black, believed to be for the American market.

'Abbey' patterned wares were produced until the Second World War when, due to government restrictions, the production of all coloured wares for the home market was prohibited; although production of coloured wares for the overseas markets was still allowed. No examples of 'Abbey' ware produced after 1940 have, as yet, been found.

Although the 'Abbey' pattern was by far the most popular of George Jones & Sons Ltd.'s underglaze blue and white patterns (being manufactured continuously for about 40 years), other blue and white patterns were also produced during the same period. The copper plate engravings for some of these patterns had been purchased when other local pottery manufacturers ceased production.

In 1902, at the sale of copper plate engravings belonging to The Old Hall Pottery, Hanley, George Jones & Sons Ltd. bought the engravings for the pattern named 'Farm'. An example of this pattern is shown in Figure 220 on a plate manufactured in 1907. At this same auction they also purchased the engravings for the pattern named 'Campanula'.

The plate, Figure 219, was produced by George Jones & Sons Ltd. in 1904, the pattern name being 'Lasso'. Although the engravings for a William Adams pattern of the same name were sold at the auction in 1861, the pattern illustrated here is not the same. An example of this pattern is shown in Williams & Weber's book, *Staffordshire II, Romantic Transfer Patterns*, and is said to be marked W. Bourne, Longton. Where George Jones acquired their pattern from, however, is uncertain.

Another set of engravings, for a pattern named 'Toro', purchased by the company, had originally belonged to Charles Allerton & Son. The example, Figure 221, is of a dinner plate produced in 1908.

A small dish manufactured by George Jones & Sons in 1912 is shown in Figure 222. There is no pattern name backstamp, but an example of this pattern has been seen on a piece produced by the Dutch pottery manufacturer Petrus Regout of Maastricht. Their pattern was named 'Indian Traffic'. How it came to be produced by both manufacturers is unclear. Interestingly Petrus Regout also produced the 'Abbey' pattern on some of his wares.

Another of the William Adams patterns bought at the bankruptcy auction by George Jones was 'Spanish Festivities'. A large meat plate manufactured in 1916 is shown in Figure 223.

Figure 521 is from a George Jones & Sons Ltd. catalogue dated 1924. It shows examples of three William Adams patterns that were available on earthenware bodies, 'Palestine', 'Cyrene' and 'Casino'. The fourth printed pattern shown was named 'Rhine'. The copper plate engravings for this pattern were purchased by George Jones & Sons Ltd. at an auction of engravings belonging to Brownfields Ltd. of Cobridge when that factory ceased production in 1900. At the same auction they also purchased the copper plate engravings for the patterns named 'Bismarck', 'Linda' and 'Pompeii'.

The 'Willow' pattern produced by George Jones & Sons Ltd. could possibly be from the copper plate engravings that were sold in William Adams' auction in 1861. Illustrated in Figure 225 is a page from a 1924 George Jones trade catalogue showing 'Willow' patterned tableware. Figure 224 shows a 'Willow' patterned compote. This shape of compote was originally produced in the mid-1880s.

An interesting little plate with a 'Willow' pattern centre was manufactured by George Jones & Sons Ltd. advertising "Goodall's Yorkshire Relish". This was a sauce that, it is believed, had been invented by the wife of Robert Goodall, a retail chemist from Leeds, in the late nineteenth century.

'Singan' was the name of another underglaze blue and white pattern produced by the company. This was a 'Willow' type pattern — an example of which has been seen on a small plate manufactured by George Jones in 1915. An auction was held on the 16 and 17 January 1861 to sell the moulds and copper plate engravings belonging to Thomas Goodfellow of the Phoenix Pottery, Tunstall. Included in the copper plate engraved patterns, at this sale, was one named 'Singan'. Was this the same pattern and did George Jones purchase it at this auction, bearing in mind that this was only three months before the William Adams auction?

Although the 'Cyrene' pattern was first used by George Jones in the 1860s and again in the early 1920s (as illustrated in the 1924 catalogue), it was not until April 1925, in an article published in *The Pottery Gazette & Glass Trade Review* describing the latest patterns produced by George Jones & Sons Ltd., that any mention had been made of the history of this pattern. An extract from the article reads:

> In searching amongst some of the old engravings of the firm, some copper-plate engravings have been found of a remarkably fine old Oriental landscape pattern, known as the 'Cyrene'. These engravings, the firm has every confidence in believing, must have formed part of the series which was purchased by Mr. George Jones - the originator of the firm - upon taking possession of what was known as the Bridge Bank Works, Stoke.

Commenting on the 'Cyrene' and 'Abbey' patterns, the article continues:

> George Jones & Sons Ltd., are certainly fortunate in having had as their founder a man such as Mr. George Jones, who had a sufficiently keen perception of the value of these old English engravings to purchase them when Mr. Wm. Adams disposed of the Bridge Bank Works.

Mention was also made in the same article of the backstamp for the 'Cyrene' pattern:

> There is a wonderful old back stamp or "semi" - to use a technical term - on the copper plate engravings which have been found ... This back stamp will still be used, so as to lend character to and authenticate the history of the century-

old pattern ... As will be seen, the trade mark embodies - if somewhat crudely - the Union Jack, the Rose, Thistle and Shamrock, the lion couchant, and in the background, what is evidently intended to be a British merchant ship.

The name of William Adams was replaced by George Jones. The first advertisement for the 'Cyrene' patterned wares appeared in *The Pottery Gazette and Glass Trade Review* in May 1925, and is shown in Figure 226.

Another old William Adams pattern that was produced by George Jones & Sons Ltd. in the 1920s and 1930s was 'Woodland'. The covered honey pot, Figure 227 (large pot), has the original William Adams backstamp on it, again with the name of George Jones replacing William Adams. The covered pâté jar, Figure 227 (small pot), bears the same pattern, but only the word 'Woodland' on the underside. This piece was produced in the mid-1930s.

An unusual patterned jug manufactured in the mid-1930s by George Jones & Sons Ltd. is shown in Figure 174. The border is a pattern seen on some 'Abbey' pieces but the main picture is of a seaside beach scene. As there is no backstamp we do not know what this pattern was called but it is certainly of twentieth century design, possibly engraved in the 1930s.

Figure 137. 'Cyrene' pattern tea plate, ca. 1870. Impressed mark 'Stone China - GJ - Stoke-on-Trent', diameter 7". £40-50; $65-80.

Figure 136. 'Casino' pattern dinner plate, ca. 1870. Impressed mark 'Stone China - GJ - Stoke-on-Trent', diameter 10.25". £50-60; $80-100.

Figure 138. 'Cyrene' pattern meat plate, ca. 1870. Impressed mark 'Stone China - GJ - Stoke-on-Trent', length 17". £110-130; $180-215.

74

Figure 139. 'Sistova' pattern soup plate, ca. 1875. Diameter 10".
Courtesy of Derek and Shirley Weyman. £50-60; $80-100.

Figure 141. 'Pastoral' pattern dinner plate, ca. 1898. Diameter 10.25".
£35-45; $60-75.

Figure 140. 'Medici' pattern dessert plate, ca. 1895. Diameter 8.5".
£35-45; $60-75.

Figure 142. 'Abbey' pattern tea pot, ca. 1910. Height 3". *Courtesy of
Fred and Joyce Moseley.* £70-90; $115-150.

Figure 143. 'Abbey' pattern oval tray, ca. 1915. Length 11". £120-140; $200-230.

Figure 146. 'Abbey' pattern sauce tureen with ladle and stand, ca. 1920. Height 5". £75-100; $120-165.

Figure 144. A rare 'Abbey' pattern tea caddy, ca. 1915. Height 5". £150-200; $250-330.

Figure 145. 'Abbey' pattern tea pot, ca. 1920. Height 5.5". £75-100; $120-165.

Figure 149. 'Abbey' pattern biscuit barrel, ca. 1920. Height 5.75". £100-120; $165-200.

Figure 147. 'Abbey' pattern plate with six egg cups, ca. 1930. £220-240; $365-400.

Figure 150. 'Abbey' pattern sauce boats. ca. 1920. Height 4" and 4.75". £60-80; $100-130 each.

Figure 148. 'Abbey' pattern biscuit barrel, ca. 1920. Height 6.5" *Courtesy of Marjorie Winters.* £100-120; $165-200.

Figure 151. 'Abbey' pattern 3-bar toast rack, ca. 1920. Length 6.5" *Courtesy of Fred and Joyce Moseley.* £100-120; $165-200.

Figure 152. 'Abbey' pattern sauce boat on fixed stand, ca. 1920. Height 3.75". *Courtesy of Fred and Joyce Moseley.* £70-90; $115-150.

Figure 153. 'Abbey' pattern cruet set, ca. 1920. Height 3.75". *Courtesy of Fred and Joyce Moseley.* £100-120; $165-200 set.

Figure 154. A set of 'Abbey' pattern 'Roman' shape tea pots, ca. 1920. Capacity 3 pint, 2 pint, 1.5 pint and 1 pint, height of 3 pint tea pot 6". £175, $290; £150, $250; £125, $210; £100, $165 respectively.

Figure 155. A set of 'Abbey' pattern cheese dishes with covers, ca. 1920. Shape name 'Carlisle', height 6.5", 6", 5.5". £180, $300; £160, $265; £140, $230 respectively.

Figure 156. 'Abbey' pattern covered vegetable dish, ca. 1920. Height 6.25". £150-170; $250-280.

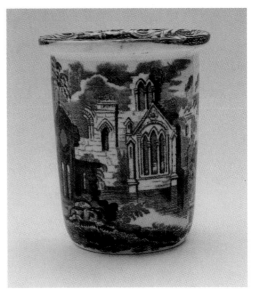

Figure 158. 'Abbey' pattern pot, ca. 1920. Height 4". *Courtesy of Fred and Joyce Moseley.* £40-60; $65-100.

Figure 157. 'Abbey' pattern oval tray, ca. 1920. Shape name 'Royal', length 10.5". £70-90; $115-150.

Figure 159. 'Abbey' pattern tea pot, ca. 1920. Height 6". *Courtesy of Fred and Joyce Moseley.* £120-140; $200-230.

Figure 160. 'Abbey' pattern tea pot, ca. 1920. Height 4.5". *Courtesy of Fred and Joyce Moseley.* £100-120; $165-200.

Figure 163. 'Abbey' pattern soup tureen, ca. 1925. Height 5.75". £160-180; $265-300.

Figure 161. 'Abbey' pattern jug, ca. 1920. Height 5.25". *Courtesy of Fred and Joyce Moseley.* £80-100; $130-165.

Figure 164. 'Abbey' pattern coffee pot, ca. 1925. Shape name 'Brighton', capacity 1.75 pints. *Courtesy of Fred and Joyce Moseley.* £120-140; $200-230.

Figure 162. 'Abbey' pattern sauce tureen, ca. 1923. Shape name 'Octagonal', height 5". £80-100; $130-165.

Figure 165. An illustration of 'Abbey' wares, from an advertisement in *The Pottery Gazette & Glass Trade Review*, July 1927. *Courtesy of Tableware International.*

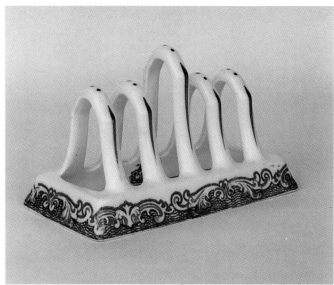

Figure 168. 'Abbey' pattern 5-bar toast rack, ca. 1930. Length 6". £120-140; $200-230.

Figure 166. 'Abbey' pattern single and double Shredded Wheat dishes, egg cups and toast rack, ca. 1930. Single Shredded Wheat dish £25-30; $40-50, double Shredded Wheat dish £30-50; $50-80, egg cups £25-30; $40-50, toast rack £120-140; $200-230.

Figure 169. 'Abbey' pattern ash tray, ca. 1930. Length 3.75". *Courtesy of Fred and Joyce Moseley.* £100-120; $165-200.

Figure 167. 'Abbey' pattern oblong plate, ca. 1930. Length 10.25". £40-60; $65-100.

Figure 170. 'Abbey' pattern coffee pot, ca. 1930. Height 8". *Courtesy of Fred and Joyce Moseley.* £120-140; $200-230.

Figure 172. 'Abbey' pattern octagonal tea pot, ca. 1933. Shape Rd. No. 777094, height 6.5". *Courtesy of Fred and Joyce Moseley.* £130-150; $215-250.

Figure 171. 'Abbey' pattern covered honey pot with fixed stand, ca. 1932. Height 5". *Courtesy of Fred and Joyce Moseley.* £50-70; $80-115.

Figure 173. Embossed 'Abbey' pattern vegetable tureen, ca. 1935. Height 5". £160-180; $265-300.

Figure 174. Jug with unusual pattern of a promenade scene and 'Abbey' border, ca. 1935. Capacity 1 pint. £40-50; $65-80.

Figure 176. 'Abbey' pattern chamber pot, ca. 1920. Height 4.75". £80-100; $130-165.

Figure 175. 'Abbey' pattern ewer and basin, ca. 1920. Shape name 'Trent', ewer height 11". £300-350; $495-580.

Figure 177. 'Abbey' pattern soap dish and brush holder, ca. 1920. Brush holder height 5". £40-60; $65-100 each.

Figure 178. 'Abbey' pattern chamber pot, ca. 1920. Height 4.75". £80-100; $130-165.

Figure 180. 'Abbey' pattern ewer and basin, ca. 1920. Basin diameter 13". £300-350; $495-580.

Figure 179. 'Abbey' pattern ewer and basin, ca. 1920. Shape name 'Olympic', basin diameter 15". £300-350; $495-580.

Figure 181. A rare 'Abbey' pattern slop pail, ca. 1920. Height 10". £500-550; $825-900.

Figure 182. 'Abbey' pattern oval trinket pots, ca. 1910. Height 3.5" and 2.5". *Courtesy of Fred and Joyce Moseley*. £60-80; $100-130 each.

Figure 184. 'Abbey' pattern vase, ca. 1915. Height 7.5". £120-150; $200-250.

Figure 183. A pair of 'Abbey' pattern vases, ca. 1915. Shape No. 341, height 6.5". £80-100; $130-165 each.

Figure 185. 'Abbey' pattern ring holder, hat pin stand and trinket box, ca. 1915. Hat pin stand height 5.5". Ring holder £30-50; $50-80, hat pin stand £80-100; $130-165, trinket box £40-60; $65-100.

Figure 186. A selection of 'Abbey' pattern candlesticks, ca. 1915. Height 7.25", 5.25". *Courtesy of Fred and Joyce Moseley.* £120-140; $200-230 each.

Figure 188. 'Abbey' pattern heart-shaped trinket box, ca. 1915. Size 3" x 2". *Courtesy of Fred and Joyce Moseley.* £80-100; $130-165.

Figure 187. 'Abbey' pattern vase, ca. 1915. Height 8.5". £110-130; $180-215.

Figure 189. 'Abbey' pattern card tray, ca. 1915. Length 12". £100-120; $165-200.

Figure 190. A pair of unusual 'Abbey' pattern vases, ca. 1920. Height 11.5". £130-150; $215-250 each.

Figure 192. A garniture of 'Abbey' pattern vases, ca. 1920. Shape no. 438, height 8" and 7". £70-100; $115-165 each.

Figure 193. 'Abbey' pattern vase, ca. 1920. Shape no. 298, height 12.5". £120-140; $200-230.

Figure 191. 'Abbey' pattern jardiniere, ca. 1920. Shape no. 402, diameter 7.5". £120-150; $200-250.

Figure 194. A garniture of 'Abbey' pattern vases, ca. 1920. Shape no. 333, height 4" and 3". £50-80; $80-130 each.

Figure 197. 'Abbey' pattern vase, ca. 1920. Shape no. 333, height 3". £50-70; $80-115.

Figure 195. Octagonal 'Abbey' pattern jardiniere, ca. 1920. Shape name 'Chinese', height 4". £60-80; $100-130.

Figure 198. 'Abbey' pattern vase, ca. 1920. Height 5.25". £60-75; $100-120.

Figure 196. 'Abbey' pattern vase, ca. 1920. Shape no. 343, height 6". £80-100; $130-165.

Figure 199. A set of 'Abbey' pattern spill vases, ca. 1920. Shape no. 433, height 12", 10", 8", 7", 6", 5". £160; $265, £140; $230, £120; $200, £100; $165, £80; $130, £60; $100 respectively.

Figure 201. 'Abbey' pattern vase, ca. 1920. Height 5". *Courtesy of Fred and Joyce Moseley.* £80-90; $130-150.

Figure 202. An unusual 'Abbey' pattern vase, ca. 1920. Shape no. 345, height 8.75". *Courtesy of Fred and Joyce Moseley.* £160-180; $265-300.

Figure 200. 'Abbey' pattern vase, ca. 1920. Shape no. 212, height 5.375". £80-100; $130-165.

Figure 203. An unusual 'Abbey' pattern vase, ca. 1920. Height 9.25". *Courtesy of Fred and Joyce Moseley.* £160-180; $265-300.

Figure 204. 'Abbey' pattern vase, ca. 1920. Shape no. 411, height 13". *Courtesy of Fred and Joyce Moseley.* £150-170; $250-280.

Figure 205. A rare 'Abbey' pattern pedestal with pot, ca. 1920. Pedestal shape no. 187, pot shape no. 322, overall height 30.5". £1500-1750; $2475-2890.

Figure 206. 'Abbey' pattern octagonal vase with lid, ca. 1921. Shape no. 444, height 8.25". *Courtesy of Fred and Joyce Moseley.* £150-175; $250-290.

Figure 208. 'Abbey' pattern plate, ca. 1926. Given as a Christmas gift to customers of James Norris Ltd., diameter 9". £30-40; $50-65.

Figure 209. Wording on back of Figure 208.

Figure 207. 'Abbey' pattern vase, ca. 1921. Shape no. 436, height 8". *Courtesy of Fred and Joyce Moseley.* £130-150; $215-250.

Figure 210. An unusual rectangular 'Abbey' pattern planter, ca. 1930. Length 8.5". £180-200; $300-330.

Figure 211. 'Abbey' pattern dressing table tray with embossed edge, ca. 1930. Length 13.5". £80-100; $130-165.

Figure 212. An illustration of 'Abbey' pattern ware, from a George Jones & Sons Ltd. 1924 trade catalogue. *Courtesy of Hanley Reference Library.*

Figure 213. An illustration of 'Abbey' pattern ware, from a George Jones & Sons Ltd. 1924 trade catalogue. *Courtesy of Hanley Reference Library.*

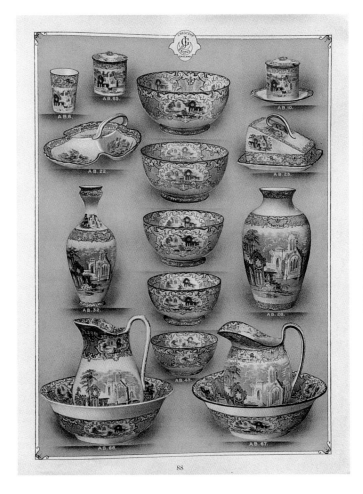

Figure 214. An illustration of 'Abbey' pattern ware, from a George Jones & Sons Ltd. 1924 trade catalogue. *Courtesy of Hanley Reference Library.*

Figure 216. Tea plate, ca. 1935. Width 6.5", centre shows King William IV coach and has the 'Abbey' border pattern. £40-50; $65-80.

Figure 215. An illustration of 'Abbey' pattern ware, from a George Jones & Sons Ltd. 1924 trade catalogue. *Courtesy of Hanley Reference Library.*

Figure 217. A rare cigarette box, match box holder and ash tray, ca. 1935. Transfer on lid of cigarette box shows King William IV coach. Length 5.25". £180-200; $300-330.

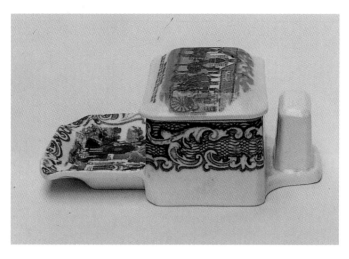

Figure 218. Side view of Figure 217.

Figure 221. 'Toro' pattern dinner plate, ca. 1908. Diameter 10.25". £35-45; $60-75.

Figure 219. 'Lasso' pattern dinner plate, ca. 1904. Diameter 10.25". *Courtesy of David and Catriona Maisels.* £50-60; $80-100.

Figure 220. 'Farm' pattern dinner plate, ca. 1907. Diameter 10.25. £35-45; $60-75.

Figure 222. 'Indian Traffic' pattern dish, ca. 1912. Diameter 5". £20-30; $35-50.

Figure 223. 'Spanish Festivities' pattern meat plate, ca. 1916. Length 14.5". £100-120; $165-200.

Figure 224. 'Willow' pattern compote, ca. 1915. Diameter 9". £60-80; $100-130.

Figure 225. An illustration of 'Blue Suez' and 'Willow' pattern wares from a 1924 George Jones & Sons Ltd. trade catalogue. *Courtesy of Hanley Reference Library.*

Figure 226. An advertisement for 'Cyrene' pattern wares from *The Pottery Gazette & Glass Trade Review*, 1 May 1925. *Courtesy of Tableware International.*

Figure 227. Two 'Woodland' pattern preserve pots, ca. 1935. Height 4.75" and 3.25". £50-75; $80-120 each.

The year 1876 was to see a complete change of emphasis on the types of wares produced by George Jones & Sons. When Llewellynn Jewitt referred to the Trent Potteries in his second, 1883, edition of *Ceramic Art of Great Britain* he stated: 'The manufacture of china in all its branches was added in 1876' The china Jewitt was referring to was not the strong stone china, which George Jones had been producing since 1862, but delicate bone china. Along with many other manufacturers, George Jones decided to move into this greatly expanding market that, up until then, had been dominated by the larger companies like Mintons, Derby, Worcester, etc.

To make way for the production of bone china, and to enable the production of their very successful majolica decorated earthenware and stone china to continue, George Jones & Sons leased a nearby vacant factory owned by the executors of Thomas Wolfe. This factory, in Welch Street, Stoke, was used for the production of earthenware. It was in this factory that George Jones & Sons manufactured some of their earthenware table and toilet wares etc. for which they were renowned. This factory continued to be leased until 1881 when all production was moved back to an expanded Trent Potteries.

Initially, bone china was used for the production of small pieces of tableware. Early dinner services were made up of bone china dinner plates with earthenware meat plates and tureens. Likewise, teasets supplied with trays had bone china tea ware and earthenware trays. This was due to the English pottery manufacturers' difficulty in producing large pieces in bone china. In a retrospect of the past forty years published in *The Pottery Gazette* in January 1913 it was stated:

> One of the most important developments in the china dinner trade was undoubtedly the introduction of the Anglo-China by George Jones & Sons, about 1884. This discovery, by the late Mr. F. R. Benham, [George Jones's eldest son] enabled the English makers to compete successfully with Haviland and other French manufacturers, who up till then had the market for cheaper china dinner ware entirely to themselves.

It is thought this article referred to Frank Jones (Benham)'s research into the manufacture of large items, such as meat plates, trays and toiletware etc. from bone china. Although no recipes for 'Anglo-China' have been discovered, it is possible that Frank Jones found that, by modifying the basic bone china recipe, he was able to produce much larger pieces in a type of bone china. Although this article referred to 'Anglo-China', that being its trade name in 1913, initially it was known as 'Anglo-French China' and pieces manufactured in this type of ware were marked 'A-F China'.

Tableware - teaware

Tableware is a collective name used to describe tea ware, dinner ware and dessert ware. The tea ware produced by George Jones & Sons, in the period commencing 1876, was, in the main, manufactured from bone china to designs produced in or after 1876. Before this period the designs for tea ware seem to have been restricted to pieces manufactured in majolica; however, George Jones most probably produced tea ware from the very beginning in 1862 — although no examples have as yet been identified prior to 1870, except for a tea plate decorated with the 'Cyrene' pattern, possibly manufactured in the late 1860s. The 'Pineapple' tea pot

registered in June 1870, the 'Wicker and Apple Blossom' tea and coffee set registered in February 1873, the attractive 'Jewel' tea pot shown in Figure 72 and manufactured in the early 1870s, and the 'Monkey' tea service registered in June 1875 are all examples of pre-bone china tea ware.

The first two designs for tea ware to be manufactured in bone china were registered on the 29 May 1876. The first design was given patent no. 300809 and was for the design of a tea cup with the shape name 'Weston'. Example of this design are shown in Figures 264, 268 and 270. The second design, given patent no. 300810, was for the design of a tea cup with the shape name 'Chad'. This shape, of which a few examples are shown in Figures 251 to 258, all decorated in hand painted patterns, was about sixty years ahead of its time. The design could be (and has been) easily mistaken as coming from the 'Art Deco' period of the 1930s. The shape is very similar to designs being produced by Christopher Dresser during the 1870s and it is possible that he might have been commissioned by George Jones to produce a design for tea ware. Could it be that the shape name 'Chad' refers, in some way, to Christopher Dresser? The 'Chad' design was produced in two shapes, the 'Low Chad' and the 'Tall Chad' - both are illustrated.

Between May 1876 and January 1886 only one design for tea ware was registered by George Jones & Sons. This design, for a tea service, was registered on 25 January 1877 and was given patent no. 307239. The pieces were all in the shape of drums and were for manufacture in earthenware and decorated in majolica.

On 30 January 1886 a design, Rd. No. 42306, was registered for various items of tableware including a tea set. The shape was named 'Kew' and a feature of this design was the moulded vertical ribbing on the lower half of the pieces. an example of this design is shown in Figure 300.

The three designs, 'Chad', 'Weston', and 'Kew', were not the only shapes of tea ware in production during this ten year period. Other designs were introduced but not registered at the Patent Office. One named 'Worcester', see Figure 279, was very similar to the 'Weston' shape but instead of the cup being angular at the base it was rounded. Another tea cup shape that was used extensively in the period up to 1900 was named 'Garnet'. Examples of this shape are shown in Figures 272, 280 and 282. They are all decorated in various patterns, the majority of which are lithographic printed patterns.

Other shapes of tea ware introduced in the early 1880s, and used extensively during the next twenty years, were named 'Warwick', 'York' (figure 262), 'Sydney' (figure 266), 'Boston', 'Sandon', 'Connaught', and 'Milford' (figure 306).

Llewellynn Jewitt, in the 1883 edition of his book, *Ceramic Art of Great Britain*, commenting on tea services from George Jones & Sons in general, and the 'York' shaped cup in particular wrote:

> In services some entirely new forms of cups and saucers - notably a scalloped shape - are of great merit and of particularly pleasing character. Thin in body, pleasant to the feel, the cup holds its place in the saucer with mechanical precision, and the "potting" and finish is faultless; this shape is all that can be wished for.

On 1 February 1888 a design, Rd. No. 92673, was registered for a tea service complete with tea kettle. The shape of the tea cup was very similar, if not the same, as the 'Weston' shape registered in May 1876, but the shape of the lid and handle on the tea pot and tea kettle were different. An example of a tea kettle to this design is shown in Figure 269. It is decorated in the very popular printed pattern, Rd. No. 826. This pattern was registered on the 25 January 1884.

A complete bone china afternoon tea set on a tray, which was found wrapped in old newspaper in a woodman's cottage in the Midlands, is illustrated in Figure 291. This tea service is interesting in that it incorporates no fewer than four different registered designs, one of which is wrong. The tray is made of earthenware, bears the impressed Rd. No. 91237, was registered on 6 January 1888, and is marked with the pattern name 'Bon Bon', which was given Rd. No. 101485 when the 'Bon Bon' pattern was registered on 8 June 1888. The tea pot and milk jug, as well as being marked with the pattern name, also have the shape Rd. No. 96154, registration date 20 March 1888. The sugar basin and cups bear the shape Rd. No. 42306, registration date 30 January 1886. This is a mistake possibly caused by the transferrer picking up the wrong registered design transfer, because, according to the design drawings, held at The Public Record Office, London, this shape of tea cup and the vertical ribs at the top of the sugar basin are features of the design Rd. No. 96154, registration date 20 March 1888 and therefore match the tea pot and jug. This particular cabaret set was manufactured in 1891.

An unusual means of securing a lid to a jug or pot was registered on 23 March 1888. The design, Rd. No. 96411, was for use on a tea pot, water jug or coffee pot. This design incorporated two "blips" moulded into the inner rim of the hole in the top of the pot or jug, one on each side of the spout. A groove was cast into part of the edge of the lid. When the lid was put into the top of the tea pot and turned, the two blips locked into the groove, thus securing the lid. Whether this design was ever used is not known as no examples have, as yet, been found.

A design for a tea pot, water jug, a large and small jug, and a two handled sugar bowl was registered on 4 October 1888, Rd. No. 109822. This design was very similar to the tea kettle shown in Figure 297. The shape of the handles, the shell shaped top and the moulded shell design at the bottom of the body, were all features of this design. Although being very similar to the tea kettle illustrated in this design held at the Public Record Office, the tea kettle shown in Figure 297 is marked with the Rd. No. 124321.

A design was registered on 5 February 1889, Rd. No. 119035, featuring a daisy pattern applied around the top half of a cup and the outer edge of a saucer. Also illustrated in this design was a sauce tureen on a stand, a vegetable dish and a dinner plate, all incorporating this same daisy pattern, applied to either the top half of the piece, as on the cup, or the outer edge, as on the saucer. It is unclear what the company was registering — was it the position of the decorated area, or was it the shape of the pieces? The tureen and dish are very similar in shape to a design registered in January 1888, Rd. No. 91237.

On 29 April 1889 a design, Rd. No. 124321, was registered for an embossed pattern. This design is illustrated on the coffee cup and tea cup in Figures 288 and 295 and shows a shell shaped moulded pattern on the lower half of the body similar to the tea kettle in Figure 297.

Another design for a tea pot, jug, sugar basin and tea cup was registered on 7 November 1889, Rd. No. 137548. The shape was named 'Anglo' and one of the features of this design was the shape of the handle, which is illustrated on the cup shown in Figure 313.

On 30 January 1890 a design, Rd. No. 143138, was registered for an embossed pattern for use on tableware. The design, now held at the Public Record Office, Kew, showed a strawberry dish complete with cream jug, sugar basin and two ladles. The embossed pattern was included on the dish, the cream jug and the sugar basin. Complete tea services were produced incorporating this design. Figures 289, 293 and 298 show various pieces featuring this design, with the embossed pattern in gold.

A design for a tea service was registered on 21 January 1891, Rd. No. 165075. The shape was named 'Bow' and various pieces are shown in Figures 290 and 292.

On 29 October 1892 a design, Rd. No. 201593, was registered for tea ware. The design, held at the Public Record Office, London, showed a tea pot, a two handled sugar box complete with lid, a jug, a cup and saucer, a tea plate, and a bread plate. The cup had tapering sides with vertical grooves moulded into it.

A design for various pieces of tableware incorporating an embossed pattern was registered on 5 January 1894, Rd. No. 225065. The design showed two shapes of cups, a milk jug, a two handled sugar box complete with lid, a muffin dish, a covered butter dish, a slop basin, a one handled bread plate, a covered jam pot, a sauce boat and a dessert plate. The shape name was 'Corea' and a sauce boat with stand to this design are shown in Figure 341.

On 23 January 1896 a design, Rd. No. 269723, was registered for a moulded shape suitable for various pieces of tableware. The design showed a cup and saucer, a large and small jug, a tea pot, a sugar box with lid, and an oval footed bowl. This shape was named 'Silver' and Figures 310 and 311 show cups and saucers to this design.

The last design to be registered for tea ware before 1900 was registered on 21 December 1897 and was given Rd. No. 311150. This design showed an embossed pattern around the rim of a cup, saucer and plate. It also featured a new shape for a tea pot.

Dinner ware

Up until 1876, all the dinner ware produced by George Jones & Sons had been manufactured in either earthenware or stone china. With the commencement of the manufacture of bone china in 1876, dinner plates were also produced in bone china but only in limited numbers. The cost of manufacturing bone china was much more expensive than of pieces made in earthenware or stone china, so consequently, the market was quite limited.

About 50% of all the company's production of earthenware and stone china was, at this time, being exported to the Americas and Africa. The export market for bone china had not yet developed, thus the market for bone china dinner ware was at home. Many of the Victorians, who were not used to such fine wares, could not afford to buy them. It was only the 'well to do' who bought such wares, the majority of the population being obliged to buy earthenware or the stronger stone china dinner ware.

In the late 1870s, vast quantities of stone china were being exported to America. An interesting backstamp has been found on some plain stone china plates taken from a ship-wreck off the coast of Delaware. The backstamp bears the Royal Arms incorporating the Lion and Unicorn with the simple quartered shield, beneath which is written 'ROYAL PATENT IRONSTONE - GEORGE JONES'. At this time a similar backstamp was used by many manufacturers on this type of ware.

Initially bone china dinner services consisted of bone china plates, with the tureens, large meat plates, and vegetable dishes etc., being made of earthenware or stone china. It was not until George Jones & Sons commenced the production of 'Anglo-French China' in the mid-1880s that complete dinner services made from china were available, at an affordable price, for the working class Victorians.

Between the beginning of 1876 and early 1884, only two designs for dinner ware were registered at the Patent Office, London, by George Jones & Sons. The first design was for a gravy dish registered on 22 January 1876 and given patent no. 297811. The second design was registered on 16 September 1881 and was given patent no. 370093. This design was for a covered vegetable dish and a sauce tureen on a stand. The shape name for this design of tureen was 'Venice'. This shape was probably based upon the gondolas of Venice and could have been designed by Horace Overton Jones, who had only recently joined the company, as a designer, after completing a world tour, which possibly included a visit to Venice. Figures 317 and 318 show examples of this shape decorated with the 'Ivy Bower' pattern. The 'Ivy Bower' pattern was registered on 29 September 1881 and was given patent no. 370636. The design for this shape of tureen, held at the Public Record Office, Kew, shows them decorated in the 'Briar' rose pattern. Although only one patent number was issued for both the shape of tureens and the 'Briar' pattern, I believe George Jones & Sons intended both the 'Venice' shape and the 'Briar' pattern to be registered as individual designs, because the majority of pieces of ware decorated with the 'Briar' pattern also bear the same lozenge mark, bearing the date code for the 16 September 1881.

On 15 March 1884, a design, Rd. No. 3657, was registered for a covered vegetable dish, a large and small tureen on a stand, and a rectangular bowl. Two examples of this design are shown in Figures 321 and 339.

It was to be two more years before another design was registered for a dinner service shape. On the 22 October 1886, a design, Rd. No. 59451, was registered for a meat plate, dinner plate and two sizes of tureens. A feature of this design, on the plates, was a ribbed border away from the edge. The tureen design incorporated three vertical ribbed sections, one at the base, one mid-way up the body of the tureen, and one around the handle on the lid.

Another design was registered, for a meat plate, a large vegetable dish and a sauce tureen on 2 May 1887, Rd. No. 73024. Embossed ribbed decorations must have been all the fashion in the 1880s, as this shape also features ribbing. Two examples of this design are shown: Figure 324 is a sauce tureen and Figure 334 is a meat plate. Figure 334 is decorated with the 'Chatsworth' pattern, a pattern that was registered on 21 October 1887, Rd. No. 84746.

On 6 January 1888, a design, Rd. No. 91237, was registered for various items of tableware including a vegetable dish with lid, sauce tureen and stand, sauce boat, and a vegetable dish. A feature of this design was, yet again, embossed vertical ribbing.

A design for a vegetable dish, sauce tureen, and gravy boat on a stand was registered on 30 January 1890, Rd. No. 143137. Figure 329 shows an example of a sauce tureen to this design.

It was to be five years before the next design, for dinner ware, was to be submitted for registration to the Patent Office. This design was registered on 29 May 1895 and was given Rd. No. 255552. It was for an embossed patterned dinner service. The pieces shown in the design, held at the Public Record Office, Kew, are a tureen, a large meat plate and a dinner sized plate.

On 12 November 1896, a design was registered for a covered vegetable dish and was given Rd. No. 288114. This dish was unusual in that it had two sections, each for different vegetables.

The next design to be registered that included dinner ware was Rd. No. 311150. This design was registered on 21 December 1897 and was for tableware. The design featured an embossed border pattern on dinner plates and a new shape of tureen with the same border pattern around the base of the tureen and around the edge of the lid.

Although this was the last design for dinner ware to be submitted for registration before 1900, the company's designers continued to produce new shapes for tureens and dishes etc. to be manufactured in earthenware, stone china or 'Anglo-French China'.

Dessert ware

Another type of ware that is included under the tableware heading is dessert ware. Dessert ware was usually sold as dessert services. A dessert service was made up of either twelve or eighteen plates together with large dishes and/or compotes. The compotes were manufactured in three sizes — low, tall, and centre. At least one of each size would be included in a complete service.

One of the earliest bone china dessert services to be manufactured by George Jones & Sons used a design registered on 26 March 1873. This design was originally produced in stone china or earthenware for decorating in majolica colours. Figure 343 shows an example of this design manufactured in bone china. This particular set was manufactured in 1877.

The first design for a bone china dessert plate was registered on 13 May 1882 and was given patent no. 380789. This plate was very similar in shape to the lily leaf design registered in March 1873 but the edge of this plate had of a more irregular, wavy shape. At one point the edge formed a 'v' section, similar to the lily leaf plate, but instead of one low relief moulded flower, this design incorporated two flowers, one on either side of the 'v' section.

Another design for a leaf shaped dessert plate was registered on 21 February 1883 and was given patent no. 394452. This shape was also similar to the lily leaf shape, but this had a serrated edge and incorporated the incised form of the veins of the leaf. The registered design shows that at the base of the leaf, two flowers were moulded in high relief, one open and one closed. Examples of this plate were also produced without these flowers. This was the last of the registered designs specifically for dessert plates. From 1884 the designs for the shape of dessert plates were usually incorporated into the registered designs for tableware, and were, for the most part, round in shape with embossed designs on the border.

In the mid-1880s, strawberry sets were still popular and were produced with ivory glazes in place of the majolica glazes. The shapes were ones that had been used during the majolica era. Examples of strawberry dishes produced during the 1880s are shown in Figures 369, 370, 371 and 387.

On 11 February 1896, Rd. No. 270717 was given to a registered design for three dessert dishes. An example of one of the dishes is shown in Figure 249. Of the two remaining dishes, one was round in shape and the other was oval, all three featuring the same embossed design.

A list of shape names for dessert plate used within this period include:

Acme, Albany, Chelsea, Duchess, Empire, Lorne, Lotus, Osbourne, Pompon, Queens, Salisbury, Sevres, Shield, Silver, and Stoke.

The compote shown in Figure 385 has an unusual token attached to the underside of it as shown in Figure 386. The token is a merchants token issued in New Zealand. The history behind these tokens is that, due to a shortage of British money, New Zealand merchants' tokens were issued from 1857. There were some 147 varieties issued in ten cities, although the majority were issued in Auckland, Christchurch, Wellington and Dunedin. The issuing of these tokens discontinued in 1881, but they continued to circulate until 1897, when British copper and silver and Australian gold became plentiful. Almost all tokens bear the name of the city and the issuing merchant; however, since few of the tokens have a stated value, the user had to rely on size and weight alone. All tokens are of copper or bronze.

The token on the base of the compote shows a working mine on the left and a 'poppet head' on the right. The wording 'Advance Thames Goldfield' is not referring to a specific goldmine, but merely promotes the goldfields of Thames, a city near Auckland in the North Island of New Zealand. On the reverse of this token is the inscription:

George McCaul
Coppersmith, Tinsmith, Plumber, Gas fitter,
Grahamstown,
1874
New Zealand (around the rim).

The value of this token was one penny. How or why this token came to be fixed to the compote is not known. Another compote bought at the same time also bears a token, but this has the head of a young Queen Victoria embossed on it.

Toilet ware

Apart from tableware, another very important type of domestic ware produced by George Jones & Sons was toilet ware. George Jones had already commenced the production of toilet ware by 1866 when he moved into his new Trent Potteries. It was usually sold as complete toilet services. Four different sizes of services were available, made up as follows:

Single Service —
1 Ewer
1 Basin
1 Soap Dish
1 Brush Holder
1 Chamber
1 Sponge Bowl - making a 6 piece service
Large Single Service —
1 Ewer
1 Basin
1 Soap Dish
1 Brush Holder
1 Chamber
1 Sponge Bowl
1 Slop Pail - making a 7 piece service
Double Service —
2 Ewers
2 Basins
1 Soap Dish
1 Brush Holder
2 Chambers
1 Sponge Bowl - making a 9 piece service
Large Double Service —
2 Ewers
2 Basins
2 Soap Dish
2 Brush Holder
2 Chambers
1 Sponge Bowl
1 Mouth Ewer
1 Mouth Basin
1 Slop Pail - making a 14 piece service

By 1884, toilet services in these four sizes were being sold. Whether earlier toilet services were sold in sets like these is unknown. Before October 1884 George Jones & Sons had only registered four designs for toilet ware, mainly designs for ewers. The first of these was in October 1868 and was for ornamentation on toiletware. The design featured a ewer and was produced in majolica, an example is shown in Figure 35. The second design was registered in March 1870 and was for a 'rope handle' for basins and chamber ware. The third design, registered in April 1874, was for the shape of a ewer similar to Figure 401 but with the lizard handle replaced with a geometrically shaped handle. The fourth design registered on the 8 November 1876, patent no. 305080, was for a bedroom service. The design held at the Public Record office, Kew, shows a ewer of similar shape to Figure 422 but with a handle that started at the top rim.

It was not until October 1884 that the design for a complete toilet service was submitted for registration by George Jones & Sons to the Patent Office in London. This design, Rd. No. 14977, was registered on 14 October 1884 and is shown in Figure 404.

It was to be three more years before another design for a toilet service was submitted for registration. This design was registered on 25 January 1888 and was given Rd. No. 92160. Examples of this design are shown in Figures 409, 410, 414, 415 and 416. A smaller ewer and basin to this design is shown in Figure 424. Although this was the next design to be registered for toilet ware, a design that was registered for dinner ware on the 22 October 1886, Rd. No. 59451, was also used for toilet ware. Figures 405 and 406 show chamber pots and Figure 412 shows a soap dish and tooth brush holder, all in this design.

On 8 November 1888, Rd. No. 113169, was given to a design for a hot water jug. The jug had a conical shaped body with a large pouring lip. It was very similar in shape to the copper beer jugs that were produced in the mid eighteenth century. The jug had a moulded handle opposite the lip, and a wicker handle attached to two moulded lugs at the top. This style of hot water jug was still available in the 1920s, as it is illustrated in a 1921 George Jones & Sons Ltd. trade catalogue that is held in the Minton Archives. This shape of jug was used in the next toilet service to be registered by the company. This design for a toilet service was registered on 20 September 1889 and was given Rd. No. 133641. An example of a ewer and a shaving mug to this design are shown in Figures 417 and 420. A ewer and basin of the same design is featured in the 1908 Army & Navy Co-operative Society Ltd. catalogue, showing the popularity of this shape some twenty years after it was first introduced.

The next design for a toilet service was registered on 26 March 1890 and was given Rd. No. 146574. The body of the two-handled ewer was similar in shape to the tea kettle shown in Figure 297. The embossed ornamentation on all the pieces in this service was also similar to the tea kettle. This shape was named 'Empress' and an example of a ewer, a basin and a chamber pot are shown in Figures 418, 419 and 421.

On 25 May 1893, Rd. No. 212635 was given to a design submitted for another toilet service. The body of the single-handled ewer, was tall and cylindrical in shape, with a ring of embossed ornamentation just below the lip. The design submitted to the Patent Office showed a ewer and basin, a chamber pot, a brush holder and a soap dish.

On 7 September 1894, Rd. No. 239437 was given to a design for a six piece toilet service. The single-handled ewer had a body with a bulbous centre section. All the pieces had an incised swirling decoration running from top to bottom. The shape was named 'Corea' and an example of this design is shown in Figure 426. This design of toilet ware was still available in the 1920s as the illustration, Figure 631, featuring this design is from a 1924 George Jones & Sons Ltd. trade catalogue held at the Hanley Reference Library.

As well as these registered designs, many other shapes of ewers were produced. Figure 403 shows a ewer, shape name 'Saxon', decorated with a pattern named 'Plevna'. This pattern was registered on 7 June 1878 and was given patent no. 322309.

A list of shape names for toiletware used within this period includes:

Athens, Cain, Doric, Empress, Egyptian, Gothic, Grecian, Guelph, Imperial, Ionic, Italian, Kew, Norman, Percy, Prah, Royal, Rustic, and Saxon.

The first interview given by Arthur Overton Jones, the recently appointed manager of the London showrooms, was published in the October 1897 edition of *The Pottery Gazette*. This also included a visit to view the latest wares available from George Jones & Sons Ltd. An extract from the report gives a good idea of what the company was well known for and how its products were viewed. It stated:

We have been favoured with an interview with Mr. A. O. Jones, at the London showrooms of the firm in Bartlett's-Buildings, and have much admired some of their recent artistic productions. In the minds of many dealers the name of George Jones & Sons is always associated with toilet ware and dinner sets. They certainly stand high for these lines, and their samples at Bartlett's-Buildings are always deserving of the attention of buyers who want good things.

Patterns

From 1876 to the beginning of 1881, most of the patterned tableware and toilet ware produced by George Jones & Sons was decorated in either underglaze transfer printed patterns, or hand painted patterns to specific designs by artists unknown. All this changed when Horace Overton Jones, George Jones fifth son, joined the company toward the end of 1880 as an artist/designer. Horace Overton Jones, who had just completed a world tour after finishing a period of training at the National Art Training School, South Kensington, London, immediately went to work in the design/decorating department of the factory. During the next fifteen years his influence on the design of patterns used for decorating the wares was enormous. In 1877, whilst at the National Art Training School, Horace Overton Jones won two prizes in a National Competition. These prizes were awarded to him in the category 'painting flowers from nature'. His natural ability for drawing and painting flowers is shown in the very many lithographed patterns bearing his initials, H.O.J. The majority of the wares produced by George Jones & Sons during the period 1881 to 1895 were decorated in these underglaze lithographed patterns.

Between July 1883 and January 1892, twenty lithographic pattern designs were submitted and given registered design numbers by the Patent Office in London. The majority of these patterns were initialled H.O.J. and the subject matter was usually flowers.

One of Horace Overton Jones's earliest pattern was registered on the 19 July 1883, and was given the name 'Overton'. Figure 365 is an example of this pattern.

The Horace Overton Jones patterns were not single patterns but were made up of a series of sketches all incorporating the same type of flower. In some cases the complete design consisted of as many as forty different sketches, all featuring different views of the flowers and their foliage. Some of his more well known patterns were of roses, sunflowers, cornflowers, pansies, and chrysanthemums. Possibly one of the most well known patterns featured pyrethrums. This pattern was registered on 25 January 1884 and was given Rd. No. 826 and usually features bees in flight above some of the flowers. Various pieces of ware decorated in this pattern are shown in Figures 269, 366, 368, 413 and 422.

Other well known patterns included 'Briar', registered on 16 September 1881, which featured the briar rose; 'Ivy Bower' registered on 29 September 1881; 'Chrysanthemums', Rd. No. 21391, registered on 3 February 1885; 'Cornflower', Rd. No. 39348, registered on 8 December 1885; 'Primroses', Rd. No. 68515, registered on 24 February 1887; and 'Azalea', Rd. No. 100,000, registered on 12 May 1888. The 'Briar' pattern turned out to be very popular and was extensively used on many different types of wares over a very long period. It was still being used to decorate dinner ware in 1923.

A pattern that was registered on 13 September 1886 and given Rd. No. 56152 was used to produce two different named patterns, each bearing the same Rd. No. The lithographed pattern, held at the Public Record Office, Kew, shows various sketches of branches laden with blossom and some separate sketches of swallows in flight. The two patterns that were to come from this were 'Birds and Bloom' and 'Peach Blow'. 'Birds and Bloom' incorporated the blossom-laden branches and the swallows, while 'Peach Blow' only featured the blossom laden branches. Figure 287 shows 'Peach Blow' and Figure 323 shows 'Birds and Bloom.

As well as these registered design patterns, Horace Overton Jones was responsible for literally thousands of other patterns. The pattern books, now held at the Wedgwood Museum, show patterns incorporating flowers and flowering shrubs of all kinds. Some of these patterns also include birds, butterflies, and other insects. A series of patterns were produced called 'Familiar Flowers H.O.J.' or 'Familiar H.O.J. Flowers'. These patterns also included bees in flight similar to pattern Rd. No. 826. Examples of dessert plates decorated in patterns from this series are shown in Figures 376 and 380.

One pattern registered on 28 March 1889 and given Rd. No. 122292 was initialled C.J.B. This pattern, of magnolia blossoms, was designed by Charles James Birbeck. Charles Birbeck had joined the company in 1877 at the age of sixteen and by 1881 was working as a china painter. Figure 416 shows a ewer decorated in this pattern.

As well as patterns featuring flowers and flowering shrubs, in the mid-1880s asymmetric designs became popular. 'Caius', see Figure 265, and 'Hawthorn' were two such named patterns.

The advantage of producing patterns as lithographic prints was that the hand tinting element of the transfer printed pattern was largely dispensed with, as the lithographic prints were produced in their correct multi-colours, although many of Horace Overton Jones's were printed in one colour and then tinted by hand. The same pattern can be seen in various colours; Rd. No. 826 is a good example. George Jones & Sons was one of the few pottery companies in 'The Potteries' to have their own lithographic printing department. This was established when Horace Overton Jones commenced his employment in 1881, and ensured that their lithographic designs were exclusive to their own wares. Many other English pottery manufacturers bought lithographic prints from specialist designers and printers, a lot of whom were in Germany. As these lithographic prints were sold to many different pottery manufacturers, they were, therefore, not exclusive to one manufacturer. The same pattern could appear on any number of different pottery manufacturers' wares.

As well as underglaze transfer printed patterns and lithographic printed patterns, George Jones & Sons also produced tableware, especially dessert ware, decorated in hand painted designs by ceramic artists. Some of these designs were painted on plain plates while others were painted on plates that had the outline of the picture embossed on the surface of the plate. Figures 359 and 362 show two plates, produced in 1883, with the pictures painted on plain plates. Figures 383 and 384 show examples of plates with the outline of the picture, of birds and foliage, embossed on the plate, and then hand painted by skilled ceramic artists.

Up until 1890, the majority of these hand painted wares were unsigned. They were produced by such people as Charles Birbeck and William Birbeck. William Birbeck, who was the half brother of Charles Birbeck, had joined George Jones & Sons in late 1880 at the age of fourteen. By April 1881, William Birbeck was employed as an artist on china, possibly working under the guidance of Charles, who was also employed as an artist on china. Another artist, who may have produced unsigned work during this period for George Jones & Sons was Charles Austin.

Around 1890, hand painted, signed work began to be produced by George Jones & Sons. A ceramic artist was only allowed to sign his own work when the art director was satisfied that he had reached a certain standard of competency. His work had to be of the highest standard, this standard only being attained after years of training. Only a certain number of artists made the grade. William Birbeck and Charles Austin were two such artists to produce signed work for George Jones & Sons.

Another artist who worked for George Jones & Sons, in the early 1890s, signed his work 'F. Bernard'. Whether this was the same artist — Bernard, the Frenchman — who in 1889 worked for

Brown Westhead, Moore & Co. is not known. An example of work signed F. Bernard is shown in Figure 397

An artist, whose painting has been seen on embossed plates, signed his work 'F. Gee'. These plates were similar to Figure 354, having a design of flowers and a humming bird.

Ornamental wares – Pâte-sur-Pâte

A description of *pâte-sur-pâte* was published in *The Pottery Gazette* in 1889. It states :

Pâte-sur-pâte is a form of decorative porcelain work in which one coloured slip is laid upon another in bands, fillets, Figures and what not, sometimes to the number of a dozen or more. Wedgwoods imitation of the Portland vase is an eminent instance of the act and Solon has also executed some remarkable work. The body is usually dark olive green, brown, turquoise blue, or black and the paste white and laid on in relief, the lights and shades partly due to the thickness of the slip which is in relief. After laying a sufficient thickness, the artist scrapes away portions according to the requirements of the design. The dark background showing through in parts, refiring renders all translucent. It is a very old process having long been used in China on porcelain and in India for common ware at the Scinde and Punjaby pottery for instance. In Scinde the pattern is pricked out on paper drawn by laying it on the surface of the jar and dusting along the prickings. The effect is good and articles are sold at from 4d to 1 shilling.

The first English pottery manufacturer to successfully produce *pâte-sur-pâte* was Mintons. This they perfected in the early 1870s when Louis Marc Emmanuel Solon, who had fled from Paris to avoid the Franco-Prussian war, joined them as an artist in 1870, having spent the previous twelve years working at Sevres. Solon's work to produce pieces of *pâte-sur-pâte* was very time consuming and the finished article was, and still is, regarded as the most perfect *pâte-sur-pâte* ever produced. Unfortunately, this made it a very expensive type of decorated ware to manufacture and consequently could only be bought by the very rich in Victorian society.

In a review of current trade conditions in the Potteries, published in the September 1879 edition of *The Pottery Gazette*, comment was made:

Messrs. George Jones & Sons, of Stoke, one of the leading firms engaged in what may be called a universal trade, are doing a good deal of *pâte-sur-pâte* work. Hitherto there has been something of a monopoly in this kind of work, but this enterprising firm, which has always tried to keep pace with older houses is successfully rivalling some of the best attempts made in the district.

If the *pâte-sur-pâte* being produced by Mintons was so expensive, how was it George Jones & Sons managed to break into the market with a product suited more to the average pocket? In the mid-1870s George Jones & Sons were producing vast quantities of high quality majolica wares, the designs of which contained many low relief mouldings. Armed with the expertise in producing these low relief moulded designs, the company commissioned Frederick Schenck to produce new models of existing designs for vases, jardinières, wall pockets and plaques, etc. and to incorporate onto these models, panels of low relief designs suitable for decorating in the *pâte-sur-pâte* style. These models were sculptured from either wax, clay or plaster — plaster being the preferred medium. From these models, plaster moulds were made. When an item was to be manufactured, the mould was filled with coloured clay slip (liquid clay). The water content was absorbed by the plaster mould until a layer of moist clay had built on the inside of the mould. The surplus slip was then poured out and the layer of clay allowed to dry. When the mould was opened, the

piece of ware (complete with its low relief moulded design but in the ground colour such as dark green or dark brown) was removed. Before firing, the low relief designs were skillfully painted with varying thicknesses of white clay slip. The piece was then fired and the designs took on the translucent effect of 'genuine' *pâte-sur-pâte*. The result of using this process was that *pâte-sur-pâte* decorated wares could be mass produced, thus lowering the cost, and consequently making the wares available to a larger market.

Frederick Schenck, the designer, was an accomplished artist and figure modeller. Before training at the National Art Training School in South Kensington, London, he had worked for one year (between 1872 and 1873), as a modeller at Wedgwood, modifying existing models and producing new ones. Frederick Schenck returned to Stoke-upon-Trent in mid-1878 after three years additional training at The Royal Scottish Academy, Edinburgh. It is believed that he worked on a free-lance basis, producing models not only for George Jones & Sons but also for other manufacturers. Most of his designs are impressed 'SCHENCK'.

Frederick Schenck's designs included nymphs, cupids, tropical foliage, birds etc. One such design on a jardinière, shows a fairy maiden teaching Cupid to play a lyre; the reverse side of the same jardinière shows Cupid playing the lyre to the maiden. The design depicting Cupid being taught to play the lyre has also been seen on a wall pocket that was once in the Wengers Ltd. Collection of Pottery in Etruria, Stoke-on-Trent. Another example of this wall pocket can be seen in G. A. Goddens' book *Victorian Porcelain* (Herbert Jenkins, London, 1961), plate 87.

At a fine art exhibition held at the Borough Hall, Stafford, in October 1883, George Jones & Sons exhibited examples of their *pâte-sur-pâte* wares. *The Staffordshire Advertiser* commenting on the exhibition, the theme of which was 'Excellence of Design', stated:

Messrs. George Jones & Sons of Stoke-upon-Trent, who since the last exhibition (in November 1878) have addressed themselves energetically to the production of *pâte-sur-pâte* at prices within the reach of persons of moderate means. They show a bright and varied selection of vases thus treated.

A plate, shown in Figure 432, shows tropical foliage with nymphs paddling in a pool. Another plate, seen in Figures 433 and 434, shows a maiden fishing and a cameo of a lady at the top. This cameo is said to be of Frederick Schenck's wife, Mary. A photograph of her is shown in Figure 435.

George Jones & Sons continued the production of *pâte-sur-pâte* until the mid-1880s when its popularity declined.

Ornamental wares

Pâte-sur-pâte was only one type of ornamental ware produced by George Jones & Sons. Many different designs of vases, jardinières and flower baskets, manufactured in majolica, were also for decorative purposes. These pieces were manufactured in either earthenware or stone china bodies. From 1876, with the commencement of the manufacture of bone china, ornamental wares of the finest quality were produced. Many of the early, bone china, pieces were to designs that were also manufactured with earthenware bodies and decorated in majolica colours. A wall bracket, registered on 30 March 1876 and given patent no. 299499, was one such piece. Shown in Figure 436 manufactured in bone china, this piece also appears in the pattern books, pattern no 3507, decorated in majolica colours. A similar example of this shape of wall bracket manufactured in bone china but with a celadon coloured body is shown in Figure 438. The shape name for this wall bracket is 'Ada'.

On 26 July 1876, patent no. 302125 was given to a design for an unusual flower holder. Called a 'Duke of Edinburgh flower holder', an example in bone china is shown in Figure 437.

A design registered on 9 October 1876 and given patent no. 304150, could be classed as either ornamental or useful ware. It was called an 'egg basket and flower holder' and was to be manufactured in either bone china or earthenware decorated in majolica colours. From the pattern book, pattern no. 3523 shows it with a turquoise ground complete with egg cups and pattern no. 3524 shows it without egg cups.

Two designs for flower baskets were registered on 25 January 1877. Patent no. 307237 was given to a design for a 'hanging basket'. This basket had an embossed wicker basket effect and was complete with a raised lid and handle. The handle was held upright between two supports attached to the sides of the basket, the basket was hung from a point between the two supports and the handle. Patent no. 307238 was given to a design for a 'handled basket'. This basket was of shallow depth and oval in shape and was complete with a raised handle.

On 2 May 1877, three designs were registered for various types of flower holders. Patent no. 309819 was given to a flower holder called a 'Moth Flower Trough'. The trough was oval in shape and had feet at both ends in the shape of an open winged moth, the moth being attached to the trough by its wings. Patent no. 309820 was given to a design for a 'Flower Bracket', the shape of which incorporated a flower similar to a Spathiphyllum (White Sails). The third design was for a 'Flower Suspender', patent no. 309821. This hanging basket had a bowl, in the shape of leaves, at each end of the bowl was a bird attached to the bowl by its wings. The whole piece was suspended by cord placed through holes in the leaf bowl.

On 30 January 1878, patent no. 318158 was given to a design for an ornamental jug. This jug, shown in Figure 230, illustrates the very high standard of not only artistic design but also workmanship of the wares being produced by George Jones & Sons. The painting of the Azaleas and the contrast between the turquoise ground and the pink of the flowers is quite stunning. A drawing of this jug in majolica colours is shown in Figure 126. This illustration came from the George Jones majolica pattern book. On the same day as the design for this jug was registered, a design for a vase was also registered. This design, which was given patent no. 318159, was for a conical shaped vase with a turned out lip, and two handles moulded on to the side of the body. The vase was decorated with small embossed flowers and the lower part of the vase had an embossed pebble effect. This design, and similar ones, were manufactured in *pâte colorée* (coloured paste). An example of a *pâte colorée* vase is shown in Figures 440 and 441.

At a Fine Arts Exhibition held at the Borough Hall, Stafford, in November 1878, George Jones & Sons exhibited examples of some of their current production of ornamental wares. A review of the exhibition published in *The Pottery Gazette* in December 1878 stated:

> The same firm have also exhibited a case of china chiefly vases with white hand moulded flowers trailing over a celadon body, which celadon is rather fresher than usual; little bits of gilding and piercing are very judiciously introduced and they are altogether in excellent good taste. Some white china vases, decorated with hand moulded primroses, tinted after nature, are very pretty and vernal looking.

In 1879, an International Exhibition was held in Sydney, Australia. George Jones & Sons were exhibitors and were awarded two prizes. One, a 'First degree of Merit', was for vases and stands, and the second, a 'First degree of Merit Special' was awarded for porcelain and majolica ware. In the *Report of Judges, and Awards*, the following comment was made on the wares exhibited by the company:

This firm shows a splendid collection of porcelain-ware of the finest description. The paintings are very fine, and the colours and shades are delicate, the gold burnishing is of a superior standard, the designs are new and exceedingly attractive; the shadings of the leaf-painting show great progress. A beautiful collection of raised flower ornaments is very artistic, the formation of the flowers and leaves is correct and finely finished, and the design unique. A great many specimens of dark-coloured-bodied ornaments with clear-cut, raised Figures, show to great advantage, and denote very great progress. This firm also shows a very good collection of earthenware, the quality of which is very fine, the painting and glazing excellent, the style new and very creditable, and the gilding exceedingly attractive.

Between 1878 and 1882, very few designs were submitted for registration. On 14 July 1882, two designs were registered for flower holders. The first, which was given patent no. 383436, was for a two-handled vase. This bulbous shaped vase was similar in shape to Figure 638 but had two vertical moulded handles placed on either side near the top. The vase had an embossed decoration consisting of a large leaf with flowers and flower buds extending beyond the leaf. The second design, which was given patent no. 383437, was a similar shape to patent no 383436; however, the two vertical handles were replaced with a single handle over the top, creating a flower basket similar to Figure 439.

Eight days later, on 22 July 1882, a design (patent no. 383802) was registered for an ornamental jug. The jug had a wavy lipped top which sloped into a bulbous body. The body of the jug was embossed with flowers and flower buds. The handle of the jug had a flower bud moulded near the top.

In October 1882, another exhibition took place at the Borough Hall, Stafford. This time the theme of the exhibition was 'Excellence of Design' and once again George Jones & Sons were exhibitors. In a report of the exhibition, published in *The Staffordshire Advertiser*, comment was made on the company's exhibits:

> The stall is distinguished for its flower baskets, modelled from nature, in which the leaves and flowers of the water lily play a prominent part. On the same stand are many meritorious examples of china painting on plaques suitable for framing and a number of striking objects decorated with flowers in high relief, the flowers being moulded in coloured clays.

In 1878 Llewellynn Jewitt published his book *Ceramic Art of Great Britain*. In his book, under the sub-heading 'Trent Pottery', he described the type of wares George Jones & Sons were producing at that time, such as majolica. By 1883, when his book was updated and re-published, his description of the wares, particularly the ornamental wares, was very vivid and complimentary. It is worth quoting this section, on ornamental wares, in full as it gives a good indication of the quality of the flower baskets being produced and also describes some of the *pâte colorée* vases:

> The ornamental productions in china ware are all characterised by the purest taste both in conception of design and in finish of decoration. A flower-basket formed of the curled-up leaf of the water-lily, has its double handle, which forms a support by passing beneath the leaf, composed of the long flower-stems of the plant twisted and plaited together, with exquisitely modelled flowers and buds at the sides. It is one of the most charming of conceptions, and is just such a careless, elegant, and surpassingly beautiful object as a naiad or a water nymph, in one of her happier moments might have improvised, as she rose from the lake, to present to some favoured mortal. Another equally charming production is a quadruple flower-basket, whose handles, crossing each other, loop up and give apparent support to the matted basket itself.

these may be classed among the most elegant of novelties, and give evidence of the purest taste on the part of the firm. They are produced in celadon and white china.

What we have said about these china flower-baskets will hold equally good with regard to the *pâte colorée* in vases, which, in their finest body of earthenware, have been recently introduced. The delicate grounding of these, the masterly way in which the groups of flowers and foliage are arranged, the judicious manner in which the relief decoration is managed, the purely artistic painting of the groups, the heightening of rims and supports with gold, and the perfect harmony and unobtrusiveness of the whole is such as becomes a joy to the educated eye, and render these productions of Messrs. Jones & Son [*sic*] acquisitions to be sought for and cherished.

By the mid-1880s flower baskets were losing their popularity. The sale of majolica decorated ornamental wares had declined, and had been replaced by ivory coloured wares with hand decorated embossed designs, utilizing the same designs and moulds that had been used for the majolica pieces. Strawberry dishes and nut dishes were quite common, not only produced in earthenware but also in bone china. Figures 369, 370 and 371 show examples of such pieces.

Vases of all shapes and sizes, jardinières large and small, were becoming popular. In the period 1885 to 1890, many of George Jones & Sons ornamental pieces were marked with the word 'FAIENCE', usually beneath the company's black backstamp. 'Faience' is not, as many people believe, the pattern name but refers to the body and decorating of the piece. Although George Jones & Sons appeared to have used the word 'faience' during the mid to late 1880s, it must have been used quite extensively for a long period afterwards, by other manufacturers. In May 1909 the *Pottery Gazette* saw fit to publish an editorial note giving a description of how the word originated. It stated:

"What is faience ?" and "How did it get its name ?" are questions that are frequently asked but seldom answered with any certainty. Persons who have been long in the trade sometimes use the word without any distinctive idea of the origin or real meaning of it. Majolica and other painted pottery was made in many Italian towns in the latter half of the fifteenth century ... one of the most celebrated manufacturers of majolica was at Faenza. But Faenza was also a place of considerable commercial importance, and had a regular trade with many foreign places. Its special majolica productions in time became known to the French by the name of the town. This name ultimately applied in the European markets to every kind of pottery, without distinction of origin, which presented any similarity to the glazed porcelain embellished with painted designs which came from "Faenza" whether majolica or not. Faience is, therefore, a word manufactured from the name of the town "Faenza", just as majolica was derived from "Majorca" in Italy [*sic*] ... Today, "faience" is by common consent understood to be something between fine porcelain and majolica - any kind of artistic pottery with painted, incised or applied embellishments ... Perhaps a short answer to the question "What is faience ?" would be - "A pottery body, between majolica and porcelain, artistically decorated and coloured." The process of evolution has given to all wares of this character the name of "faience". We admit this is a very wide - far too wide - definition, but the indiscriminate, the injudicious, use of the term - without remonstrance - seems to justify it.

In June 1888, *The Pottery Gazette* stated: '...During the past twelve months a considerable number of manufacturers were now producing art pottery...' What is art pottery? The term was adopted in the 1880s to describe ornamental and useful wares used to achieve a particular look to the interior design and decoration of Victorian homes. It was eventually used to describe wares produced, from the 1870s to the art deco period of the 1930s, that reflected the artistic taste of the times.

It was around 1891 when George Jones & Sons commenced the production of their interpretation of art pottery. Art pottery, of the 1890s, incorporated many features, one of which was the use of brightly coloured glazes to create contrast. The designers at George Jones & Sons used these to very good effect, featuring grounds in beautiful reds, yellows, blues, greens etc. with flowers painted in sharp contrast to the ground colours. The various shapes of vases and jardinières, 'gracefully modelled on true art lines', represented another feature of 1890s art pottery.

One thing that was unique to the art pottery produced during this period was that the pattern or style name included the word 'ware' and was usually incorporated into the manufacturers' backstamp. This is a list of pattern or style names used by George Jones & Sons up to 1900.

Athenian Ware
Azure Ware
Burmese Ware
Cerutean Ware
Crescentine Ware
Madras Ware
Melrose Ware
Orient Ware
Peconia Ware
Prahsa ware
Ruby Ware
Tyrean Ware

After 1900 Imperial Ware and Morrish Ware were added to the list of names.

The only article to appear in *The Pottery Gazette,* reporting on the art pottery of George Jones & Sons Ltd., was published in October 1897. It stated:

there is another branch of the firm's business which also merits special attention. We refer to their art wares. The upper rooms of their premises constitute an art exhibition in themselves. They are filled with the most interesting assortment of the firm's artistic and fancy goods. We are not proposing to institute comparisons between Messrs. Jones's productions and those of other firms making art pottery. Nowhere would comparison be so out of place. Different productions of high-class pottery are not comparable. Each firm has distinctive characteristics of it's [*sic*] own ... They have a number of vases of noble proportions, and a varied assortment of quaint and fancy shapes. There are several of their decorations that are decidedly unique, and that illustrate in a pronounced manner the individuality we have referred to.

The article went on to feature 'Melrose' ware, 'Ruby' ware, and 'Crescentine' ware. It also showed photographs of vases in both 'Melrose' and 'Crescentine' ware.

A large proportion of the early art pottery, especially the 'Madras' and 'Melrose' ware, was decorated with patterns designed by Horace Overton Jones. Many of these were lithographic patterns and were all of flowers or flowering shrubs. None of the art pottery wares bear any pattern numbers on the base and, up to the present time, no pattern or shape books showing examples of the art pottery manufactured during this period have been found.

Figure 474 shows a 'Madras' ware jardinière. A feature of this piece is the superb modelling of the feet rising up the side of the body toward a border of moulded flowers and leaves.

The first design for a vase to be registered since the end of the majolica era was registered on the 17 March 1899 and was given Rd. No. 335404. An example of this design is shown in

Figure 486. This elegant vase is decorated in the 'Madras' ware and the pattern consists of sprigs of Hawthorn.

Two different styles of decorating a large 'Madras' ware vase are shown in Figures 469 and 470. The vase weighs 31 pounds and has moulded flower buds around the top with stems that wind around the rim and are then intertwined to form the two handles. From the base, moulded bulrushes rise to meet the handles. Both pieces are marked with the initials H.O.J. The 'Madras' ware vase shown in Figure 472 is also illustrated in *The Pottery Gazette* article of October 1897 in 'Crescentine' ware and shown in Figure 478. The three handled 'Madras' ware jardinière shown in Figure 459 is quite rare. The red flowers contrast well with the dark yellow ground.

Two different examples of the same shaped vase are shown in Figures 466 and 467. Figure 466 is 'Melrose' ware and Figure 467 is 'Madras' ware. The embossed scaling effect at the base of the vase shows up well on the 'Melrose' piece as does the contrast between the yellow ground and the brown underglaze transfer printed flowers. The 'Madras' vase has the characteristic underglaze transfer printed border around the top. The conical shaped vase, shown in Figure 481, is in 'Melrose' ware. The embossed chrysanthemums painted in brown contrast well with the yellowy green ground. A finely moulded 'Melrose' ware jug is shown in Figure 482. The sweeping handle adds to the graceful design. The embossed brown chrysanthemums and the yellowy green ground again create a pleasing contrast. An amusingly shaped 'Melrose' ware vase is shown in Figure 484 — note the unusual border pattern around the rim. Although I stated earlier that none of the art pottery pieces bear any pattern numbers, this border pattern appears in the pattern book under the pattern number A1710.

A rare piece of 'Orient' ware is shown in Figure 468. A feature of this vase is the unusual way the ground colour changes from light turquoise at the top to dark turquoise at the base.

A pair of 'Tyrean' ware vases are shown in Figure 476. The burgundy ground contrasts beautifully with the gold decorated scenes of deer and highland cattle in raised paste. Interestingly, the gold backstamp incorporates a crown. These vases were also produced with various coloured grounds including a blue/green ground.

A 'Cyprian' ware vase is shown in Figure 485. The raised paste, hand painted landscape scene is quite unusual.

As well as producing their interpretation of art pottery, George Jones & Sons Ltd. also produced other designs for vases and jardinières. Many were marked A-F China (Anglo-French China). One particular type of decoration is shown on the vases in Figures 454, 455 and 456. The majority of these underglaze pictures are of rural scenes or seascapes. This type of decoration was also used to decorate tableware. Figure 305 shows a coffee cup and saucer decorated in a similar style.

In September 1899, a comment was noted in the Information Book of the Stoke-upon-Trent branch of The Manchester and Liverpool Bank that Mr. G. H. Jones had informed the bank that George Jones & Sons Ltd.: 'were doing well with the speciality - 'Anglo-French China' - for which they were mainly increasing their works'

Commenting on the wares of George Jones & Sons Ltd. in 1902, W. P. Jervis wrote in his book *Encyclopaedia of Ceramics*:

There has been a laudable effort to produce only the best goods it was possible to make, whether in china, earthenware or majolica; and the same relative care is taken with a sponged bowl as with some of those beautiful creations in which underglaze painting is combined with rich and original glazes. The beautiful 'Melrose' ware is of this nature. The pieces are finely modeled, graceful in shape, and present some brilliant colorings, the ground varying from warm crimson to a brilliant yellow. About all these pieces there is an individuality that never descends to a mannerism which is not easy to describe.

Figure 228. Earthenware bread plate, ca. 1876. Shape name 'Hawthorn', length 13". £60-80; $100-130. Also produced in majolica.

Figure 229. Bone china broth set, ca. 1877. Broth bowl is marked with backstamp 'T. Goode', tray impressed GJ, tray diameter 10". £150-200; $250-330.

Figure 230. A rare bone china jug, ca. 1878. Registered design 30 January 1878, pattern no. 4533, height 7.5". £350-400; $580-660. Also produced in majolica, see Figure 126.

Figure 231. A rare earthenware wine cooler, ca. 1884. Pattern no. 7551, marked 'Faience', height 8.5". £400-450; $660-750.

Figure 232. Earthenware cheese dish and cover, ca. 1885. Shape Rd. No. 14976, pattern no. 7884, height 7.5". *Courtesy of Fred and Joyce Moseley.* £200-250; $330-415.

Figure 234. Earthenware sweetmeat dish, ca. 1886. Pattern no. 6856, diameter 6.5". *Courtesy of Derek and Shirley Weyman.* £40-50; $65-80.

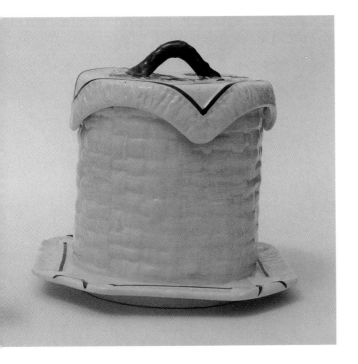

Figure 233. Earthenware preserve pot on fixed stand, ca. 1886. Shape Rd. No. 9725, pattern no. 7838, height 5". *Courtesy of Derek and Shirley Weyman.* £120-140; $200-230.

Figure 235. An unusually shaped bone china dish, ca. 1886. Pattern Rd. No. 826, pattern no. 7185, diameter 6.75". £75-100; $120-165.

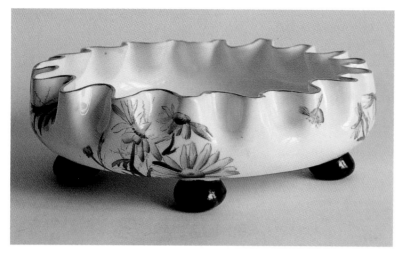

Figure 236. Side view of Figure 235 showing foot pads.

Figure 239. Earthenware cheese dish and cover, ca. 1886. Pattern no. 6227, height 8.5". *Courtesy of Derek and Shirley Weyman.* £180-200; $300-330.

Figure 237. Earthenware jug, ca. 1886. Pattern name 'Primrose', height 6.75". £120-140; $200-230.

Figure 238. Earthenware jug, ca. 1886. Pattern name 'Chrysanthemum', height 6.75". *Courtesy of Mike and Jenny Dunn.* £120-140; $200-230.

Figure 240. Earthenware muffin dish, ca. 1888. Pattern no. 8133, pattern name 'Almonds', marked 'Faience', width 7.5". £60-80; $100-130.

Figure 243. Earthenware marmalade pot on fixed stand, ca. 1890. Shape Rd. No. 124120, pattern no. 9504, height 5.5". *Courtesy of Derek and Shirley Weyman.* £80-100; $130-165.

Figure 241. Earthenware cheese dish and cover, ca. 1890. Pattern name 'Peach Blow', marked 'Faience', height 8". *Courtesy of Derek and Shirley Weyman.* £180-200; $300-330.

Figure 242. Earthenware candlestick, ca. 1890. Pattern name 'Briar', pattern no. 7371, height 3.25". *Courtesy of Derek and Shirley Weyman.* £80-100; $130-165.

Figure 244. Earthenware marmalade pot on fixed stand, ca. 1892. Shape Rd. No. 124120, pattern name 'Chrysanthemum', Rd. No. 21391, height 7". *Courtesy of Fred and Joyce Moseley.* £80-100; $130-165.

Figure 245. Earthenware cheese dish and cover, ca. 1893. Pattern Rd. No. 122293, initialled H.O.J, height 7". £180-200; $300-330.

Figure 247. Bone china leaf-shaped dish, ca. 1894. Pattern no. A1181, diameter 5.25". *Courtesy of Marjorie Winters.* £40-50; $65-80.

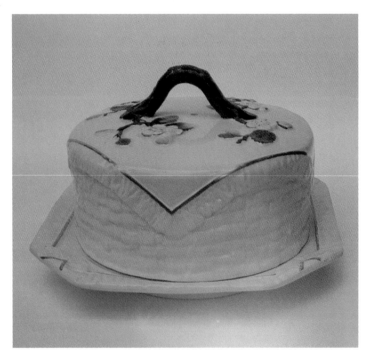

Figure 246. Earthenware cheese dish and cover, ca. 1894. Shape Rd. No. 9725, height 5". *Courtesy of Marjorie Winters.* £150-170; $250-280.

Figure 248. Bone china jug, ca. 1895. Pattern no. A1194, height 6.75". £70-90; $115-150.

Figure 249. Bone china dessert dish, ca. 1897. Shape Rd. No. 270717, pattern no. A2601, width 8.5". £70-90; $115-150.

Figure 251. Bone china tea cup, coffee cup and saucer, ca. 1877. Shape registered design 29 May 1876, shape name 'Tall Chad', pattern no. 4588, saucer diameter 5.375". £90-100; $150-165.

Figure 250. Earthenware biscuit barrel, ca. 1899. Pattern no. E315, initialled H.O.J, height 9". £180-200; $300-330.

Figure 252. Bone china tea cup, coffee cup and saucer, ca. 1877. Shape registered design 29 May 1876, shape names 'Low Chad' and 'Tall Chad', pattern no. 5746, saucer diameter 5.375". £90-100; $150-165.

Figure 253. Bone china tea cup and saucer, ca. 1878. Shape registered design 29 May 1876, shape name 'Tall Chad', pattern no. 4649, saucer diameter 5.25". £70-90; $115-150.

Figure 254. Bone china cup and saucer, ca. 1878. Shape registered design 29 May 1876, shape name 'Tall Chad', pattern no. 5014, saucer diameter 5.25". £70-90; $115-150.

Figure 255. Bone china cup and saucer, ca. 1880. Shape registered design 29 May 1876, shape name 'Tall Chad', pattern no. 4642, saucer diameter 6.125". £70-90; $115-150.

Figure 256. Drawing of pattern no. 4642 on a 'Tall Chad' cup, Figure 255, taken from the George Jones pattern books. *Courtesy of Trustees of the Wedgwood Museum.*

Figure 257. Bone china cup and saucer, ca. 1880. Shape registered design 29 May 1876, shape name 'Tall Chad', pattern no. 5818, saucer diameter 5.25". £70-90; $115-150.

Figure 258. Bone china cup and saucer, ca. 1881. Shape registered design 29 May 1876, shape name 'Tall Chad', pattern no. 5750, saucer diameter 5.25". £70-90; $115-150.

Figure 259. Bone china cup and saucer, ca. 1879. Shape registered design 29 May 1876, pattern no. 5922, saucer diameter 5.625". £40-60; $65-100.

Figure 261. An unusual and early embossed bone china tea cup and saucer, ca. 1880. Saucer diameter 5.5". *Courtesy of Marjorie Winters.* £70-90; $115-150.

Figure 260. Bone china two-handled plate, ca. 1877. Pattern no. 4533, diameter 9.5". £60-80; $100-130.

Figure 262. Bone china cup and saucer, ca. 1880. Shape name 'York', pattern no. 6011, saucer diameter 5.5". £40-60; $65-100.

Figure 263. Earthenware cup and saucer, ca. 1880. Pattern name 'Our Roses', pattern no. 7791, saucer diameter 5.125". £40-60; $65-100.

Figure 265. Earthenware tea plate, ca. 1882. Pattern name 'Caius', diameter 7.5". £15-25; $25-40.

Figure 264. Bone china cup and saucer, ca. 1881. Shape registered design 29 May 1876, shape name 'Weston', pattern no. 5975, saucer diameter 5". £40-60; $65-100.

Figure 266. Earthenware cup and saucer, ca. 1882. Shape name 'Sydney', pattern no. 6001, saucer diameter 5.75". £30-40; $50-65.

115

Figure 267. An unusual bone china coffee cup, saucer, jug and basin, ca. 1883. Shape name 'York', pattern registered design 16 September 1881, pattern name 'Briar', pattern no. 6035, saucer diameter 5". Jug and basin £30-40; $50-65 each, cup and saucer £50-60; $80-100.

Figure 268. Bone china cup, saucer and milk jug, ca. 1884. Cup shape registered design 29 May 1876, shape name 'Weston', pattern Rd. No. 826, pattern no. 6264, saucer diameter 5.5", jug height 4". £30-40; $50-65 each piece.

Figure 269. A rare bone china tea kettle, ca. 1884. Pattern Rd. No. 826, pattern no. 6264, height 7.5". £130-150; $215-250.

Figure 270. Bone china cup and saucer, ca. 1884. Shape registered design 29 May 1876, shape name 'Weston', saucer diameter 5.625". £40-60; $65-100.

Figure 272. Bone china cup and saucer, ca. 1884. Shape name 'Garnet' pattern registered design 16 September 1881, pattern name 'Briar', pattern no. 6275, saucer diameter 5.5". £40-60; $65-100.

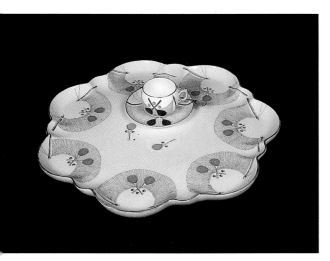

Figure 271. An unusual earthenware revolving tray for an afternoon tea set, ca. 1884. Pattern no. 6227, depicting tennis rackets, balls and nets, revolving tray approximate diameter 20". *Courtesy of The Gurney Collection*. £600-650; $990-1070 for complete set.

Figure 273. Bone china cup and saucer, ca. 1885. Pattern no. 6342, saucer diameter 5.75". £40-60; $65-100.

117

Figure 274. Graduated set of three earthenware jugs, ca. 1885. Pattern name 'Briar', pattern no. 7359, height 8", 7.5", 6.75". *Courtesy of Derek and Shirley Weyman.* £150-170; $250-280 for set.

Figure 275. Bone china coffee cup, saucer and milk jug, ca. 1885. Pattern Rd. No. 826, pattern no. 6265, saucer diameter 3.25". £30-40; $50-65 each piece.

Figure 276. Bone china cup and saucer, ca. 1886. Shape name 'York', pattern Rd. No. 39348, pattern name 'Cornflower', pattern no. 6434, saucer diameter 5.5". £40-60; $65-100.

118

Figure 277. Bone china cup and saucer, ca. 1886. Shape name 'Garnet', pattern no. 6155, saucer diameter 5.75". £40-60; $65-100.

Figure 278. Bone china cup and saucer, ca. 1886. Shape name 'Garnet', pattern registered design 29 September 1881, pattern name 'Ivy Bower', pattern no. 6099, saucer diameter 5.75". £40-60; $65-100.

Figure 279. Bone china cup and saucer, ca. 1886. Shape name 'Worcester', pattern registered design 16 September 1881, pattern name 'Briar', pattern no. 6327, saucer diameter 5.625". £40-60; $65-100.

Figure 280. Bone china tea pot, jug and basin, ca. 1887. Shape name 'Garnet', pattern Rd. No. 68515, pattern name 'Primrose', tea pot height 5.5". *Courtesy of Derek and Shirley Weyman.* £110-130; $180-215.

Figure 281. Partially complete afternoon tea set, ca. 1887. Cup shape M/S, pattern name 'Peach Blow', pattern no. 9003, tray diameter 23.25". *Courtesy of Marjorie Winters.* £400-450; $660-750 complete set.

Figure 282. Bone china cup and saucer, ca. 1887. Shape name 'Garnet', pattern name 'Eden', pattern no. 6371, saucer diameter 5.75". £40-60; $65-100.

Figure 283. Bone china cup and saucer, ca. 1888. Shape Rd. No. 96154, pattern no. 9142, initialled H.O.J, saucer diameter 5.625". £40-60; $65-100.

Figure 284. Bone china two-handled cup and saucer, ca. 1888. Cup shape Rd. No. 96154, saucer diameter 5.75". £50-70; $80-115.

Figure 285. Bone china covered breakfast cup and saucer, ca. 1888. Shape Rd. No. 42306, shape name 'Kew', pattern no. 6490, saucer diameter 6.5". £50-70; $80-115.

Figure 286. Bone china cup and saucer, ca. 1890. Pattern no. 9043, saucer diameter 5.5". £40-60; $65-100.

Figure 287. Bone china cup and saucer, ca. 1890. Shape name 'Garnet', pattern Rd. No. 56152, pattern name 'Peach Blow', pattern no. 9004, saucer diameter 5.5". £40-60; $65-100.

Figure 288. Bone china cup and saucer, ca. 1891. Shape Rd. No. 124321, saucer diameter 5.5". £50-70; $80-115.

Figure 289. Bone china tea pot, jug and basin, c. 1891. Shape Rd. No. 143138, tea pot height 5.5". *Courtesy of Fred and Joyce Moseley.* £110-130; $180-215.

Figure 290. Bone china tea pot, jug and basin, ca. 1891. Shape Rd. No. 165075, shape name 'Bow', pattern no. A291, tea pot height 5". *Courtesy of Derek and Shirley Weyman.* £110-130; $180-215 set

Figure 291. Afternoon tea service consisting of an earthenware tray with a bone china tea set, ca. 1891. Teapot shape name Ionic, pattern name 'Bon Bon', tray length 17". £450-500; $750-825.

Figure 292. Bone china coffee cup and saucer, ca. 1891. Shape Rd. No. 165075, shape name 'Bow', pattern no. A1630, initialled H.O.J., saucer diameter 4.75". £50-60; $80-100.

Figure 294. Earthenware coffee pot, ca. 1892. Shape registered design 1 August 1883, pattern no. 7747, height 7.5". *Courtesy of Derek and Shirley Weyman.* £100-120; $165-200.

Figure 293. Bone china cup and saucer, ca. 1892. Shape Rd. No. 143138, pattern no. A91, saucer diameter 5.625". £50-70; $80-115.

Figure 295. Bone china coffee cup and saucer, ca. 1892. Shape Rd. No. 124321, pattern Rd. No. 122293, saucer diameter 5". £60-70; $100-115.

Figure 296. Bone china coffee cup and saucer, ca. 1891. Shape Rd. No. 124321, pattern no. A14, saucer diameter 4.75". £50-60; $80-100.

Figure 298. Bone china cup and saucer, ca. 1893. Shape Rd. No. 143138, pattern no. A90, saucer diameter 5.625". £50-70; $80-115.

Figure 297. Bone china tea kettle, ca. 1892. Shape Rd. No. 124321, height 7.5". £100-120; $165-200.

Figure 299. Bone china coffee cup and saucer, ca. 1893. Pattern no. 7106, saucer diameter 5.625". £50-70; $80-115.

Figure 300. Bone china cup and saucer, ca. 1894. Shape Rd. No. 42306, shape name 'Kew', pattern Rd. No. 8851, pattern name 'Blantyre', pattern no. 6441, saucer diameter 5.5". £40-60; $65-100.

Figure 302. Bone china single-handled plate, ca. 1894. Shape Rd. No. 143138, pattern no. A16, diameter 8.5". £60-80; $100-130.

Figure 301. Bone china cup and saucer, ca. 1894. Pattern Rd. No. 56152, pattern name 'Birds and Bloom', pattern no. 9001, saucer diameter 5.625". £40-60; $65-100.

Figure 303. Bone china single-handled plate, ca. 1897. Shape Rd. No. 269723, shape name 'Silver', pattern no. A2570, diameter 9". *Courtesy of Derek and Shirley Weyman.* £60-80; $100-130.

Figure 304. Bone china tea cup and saucer, ca. 1897. Shape name 'Sterling', pattern no. A3113, saucer diameter 5.5". *Courtesy of Derek and Shirley Weyman.* £50-70; $80-115.

Figure 306. Bone china tea cup, coffee cup and saucers, ca. 1898. Tea cup shape name 'Milford', cup height 2.5". *Courtesy of Derek and Shirley Weyman.* Tea cup £50-70; $80-115, coffee cup £40-50; $65-80.

Figure 305. Bone china coffee cup and saucer, ca. 1898. Pattern no. A1427, saucer diameter 4.5". £50-70; $80-115.

Figure 307. Bone china plate with handles, ca. 1898. Diameter 9.5". *Courtesy of Derek and Shirley Weyman.* £60-80; $100-130.

Figure 308. Bone china cup and saucer, ca. 1898. Shape name 'Sterling', pattern no. A3123, saucer diameter 5.25". £40-60; $65-100.

Figure 309. Bone china cup and saucer, ca. 1898. Pattern no. TC 323, saucer diameter 5.5". *Courtesy of Marjorie Winters.* £50-60; $80-100.

Figure 310. Bone china cup and saucer, ca. 1899. Shape Rd. No. 269723, shape name 'Silver', pattern no. A2751, saucer diameter 5.5". £40-60; $65-100.

Figure 311. Bone china cup and saucer, ca. 1899. Shape Rd. No. 269723, shape name 'Silver', pattern no. A2758, saucer diameter 5.5". £40-60; $65-100.

Figure 312. Bone china jug and basin, ca. 1899. Shape Rd. No 269723, shape name 'Silver', height 2.5". £25-35; $40-60 each piece.

Figure 313. Bone china cup and saucer, ca. 1899. Shape name 'Anglo', pattern no. A4627, saucer diameter 5.5". £40-60; $65-100.

Figure 314. Bone china cup and saucer, ca. 1899. Pattern no. A1692, saucer diameter 5.5". £40-60; $65-100.

Figure 316. Bone china dinner plate, ca. 1880. Pattern no. 5864, diameter 9.75" £40-60; $65-100.

Figure 315. Stone china dinner plate, ca. 1875. Pattern name 'Brighton', pattern no. 4902, diameter 10.25". *Courtesy of Derek and Shirley Weyman.* £30-40; $50-65.

Figure 317. An unusual earthenware sauce tureen with stand, ca. 1881. Shape registered design 16 September 1881, shape name 'Venice', pattern registered design 29 September 1881, pattern name 'Ivy Bower', pattern no. 6787, length 9.5". £110-130; $180-215.

Figure 318. An unusual earthenware vegetable dish, ca. 1881. Shape registered design 16 September 1881, shape name 'Venice', pattern registered design 29 September 1881, pattern name 'Ivy Bower', pattern no. 6787, length 13.25". £140-160; $230-265.

Figure 319. Earthenware dinner plate, ca. 1881. Pattern no. 6714, diameter 10.5". £30-40; $50-65.

Figure 320. Earthenware sauce tureen with stand and ladle, ca. 1882. Pattern registered design 13 October 1873, pattern name 'Cuba', length 9". £100-120; $165-200.

Figure 321. Earthenware sauce tureen with stand and ladle, ca. 1884. Shape Rd. No. 3657, pattern name 'Kent', length 9". *Courtesy of Derek and Shirley Weyman.* £100-120; $165-200.

Figure 322. Earthenware gravy dish, ca. 1886. Pattern Rd. No. 21391, pattern name 'Chrysanthemum', pattern no. 8636, length 19.5". £130-150; $215-250.

Figure 323. Earthenware meat plate, ca. 1887. Pattern name 'Birds and Bloom', length 18". £60-80; $100-130.

Figure 324. Earthenware sauce tureen with stand, ca. 1888. Shape Rd. No. 73024, pattern no. 9294, length 7.5". *Courtesy of Marjorie Winters.* £100-120; $165-200.

Figure 325. Earthenware covered broth bowl with stand, ca. 1888. Pattern Rd. No. 100,000, pattern name 'Azalea', pattern no. 9501, height 4.5". *Courtesy of Derek and Shirley Weyman.* £60-80; $100-130.

Figure 326. Earthenware dinner plate, ca. 1888. Pattern Rd. No. 84746, pattern name 'Chatsworth', pattern no. 6494, diameter 10.5". £30-40; $50-65.

Figure 327. Earthenware game pie dish, ca. 1889. Registered design 27 December 1873, pattern no. 6889, marked 'Faience', length 11". *Courtesy of Derek and Shirley Weyman.* £400-450; $660-750.

Figure 328. Earthenware vegetable dish, ca. 1888. Pattern name 'Congo', length 12". £50-70; $80-115.

Figure 329. Earthenware sauce tureen with stand, ca. 1890. Shape Rd. No. 143137, pattern name 'Charm', length 8.5". *Courtesy of Derek and Shirley Weyman.* £50-60; $80-100.

Figure 330. A-F china tureen, ca. 1890. Pattern no. 9711, length 11". *Courtesy of Marjorie Winters.* £60-80; $100-130.

Figure 332. Earthenware dinner plate, ca. 1890. Pattern Rd. No. 134138, pattern no. 9294, diameter 10.375". £40-60; $65-100.

Figure 331. Bone china dinner plate, ca. 1890. Pattern Rd. No. 826, pattern no. 6496, diameter 9.75". £40-60; $65-100.

Figure 333. A-F china covered vegetable dish, ca. 1892, Pattern Rd. No. 166458, pattern name 'Dual', length 12". *Courtesy of Derek and Shirley Weyman.* £70-90; $115-150.

Figure 334. Earthenware meat plate, ca. 1892. Shape Rd. No. 73024, pattern Rd. No. 84746, pattern name 'Chatsworth', length 15.75". £60-80; $100-130.

Figure 335. Earthenware dinner plate, ca. 1893. Pattern name 'Kio', pattern no. 9866, diameter 10.25". £40-50; $65-80.

Figure 336. Earthenware meat plate, ca. 1893, Pattern name 'Belfast', length 13.25". £30-40; $50-65.

Figure 337. A-F china soup dish, ca. 1895. Pattern name 'Kio', pattern no. 9704, diameter 10". *Courtesy of Derek and Shirley Weyman.* £25-30; $40-50.

Figure 338. A-F china covered vegetable dish, ca. 1895. Pattern no. 9774, length 10". *Courtesy of Fred and Joyce Moseley.* £70-90; $115-150.

Figure 339. Earthenware vegetable dish, ca. 1895. Shape Rd. No. 3657, pattern name 'Colony', length 10.5". £50-70; $80-115.

Figure 340. Earthenware salmon platter, ca. 1897. Shape Rd. No. 225065, painting of fish signed W. Birbeck, length 22.75". £350-400; $580-660.

Figure 341. A-F china sauce boat with stand, ca. 1897. Shape Rd. No. 225065. Painting of fish signed W. Birbeck, height 4.5". £150-180; $250-300.

Figure 342. Earthenware covered vegetable dish, ca. 1899. Pattern name 'Kent', pattern no. 7920, length 13". *Courtesy of Derek and Shirley Weyma*n. £70-90; $115-150.

Figure 343. Four bone china dessert plates and a compote, ca. 1877. Registered design 26 March 1873, pattern no. 4784, length 8.75". £60-80; $100-130 each plate. £100-120; $165-200 compote.

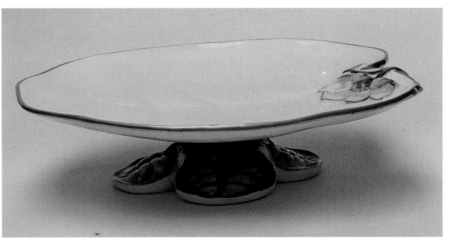

Figure 346. Bone china dessert plate, ca. 1878. Pattern registered design 13 October 1873, pattern name 'Cuba', pattern no. 4790, diameter 8.75". £50-70; $80-115.

Figure 344. Bone china strawberry dish, ca. 1877. Pattern no. 4476, diameter 10". *Courtesy of Derek and Shirley Weyman.* £350-400; $580-660.

Figure 345. An unusual bone china low comport, ca. 1877. Registered design 26 March 1873, pattern no. 4784, height 2.25". £80-100; $130-165.

Figure 347. Bone china dessert plate, ca. 1878. Back marked 'R. Judd', G. Godden's *Staffordshire Porcelain* shows a similar piece. £70-90; $115-150.

Figure 349. Bone china dessert plate, ca. 1880. Pattern no. 5390, diameter 8.5". £60-80; $100-130.

Figure 348. Bone china dessert plate, ca. 1880. Pattern no. 5363, width 8". *Courtesy of Marjorie Winters.* £80-100; $130-165.

Figure 350. Bone china dessert plate, ca. 1881. Pattern no. 5467, diameter 9". *Courtesy of Derek and Shirley Weyman.* £60-80; $100-130.

Figure 351. Bone china dessert plate, ca. 1881. Pattern no. 5468, diameter 8.75". £60-80; $100-130.

Figure 353. An unusually decorated bone china dessert plate, ca. 1882. Pattern no. 5441, diameter 9". £80-100; $130-165.

Figure 352. Bone china dessert plate, ca. 1882. Pattern no. 5428, diameter 9". £60-80; $100-130.

Figure 354. Bone china dessert plate, ca. 1882. Pattern no. 5395, diameter 9". £80-100; $130-165.

Figure 355. Drawing of pattern no. 5395, as on Figure 354, taken from a George Jones & Sons Ltd. pattern books. *Courtesy of Trustees of the Wedgwood Museum.*

Figure 357. Bone china dessert plate, ca. 1883. Pattern Rd. No. 826, pattern no. 8249, diameter 9". *Courtesy of Derek and Shirley Weyman.* £60-80; $100-130.

Figure 356. Bone china dessert plate, ca. 1882. Picture of Kelso Abbey, Roxburghshire, diameter 9". £110-130; $180-215.

Figure 358. An unusual earthenware triple tray, ca. 1883. Length 12.5". *Courtesy of Derek and Shirley Weyman.* £200-220; $330-365.

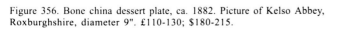

142

Figure 359. Bone china dessert plate, ca. 1883. Pattern no. 7029, diameter 9". *Courtesy of Marjorie Winters.* £60-80; $100-130.

Figure 361. Earthenware tall compote and dessert dish, ca. 1883. Compote height 5". £40-60; $65-100 each piece.

Figure 360. Bone china dessert plate, ca. 1883. Pattern registered design 16 September 1881, pattern name 'Briar', pattern no. 7012, diameter 9". £50-70; $80-115.

Figure 362. Bone china dessert plate, ca. 1883. Pattern no. 7028, diameter 8.75". £50-70; $80-115.

Figure 363. Earthenware dessert plate, ca. 1884. Pattern name 'Congo', pattern no. 7993, diameter 9". *Courtesy of Fred and Joyce Moseley.* £30-40; $50-65.

Figure 365. Bone china dessert plate, ca. 1884. Pattern no. 6313, pattern name 'Overton', diameter 9". £60-80; $100-130.

Figure 364. Bone china dessert plate, ca. 1884. Pattern name 'Lilium', pattern no. 7056, diameter 8.75". £60-80; $100-130.

Figure 366. Earthenware tall compote, ca. 1884. Pattern Rd. No. 826, pattern no. 7986, height 5". £40-60; $65-100.

Figure 367. An attractive bone china dessert plate, ca. 1884. Diameter 9". £100-120; $165-200.

Figure 368. An unusual earthenware fruit bowl, ca. 1884. Pattern Rd. No. 826, pattern no. 7499, length 12.25". £60-80; $100-130.

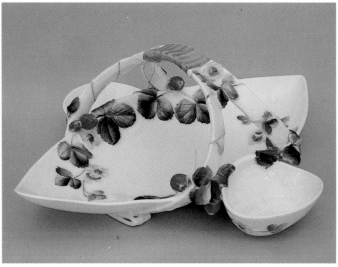

Figure 369. Bone china strawberry and fruit basket, ca. 1885. Registered design 10 March 1877, pattern no. 5621, length 14". *Courtesy of Derek and Shirley Weyman*. £400-450; $660-750.

Figure 370. Earthenware strawberry dish with ladle, ca. 1885. Registered design 11 April 1882, pattern name 'Strawberry', pattern no. 7803, length 13". *Courtesy of Fred and Joyce Moseley*. £550-600; $900-990.

145

Figure 371. Earthenware strawberry dish with cream jug and sugar bowl, ca. 1885. Registered design 16 February 1872, length 14.875". *Courtesy of Christopher Phillips.* £550-600; $900-990.

Figure 373. Bone china dessert plate, ca. 1885. Pattern no. 8332, diameter 9". *Courtesy of Derek and Shirley Weyman.* £70-90; $115-150.

Figure 372. Bone china dessert plate, ca. 1885. Pattern no. 8332, diameter 9". *Courtesy of Derek and Shirley Weyman.* £70-90; $115-150.

Figure 374. Earthenware dessert plate, ca. 1885. Pattern Rd. No. 21391, pattern name 'Chrysanthemum', pattern no. 7996, diameter 8.75". £30-50; $50-80.

146

Figure 375. Earthenware dessert plate, ca. 1885. Pattern no. 8623, diameter 9.25". £30-40; $50-65.

Figure 377. Bone china dessert plate, ca. 1886. Picture of 'Phalenopsis Grandiflora', monogram on back E.W.J. Could this be Elizabeth Walmsley Jones, George Henry Jones wife? £60-80; $100-130.

Figure 376. Bone china dessert plate, ca. 1886. Pattern name 'H.O.J. Familiar Flowers', pattern no. 8230, width 9". £70-90; $115-150.

Figure 378. Bone china tall compote, ca. 1886. Pattern Rd. No. 56152, pattern name 'Birds and Bloom', height 5". £50-70; $80-115.

Figure 379. Bone china dessert plate, ca. 1886. Pattern initialled H.O.J., diameter 9". £60-80; $100-130.

Figure 381. Earthenware low compote, ca. 1887. Pattern name 'Almonds', height 2.75". £30-50; $50-80.

Figure 380. Bone china dessert plate, ca. 1887. Pattern name 'H.O.J. Familiar Flowers', pattern no. 8212, diameter 9". £70-90; $115-150.

Figure 382. Earthenware centre compote, ca. 1887. Pattern name 'Almonds', height 6". £40-60; $65-100.

Figure 383. Bone china dessert plate, ca. 1887. Pattern no. 5496, diameter 9". £80-100; $130-165.

Figure 385. Bone china low compote, ca. 1885. Pattern registered design 13 October 1873, pattern name 'Cuba', height 2.5". £60-80; $100-130.

Figure 384. Bone china dessert plate, ca. 1887. Pattern no. 5496, diameter 9". £80-100; $130-165.

Figure 386. Photograph of a token attached to the underside of the compote, Figure 385. For an explanation of the token's use, see dessert ware text.

Figure 387. Earthenware strawberry dish, c. 1888. Registered design 19 February 1876, pattern 6877, width 10". £270-300; $445-495.

Figure 388. Earthenware dessert plate, ca. 1888. Pattern no. 9280, diameter 8.75". £40-60; $65-100.

Figure 389. Bone china dessert plate, ca. 1888. Pattern no. 8438, initialled H.O.J., diameter 8.75". £60-80; $100-130.

Figure 390. Bone china dessert plate, ca. 1889. Pattern Rd. No. 122293, pattern no. 8452, initialled H.O.J., diameter 8.75". £50-70; $80-115.

Figure 392. Bone china dessert plate, ca. 1891. Shape Rd. No. 124120, pattern is of Clematis, initialled H.O.J., diameter 8.75". £70-90; $115-150.

Figure 391, Bone china dessert plate, ca. 1890. Pattern no. A1111, initialled H.O.J., diameter 8.25". £50-70; $80-115.

Figure 393. Bone china dessert plate, ca. 1891. Shape Rd. No. 124120, pattern no. 8440, diameter 9". £70-90; $115-150.

Figure 394. Bone china dessert plate, ca. 1892. Shape Rd. No. 143138, pattern initialled H.O.J., length 11.5". £70-90; $115-150.

Figure 396. Bone china dessert plate, ca. 1893. Shape Rd. No. 143138, diameter 8.75". £70-90; $115-150.

Figure 395. Bone china dessert plate, ca. 1893. Shape Rd. No. 143138, picture of Virginian Partridge signed C. Austin, diameter 8.75". £130-150; $215-250.

Figure 397. Bone china dessert plate, ca. 1894. Shape Rd. No. 143138, pattern no. A316, signed F. Bernard, diameter 8.75". £130-150; $215-250.

152

Figure 398. Earthenware compote, ca. 1894. Pattern no. 9889, initialled H.O.J., height 5". £40-60; $65-100.

Figure 399. Bone china dessert plate, ca. 1899. Pattern no. D266, diameter 9". £60-80; $100-130.

Figure 400. Bone china dessert plate, ca. 1899. Pattern no. D248, painting of Roach signed W. Birbeck, diameter 9". £130-150; $215-250.

Figure 401. A rare earthenware ewer, ca. 1874. Shape name Prah, shape registered design 19 February 1874, pattern registered design 21 April 1874, pattern name 'Adansi', height 7.25". £150-175; $250-290.

Figure 403. Earthenware ewer, ca. 1881. Shape name 'Saxon', pattern registered design 7 June 1878, pattern name 'Plevna', pattern no. 6613, height 11.5". £70-90; $115-150.

Figure 402. A rare earthenware chamber pot, ca. 1874. Shape registered design 19 February 1874, pattern registered design 21 April 1874, pattern name 'Adansi', diameter 8.75". £60-80; $100-130.

Figure 404. Design of toilet set registered 14 October 1884, Rd. No. 14977. *Courtesy of the Public Record Office.* Reference no. BT50/19.

Figure 405. Earthenware chamber pot, ca. 1886. Shape Rd. No. 59451, pattern no. 9336, diameter 9". *Courtesy of Fred and Joyce Moseley.* £40-60; $65-100.

Figure 406. Earthenware chamber pot, ca. 1886. Shape Rd. No. 59451, pattern no. 9915, initialled H.O.J., diameter 9". £40-60; $65-100.

Figure 407. Earthenware ewer and basin, ca. 1886. Pattern name 'Cairo', pattern no. 7638, basin diameter 10". £130-150; $215-250.

Figure 409. Earthenware chamber pot, ca. 1887. Shape Rd. No. 92160, shape name 'Imperial', pattern Rd. No. 826, diameter 9". *Courtesy of Derek and Shirley Weyman.* £40-60; $65-100.

Figure 408. Earthenware ewer, ca. 1887. Pattern Rd. No. 68515, pattern name 'Primrose', height 11.25". £70-90; $115-150.

Figure 410. Earthenware ewer, basin, soap dish and shaving mug, ca. 1887. Shape Rd. No. 92160, shape name 'Imperial', pattern Rd. No. 826, basin diameter 16". *Courtesy of Derek and Shirley Weyman.* £400-450; $660-750, complete set including chamber pot Figure 409.

Figure 411. Earthenware chamber pot, ca. 1887. Pattern name 'Anemone', pattern no. 8919, diameter 9". £40-60; $65-100.

Figure 412. Earthenware soap dish and tooth brush holder with stand, ca. 1887. Shape Rd. No. 59451, pattern registered design 16 September 1881, pattern name 'Briar', pattern no. 8979, brush holder height 6". £30-50; $50-80 each piece.

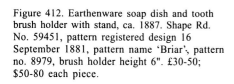

Figure 413. Earthenware ewer and basin, ca. 1887. Pattern Rd. No. 826, pattern no. 8642, basin diameter 15.5". *Courtesy of Derek and Shirley Weyman.* £220-250; $365-415.

157

Figure 414. Earthenware chamber pot, ca. 1888. Shape Rd. No. 92160, pattern Rd. No. 100,000, pattern name 'Azalea', pattern no. 9322, diameter 9". £40-60; $65-100.

Figure 415. Earthenware shaving mug, ca. 1888. Shape Rd. No. 92160, pattern no. 9309, height 5". *Courtesy of Marjorie Winters*. £40-60; $65-100.

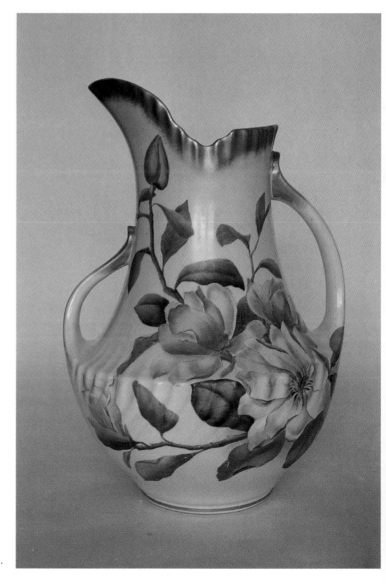

Figure 416. An attractive earthenware ewer, ca. 1889. Shape Rd. No. 92160, shape name 'Imperial', pattern Rd. No. 122292, pattern initialled C.J.B., pattern no. 9340, height 14". £100-120; $165-200.

Figure 417. Earthenware ewer, ca. 1889. Shape Rd. No. 133641, pattern Rd. No. 100,000, pattern name 'Azalea', initialled H.O.J., pattern no. 9375, height 12.75". £130-150; $215-250.

Figure 419. Earthenware chamber pot, ca. 1890. Shape Rd. No. 146574, shape name 'Empress', pattern Rd. No. 39348, pattern name 'Cornflower', diameter 9.5". *Courtesy of Marjorie Winters.* £40-60; $65-100.

Figure 418. Earthenware ewer, ca. 1890. Shape Rd. No. 146574, shape name 'Empress', pattern Rd. No. 39348, pattern name 'Cornflower', height 12". *Courtesy of Marjorie Winters.* £100-120; $165-200

Figure 420. Earthenware shaving mug, ca. 1890. Shape Rd. No. 133641, pattern Rd. No. 76274, pattern name 'Charm', pattern no. 9376, height 4.25". £40-60; $65-100.

Figure 422. Earthenware ewer, ca. 1892. Pattern Rd. No. 826, height 11.25". £70-90; $115-150.

Figure 421. Earthenware basin, ca. 1891. Shape Rd. No. 146574, pattern name 'Kio', diameter 16". *Courtesy of Marjorie Winters.* £80-100; $130-165.

Figure 423. Earthenware chamber pot, ca. 1893. Pattern name 'Almonds', diameter 9". £40-60; $65-100.

Figure 424. Earthenware ewer and basin, ca. 1893. Shape Rd. No. 92160, shape name 'Imperial', pattern Rd. No. 122292, pattern no. 9257, basin diameter 10.5". £130-150; $215-250.

Figure 426. Earthenware ewer and basin, ca. 1898. Shape Rd. No. 239437, shape name, 'Corea', basin diameter 16". *Courtesy of Derek and Shirley Weyman.* £220-250; $365-415.

Figure 425. Earthenware ewer, ca. 1895. Shape Rd. No. 92160, shape name 'Imperial', pattern no. A1258, height 14". *Courtesy of Marjorie Winters.* £100-120; $165-200.

Figure 427. Earthenware jardiniere with *pâte-sur-pâte* panels, impressed 'Schenck', ca. 1878. Shape registered design 31 October 1877, shape name 'Ribbon', pattern no. 5646, height 7". £900-1100; $1485-1815.

Figure 430. Earthenware vase with *pâte-sur-pâte* panel, ca. 1880. Pattern no. 5658, height 9.5". *Courtesy of Derek and Shirley Weyman.* £900-1100; $1485-1815.

Figure 428. Reverse side of Figure 427.

Figure 429. Earthenware vase with *pâte-sur-pâte* panel, impressed 'Schenck', ca. 1880. Height 6.25". *Courtesy of The Hanley Museum.* £900-1100; $1485-1815.

Figure 431. Earthenware vase with *pâte-sur-pâte* panel, ca. 1880. Pattern no. 5662, height 10.75". *Courtesy of Derek and Shirley Weyman.* £1000-1200; $1650-1980.

Figure 433. Earthenware plate with *pâte-sur-pâte* decoration, impressed 'Schenck', ca. 1880. Diameter 10". *Courtesy of David and Mavis Schenck. Photograph by Keith Wakeley Studios, Wimbledon.* £800-1000; $1320-1650.

Figure 434 Enlarged detail of cameo at top of figure 433. It is believed that Frederick Schenck's wife, Mary Ann, modelled for this design. *Courtesy of David and Mavis Schenck. Photograph by Keith Wakeley Studios, Wimbledon.*

Figure 432. Earthenware wall plaque with *pâte-sur-pâte* decoration, impressed 'Schenck', ca. 1880. Diameter 12". *Courtesy of Jonathan and Louise Schenck. Photograph by Keith Wakeley Studios, Wimbledon.* £1000-1200; $1650-1980.

Figure 435. Photograph (ca. 1872) of Mary Ann Schenck at the age of nineteen. *Courtesy of David and Mavis Schenck. Photograph by Keith Wakeley Studios, Wimbledon.*

Figure 436. Bone china wall bracket, ca. 1876.
Shape registered design 30 March 1876,
pattern no. 4432, length 11.5". £275-300;
$455-495.

Figure 438. Bone china wall bracket with
moulded flowers, ca. 1877, length 11.5".
Courtesy of Derek and Shirley Weyman. £275-
300; $455-495.

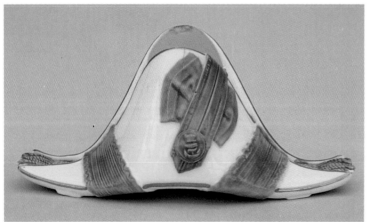

Figure 437. A rare bone china 'Duke of Edinburgh' flower holder, ca.
1876. Registered design 26 July 1876, height 3.25". *Courtesy of Derek
and Shirley Weyman.* £120-150; $200-250.

Figure 439. A rare bone china flower basket, ca. 1882. Pattern no. 7142,
height 9.25". £400-450; $660-750.

Figure 442. Earthenware vase, ca. 1886. Pattern name 'Azalea', pattern no. 5125, marked 'Faience', height 29". *Courtesy of Fred and Joyce Moseley.* £300-350; $495-580.

Figure 440. A very attractive earthenware *pâte colorée* vase, ca. 1883. Pattern no. 7524, height 9.5". *Courtesy of Derek and Shirley Weyman.* £200-220; $330-365.

Figure 443. Earthenware vase, ca. 1886. Pattern name 'Tulip', marked 'Faience', height 24.5". *Courtesy of Marjorie Winters.* £300-350; $495-580.

Figure 441. Reverse side of Figure 440.

Figure 444. Earthenware vase, ca. 1886. Pattern name 'Kio', pattern no. V100, vase marked 'Faience', height 9.5". £150-180; $250-300.

Figure 446. Earthenware vase, ca. 1887. Vase marked 'Faience', height 6". £70-90; $115-150.

Figure 445. Earthenware vase, ca. 1886. Pattern Rd. No. 21391, pattern name 'Chrysanthemum', vase marked 'Faience' height 9.75". £150-180; $250-300.

Figure 447. Earthenware vase, ca. 1887. Vase marked 'Faience', height 6.75". £70-90; $115-150.

Figure 448. A pair of earthenware candlesticks, ca. 1887. Shape Rd. No. 9725, pattern Rd. No. 826, pattern no. 7293, height 6.5". *Courtesy of Fred and Joyce Moseley*. £80-100; $130-165.

Figure 450. Reverse side of Figure 449.

Figure 449. An attractive bone china vase, ca. 1888. Height 10". *Courtesy of Derek and Shirley Weyman*. £150-175; $250-290.

Figure 451. A pair of earthenware vases, ca. 1888. Pattern no. 9425, vase marked 'Faience', height 16". £300-350; $495-580 pair.

167

Figure 452. Earthenware vase, ca. 1888. Pattern Rd. No. 100,000, pattern name 'Azalea', initialled H.O.J., vase marked 'Faience', height 5.5". *Courtesy of Marjorie Winters*. £60-80; $100-130.

Figure 454. A pair of A-F china vases, ca. 1893. Height 8.5". £400-450; $660-750 pair.

Figure 455. A pair of A-F china vases, ca. 1893. Height 7.25". £350-400; $580-660 pair.

Figure 453. Earthenware vase, ca. 1891. Pattern Rd. No. 166458, pattern name 'Dual', pattern no. 9690, height 12". *Courtesy of Derek and Shirley Weyman*. £130-160; $215-265.

Figure 456. A-F china vase, ca. 1893. Height 8.25". £100-120; $165-200.

Figure 458. 'Madras' ware jardinière, ca. 1895. Height 9". *Courtesy of Derek and Shirley Weyman.* £150-175; $250-290.

Figure 457. 'Crescentine' ware vase, ca. 1895. Height 3.75". *Courtesy of Fred and Joyce Moseley.* £80-100; $130-165.

Figure 459. A three handled 'Madras' ware vase, ca. 1895. Pattern initialled H.O.J., height 7.5". £400-450; $660-750.

Figure 460. A pair of 'Madras' ware vases, ca. 1895. Height 12". *Courtesy of Fred and Joyce Moseley.* £350-375; $580-620.

Figure 462. Earthenware vase, ca. 1895. Height 12.5". *Courtesy of Derek and Shirley Weyman.* £120-150; $200-250.

Figure 461. 'Madras' ware vase, ca. 1895. Height 17". *Courtesy of Derek and Shirley Weyman.* £250-270; $415-445.

Figure 463. Earthenware vase, ca. 1895. Height 9.5" *Courtesy of Derek and Shirley Weyman*. £80-100; $130-165.

Figure 465. Enlarged picture of signature of C. Austin on Figure 464.

Figure 466. 'Melrose' ware vase, ca. 1895. Height 12". *Courtesy of Fred and Joyce Moseley*. £350-375; $580-620.

Figure 464. 'Crescentine' ware vase with attractive hand painted decoration, ca. 1895. Painting signed C. Austin, height 12". *Courtesy of Jane Winkle*. £450-500; $750-825.

171

Figure 467. 'Madras' ware vase, ca. 1895.
Height 12". £350-375; $580-620.

Figure 469. An impressive 'Madras' ware, two-handled vase, ca. 1895. Height 22". *Courtesy of Derek and Shirley Weyman.* £1100-1300; $1815-2145.

Figure 468. A rare 'Orient' ware vase, ca. 1895. Pattern initialled H.O.J., height 12.25". £400-450; $660-750.

Figure 470. 'Madras' ware vase, ca. 1895. Pattern initialled H.O.J., height 22". £1100-1300; $1815-2145.

Figure 472. 'Madras' ware vase, ca. 1895. Height 14.75". £400-450; $660-750.

Figure 471. Enlarged view, showing high relief decoration of bulrushes on the side of Figure 470.

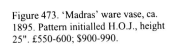

Figure 473. 'Madras' ware vase, ca. 1895. Pattern initialled H.O.J., height 25". £550-600; $900-990.

Figure 477. Illustration of 'Melrose' ware vases, from *The Pottery Gazette*, October 1897. *Courtesy of Tableware International.*

Figure 474. A superb 'Madras' ware jardiniere, ca. 1895. Pattern initialled H.O.J., height 12". £650-700; $1070-1155.

Figure 478. Illustration of 'Crescentine' ware vases, from *The Pottery Gazette*, October 1897. *Courtesy of Tableware International.*

Figure 475. Bone china jardinière, ca. 1896. Shape Rd. No. 269723, shape name 'Silver'. This piece has naively painted panels showing a soldier, cat, owl, butterflies and grasses. *Courtesy of Derek and Shirley Weyman.* £60-80; $100-130.

Figure 476. A pair of 'Tyrean' ware vases, with raised paste gilded panels of highland cattle and deer, ca. 1897. Height 8". £350-400; $580-660.

Figure 479. 'Tyrene' ware 'loving-cup', ca. 1898. Height 5.25".
Courtesy of Fred and Joyce Moseley. £80-100; $130-165.

Figure 481. 'Melrose'
ware vase, ca. 1898.
Height 12". £160-180;
$265-300.

Figure 480. 'Melrose' ware vase and decorative lamp, ca. 1898. Vase
height 10.25". *Courtesy of Derek and Shirley Weyman.* £200-250; $330-
415 each piece.

Figure 482. 'Melrose' ware vase, ca. 1898. Height 12.75". £350-400;
$580-660.

Figure 483. 'Melrose' ware vase, ca. 1898. Height 10.5". £300-350; $495-580.

Figure 485. A rare 'Cyprian' ware vase, ca. 1899. Low relief, hand-painted panel, height 9.75". £250-300; $415-495.

Figure 484. An unusually shaped 'Melrose' ware vase, ca. 1898. Height 9.25". £400-450; $660-750.

Figure 486. 'Madras' ware vase, ca. 1899. Shape Rd. No. 335404, height 13.75". £300-350; $495-580.

Charles Birbeck, the art director of George Jones & Sons Ltd. who was appointed to succeed Horace Overton Jones when he left the company in about 1895, was by 1900 greatly influencing the design of wares being produced by the company. His natural artistic talents were becoming evident from the design of patterns and shapes of wares being produced in the decorating department.

In March 1904, after a visit to the company's London showrooms, *The Pottery Gazette* commented:

From some of the ornamental schemes it is clear the company have artists who are quick to perceive the trend "fashion" in art (for there is always one), and to apply it to pottery.

When the *art nouveau style* became popular in the early 1900s, the designers at George Jones & Sons Ltd. refrained from producing some of the more outlandish designs created by other manufacturers. They tended to be rather conservative in the design of wares. This was born out in a report published in *The Pottery Gazette* in July 1905, after another visit to the London showrooms:

The company submit a large variety of forms and decorations in the styles that are now popular. They do not, however, go to some of the extremes that the fickleness of the public seems to like. All their shapes and ornamentation's are in accordance with good taste. It is to the credit of the trade that manufacturers of really good pottery - whether earthenware or china - do not yield to the demands which public fancy often makes, for eccentricities in either form or ornamentation. They come as near to what are termed "popular styles" as good taste will allow them but they rarely go beyond its limits. It may be safely said that Messrs. George Jones & Sons never do.

During the early part of the 1900s, the company rarely advertised their wares, but tended to rely on their reputation for producing good quality products at popular prices. Advertisements that did appear in *The Pottery Gazette* merely featured the name 'Crescent Ware' and stated: 'This well known registered trade mark is the sole property of George Jones & Sons Ltd.'.

By 1913 George Jones & Sons Ltd. had become well known for high quality table and toilet ware in bone china. *The Pottery Gazette* commented in December 1913:

Whilst they produce very extensive quantities of earthenware of a really capital quality, and have a wonderful variety of smart and appealing designs in earthenware dinner and toilet sets, it is ... to their china that they principally look for purposes of revenue. Many royal orders have from time to time found their way to the "Crescent" Potteries including commissions from his late Majesty King Edward when Prince of Wales, H. M. Queen Mary when Princess of Wales, the Queen of Siam, and the Crown Prince of Siam.

Another area of production that was highlighted in this article was the company's association with the metal industries of Sheffield, Birmingham and other centres:

on account of the variable lines they supply to meet the exigencies of the mounting trade, a connection which they have always done their best to foster, and by reason of consistent and sustained efforts in this direction they are now reaping a rich harvest.

Between 1905 and 1915, apart from a couple of articles, virtually no publicity was given to the company or its wares. This was obviously by intention, but after a couple of difficult years, when trade was bad and the fortunes of the company took a dive, Thomas Hammersley was appointed managing director in May 1915. As a result, the company's attitude toward advertising changed, and a more open policy was adopted. Thomas Hammersley had been a traveller for George Jones & Sons Ltd. for over 20 years, and knew the advantages to be gained by advertising extensively the wares on offer. With this change in policy, the advertisements in *The Pottery Gazette* became quite extensive and, as a result, visits by reporters from the magazine to the London showrooms became more frequent. This policy continued well into the 1930s.

As well as advertising the company's products in trade magazines, Thomas Hammersley also decided that the company should start exhibiting their wares. In early 1915 they were exhibitors at the Board of Trade Exhibition held at the Victoria & Albert Museum in London. A report of the exhibition was published in *The Pottery Gazette* in June 1915 and, apart from featuring a full range of 'Old English Abbey' ware, the company also showed:

a full range of high-class earthenware and china for the home market ... a line of white granite and inexpensive wares, such as sponged and painted, for the Colonial markets, as well as hotel badged goods and CC wares.

To give an indication of the range and scale of production by George Jones & Sons Ltd. at this time, I quote from a report published in *The Pottery Gazette* in July 1915:

The range of their production is so far reaching that it really covers everything needed in the home or in the institution. Truly this is a house that the dealer can approach for almost anything, and at the same time be pretty sure of getting it.

During February - March 1916, the company exhibited for the second year running at the Board of Trade Exhibition. Again their stand featured new examples of services in both china and earthenware for the home market and white granite, sponged and C.C. wares.

Although the First World War had been raging in Europe for nearly two years, no restrictions had been placed on the pottery manufacturers, as to the types of wares they could produce. The company was still producing china goods for all markets, including the luxury trade, which was mainly for the home market, as overseas buyers were more interested in earthenware at that time.

In March 1916, the advertisement, shown in Figure 642, was placed in *The Pottery Gazette;* in the following June a similar advertisement was placed in *The Pottery Gazette*, showing the same pieces but with a note added which demonstrated that Thomas Hammersley's enthusiasm for advertising the company's wares was paying dividends. The note read:

Our previous advertisement of these goods (March issue) brought us many orders and enquiries from America, Australasia, Canada, and the Home Market, showing the value of advertising when you have something good to offer. May we hear from you?

Another innovation, introduced by Thomas Hammersley, was to advertise tours of the country by the company's travellers. The first of these advertisements appeared in *The Pottery Gazette* in August 1916 and is shown in Figure 643.

Another Board of Trade Exhibition was held in early 1917 and again George Jones & Sons Ltd. were exhibitors. Their stand, which was one of the larger ones, was filled with tea, dinner, dessert services and toilet sets in both china and earthenware. Ornamental wares of all shapes and sizes were also on display. Many of the wares had decorations which included roses and *The Pottery Gazette,* commenting on the company's wares, stated:

> In black and white ware, which has been fashionable of late, the rule has generally been "roses, roses all the way."

By mid-1917 the war was taking its toll. Men were being killed in the thousands and more were needed to sustain the effort to keep Europe free, causing acute shortages of labour. This was reflected in two advertisements placed in *The Pottery Gazette* by George Jones & Sons Ltd. in May and June 1917. The May advertisement highlighted the shortage of labour and how it was affecting production, and the June advertising copy reflected on the hatred that was felt for the enemy at that time. These advertisements are shown in Figures 506 and 578.

In 1917 an exhibition took place that was to have quite an effect on the sales of the company. The exhibition was held at the Royal Academy and was organised by the Arts and Crafts Society. One of the stands was occupied by the Design Industries Association on which they exhibited examples of manufactured items that they felt conformed to their formula, which was 'fitness for purpose, simplicity of form and economy of decoration'. Among the items on display were some examples of sponged and brushwork patterns by George Jones & Sons Ltd., which the company produced for export to West Africa. This type of ware was amongst the cheapest produced by the company, being of indifferent quality, for export to what are now called the third world nations. One of the visitors to this exhibition was Harry Trethowan, chief buyer for Heals of London. He was quite taken with these designs and managed to persuade the company to produce similar designs, but on better quality wares. These were subsequently sold at Heals department store in London and a lucrative trade developed between Heals and George Jones & Sons Ltd. that was to last well into the 1930s. They supplied Heals with large quantities of earthenware and china decorated with underglaze patterns. At one time, the company employed over forty paintresses working specifically on products for Heals. Some of the designs used were 'Country Bunch', 'Blue Leaf' and 'Hedgerow'.

In early 1918, due to lack of staff, again as a result of the war effort, the company was unable to exhibit at the British Industries Fair; however, in 1919 they once again exhibited at this Fair. They had a full range of all their usual production in earthenware and china on display. In earthenware they showed inexpensive patterns of refined characteristics suitable for the foreign markets and capable of competing with continental makers. They also showed a range of sponged ware, a line the company was noted for. George Jones & Sons Ltd. exported to most countries and they produced catalogues not only in English but in French, Spanish and Portuguese. Much of their cheaper wares were exported to 'third world' countries.

The year 1919 was the last year the company exhibited at the British Industries Fair for some years. March 1919 saw the opening of their new showrooms at 47, Holborn Viaduct, London. Here they decided to hold their own Spring exhibition, timed to coincide with the British Industries Fair.

In March 1920 *The Pottery Gazette and Glass Trades Review* gave a good account of how varied the production was from the company at this time. It stated:

> George Jones & Sons Ltd., are one of the comparatively few firms of domestic potters who are able to supply almost everything that the trade is likely to demand, no matter whether it be in the realm of distinctly useful, everyday wares,

or in the region of rich and exclusive bone china for tea, dinner or toilet table. They are equally at home with any of these phases of the trade.

In the spring of 1921, the company again held an exhibition at their London showrooms. They placed great importance on these exhibitions, and this was emphasised by the fact that Thomas Hammersley (managing director), Arthur Overton Jones (deputy chairman and showroom manager), and their provincial travellers, were all in attendance to assist customers. *The Pottery Gazette and Glass Trades Review* commented: 'The exhibition was a powerful one and included some fine examples of the very latest products of the Crescent Potteries in all branches of the domestic trade.

As had been the case since Thomas Hammersley took control of George Jones & Sons Ltd. in 1915, the company advertised extensively during the year in *The Pottery Gazette and Glass Trades Review*. The advertisements in 1921 featured new shapes for dinner and tea ware and new styles of decorations.

The exhibition mounted in March 1922 at their London showrooms, was again reviewed by *The Pottery Gazette and Glass Trades Review:*

> Ever since the firm opened out their present showrooms, which ... are now second to none in the pottery salesmanship arrangements of the metropolis, they have lived up to a programme of bringing out some really smart new productions with the commencement of each season. This year is no exception to the rule ... a feature of this year's samples is the introduction of a greater element of actual brushwork in the decorations offered.

A comment was also made in the same article, about the company's art director:

> Mr C. J. Birbeck, the firm's designer, seems quite as much actuated by inventiveness as any of the more youthful members of his particular profession, and it is clear that the firm's customers have only to give the works a lead to get any sort of decorative treatment they require, providing that it is commercially manageable, and that it has reasonable prospects of success.

In the spring of 1923, George Jones & Sons Ltd. exhibited at the British Industries Fair which was held at Shepherd's Bush, London. As previously stated, the company, since 1919, had held their own exhibitions at their London showrooms, which apparently were, at that time, the best in the trade. This change of policy may have been due to poor trade in 1922. The company may have determined that exhibiting at this fair would gain them a wider audience.

They had two stands at this two week exhibition. A photograph of the stand featuring their display of china ware is shown in Figure 515. Once again both the Managing Director and Deputy Chairman were in attendance. *The Pottery Gazette & Glass Trade Review,* commenting on the display by George Jones & Sons Ltd., stated:

> It was one of the most dignified exhibits in the whole Fair, and the tables and shelves were arrayed with a very representative selection of the company's production in the numerous branches which they cover, from white granite for export to fine bone china in tea and dessert sets. There was a magnificent range of toilets ... For a luxury toilet set we can conceive of nothing finer than one of these "Crescent" china services.

By the end of 1923 the company was beginning to advertise their very popular blue and white 'Abbey' pattern; a line they had been producing for over 20 years.

In 1924, no mention was made of George Jones & Sons Ltd. exhibiting at any major exhibitions, even though the British Empire Exhibition was held at Wembley, at which many of the major British pottery manufacturers exhibited. Instead, in February 1924, the company advertised:

24 pudding plates
12 soup plates
4 dishes 10"
2 dishes 12"
2 dishes 14"
1 dish 16"
1 dish 18"
1 soup tureen
1 cover for soup tureen
1 stand for soup tureen
1 salad bowl
2 sauce tureens
2 covers for sauce tureens
2 stands for sauce tureens
4 vegetable dishes
4 covers for vegetable dishes
1 white fish drainer - making a 101 piece set

Many of the large department stores in England, particularly in London, were stockists of 'Anglo China' dinner services. The Army & Navy Co-operative Society Ltd. was one and examples of 'Anglo-China' dinner services appear in their catalogues. There are also examples of designs available for earthenware dinner services. Figure 569 shows an example of a tureen, manufactured in 'Anglo-China', that was illustrated in the 1908 Army & Navy Co-operative Society Ltd. catalogue. Figure 725 shows an example of a pattern, named 'Enfield', that was used to decorate 'Anglo-China' dinner services and was also illustrated in the same catalogue.

Earthenware dinner services were available in three different sizes:

	52 piece set	76 piece set	105 piece set
dinner plates	12	24	36
soup plates	-	8	12
pudding plates	12	8	12
cheese plates	12	8	12
dish 9"	2	2	2
dish 10"	1	1	2
dish 12"	1	1	2
dish 14"	1	1	2
dish 16"	1	1	1
dish 18"	-	1	1
gravy dish	-	-	2
soup tureen	-	1	1
cover for soup tureen	-	1	1
stand for soup tureen	-	1	1
sauce tureen	2	2	2
cover for sauce tureen	2	2	2
stand for sauce tureen	2	2	2
vegetable dish	2	4	4
cover for vegetable dish	2	4	4
salad bowl	-	1	1
pie dish 9" (white)	-	1	1
pie dish 11" (white)	-	1	1
fish drainer	-	1	1

The Army and Navy Co-operative Society Ltd. catalogue also featured the 'kitchen outfit'. This comprised of a combination of earthenware table and kitchen ware; consisting of 134 pieces it was made up as follows:

1 dinner service 52 pieces
1 breakfast set 29 pieces
6 plain basins of various sizes
6 lipped basins of various sizes
6 pudding basins of various sizes
6 white store jars of various sizes
4 tankard jugs of various sizes
4 kitchen pans of various sizes
2 jelly moulds of various sizes
8 pie dishes of various sizes
1 Rockingham tea pot
1 pepper box
1 mustard pot
2 glass salt cellars
6 tumblers

In 1913, a pottery exhibition was held in Stoke-on-Trent to celebrate the visit of King George V and Queen Mary to the town. *The Pottery Gazette* wrote of this exhibition:

George Jones & Sons Ltd ... had a table arrayed with a capital assortment of "Crescent" china, a choice neat dinner pattern with gold band and medallions of raised gold spots, enclosing a bunch of roses ... Sample pieces of a dinner service made for King Edward VII when Prince of Wales, and also samples of a service supplied to the King of Siam at the [his] Coronation, were included, also others made for the same monarch at a later period, together with samples of ware made for the Crown Prince of Siam produced from a water-colour drawing which Her Majesty had seen.

At this same exhibition, F. Winkle & Co. Ltd,. pottery manufacturers of Stoke-upon-Trent exhibited an array of domestic items decorated in their 'Pheasant' pattern. When the company closed down, George Jones & Sons Ltd. acquired the engravings for this pattern and reproduced it on dinner ware in the mid-1920s and again in the 1930s.

By the end of 1913 George Jones & Sons Ltd. were reputed to be one of the largest English manufacturers of china dinner services. After a visit to their warehouses, a reporter from *The Pottery Gazette* commented:

I have heard it said many times that a china dinner service is merely a luxury of the well-to-do. It [sic] that be so, judging by the warehouses of George Jones & Sons, Ltd., this must be a very luxurious age, and the well-to-do classes are by no means a negligible quantity. But I should rather imagine that this firm is so well equipped industrially, that it is able to supply its china at a popular price, consistent with good quality and many people can be persuaded that 'Crescent' china is value for money that it will be to their interest to pay rather more than they intended, and go in for a real china service calculated to have a longer life, than to purchase an earthenware one, which may possibly require replacing much earlier.

During the First World War, although the company still produced large quantities of china dinner services, it was the cheaper earthenware services that they advertised. Toward the end of the war, as was said earlier in the tea ware section, shapes produced by the design department were not specifically for dinner or tea ware, but were available as a full suite of tableware. The 'Carlisle' shape shown in Figure 506 was the first to be introduced, in 1917. In 1921 the 'Octagon' shape was introduced and a sauce tureen in this shape, decorated with the 'Abbey' blue and white pattern, is shown in Figure 162, and a meat plate with a hand decorated pattern is shown in Figure 580. The 'Octagon' shape was produced in their Ivory earthenware body.

Another tableware shape, introduced toward the end of 1921, was named 'Mount Vernon'. Examples of dinner ware in this shape are shown in Figure 516 (top). In early 1922, two more designs for tableware were introduced. One named 'Monmouth' had an embossed decoration and examples of this shape of tureen are shown in Figure 519. The second design was named 'Cardiff'; an example of this design is shown in Figure 524.

Below is a list of bone china dinner ware shapes available in 1923:

Carlisle, Crescent, Douglas, Dover, Enid, Granada, Hereford, Madrid, Majestic, Naples, Paris, Riga, and Truro.

Various illustrations of dinner ware available in 1924 are shown in Figures 581 to 583. These are taken from a George Jones & Sons

Ltd. catalogue of that year. The same shapes were still available in 1927.

During the mid-1920s, the 'Abbey' blue and white pattern was extensively advertised. Some advertisements featured dinner ware. Figure 165 shows an earthenware vegetable dish and sauce tureen with the shape name 'Willow' decorated in this pattern.

In March 1927 a new Ivory earthenware body shape for tableware was introduced. Named 'Bouquet', a vegetable dish and meat plate in this shape are shown in Figure 528. In August 1927, a new shape for bone china tableware was introduced named 'Sandringham'. A vegetable dish in this shape is shown in Figure 529.

Dessert ware

According to the Army & Navy Co-operative Society Ltd. catalogues of the early 1900s, a dessert service for twelve people was made up of twelve dessert plates and six comports. The difference between a dinner plate and a dessert plate was its size. A dinner plate was usually about 10.5" in diameter, whereas a dessert plate was about 9.5" in diameter. Comports came in three sizes, low, tall, and centre. The average size of these was: low compote — 9.5" in diameter x 2.5" high, tall compote — 9.5" in diameter x 4.5" high, and a centre compote — 10" in diameter x 6" high. Sometimes compotes were square or oval instead of round.

In the 1870s, George Jones & Sons produced many different shapes of majolica decorated comports. Some had animals entwined around the stem, but by the mid-1880s this style of compote no longer 'appealed to the buying public. The designs for the comports of the 1900s had been around for about twenty years. Figures 381 and 382 show a low and centre compote manufactured in the early 1880s, and Figure 224 shows a similar low compote manufactured in 1915.

The majority of plates bought by collectors today are dessert plates. They are more highly decorated than dinner plates and, while dinner plates are usually round with plain edges, dessert plates can be found in more attractive shapes.

Dessert ware was manufactured in earthenware, but the majority of very ornate and sometimes hand painted plates were made from bone china. George Jones & Sons Ltd. was well known for its dessert services. Although not sold in such large quantities as dinner and tea services, they were still very much sought after, being rather a luxury for the majority of the population. The Americans were large purchasers of the company's dessert services. At all the exhibitions at which the company appeared and in their London showrooms, they always had fine specimens of their high class dessert ware on display.

This type of ware was very rarely advertised, and only occasionally would a reference be made, by a reporter from *The Pottery Gazette and Glass Trades Review*, usually following a visit to the London showrooms or to the works.

Toilet ware

By 1904 George Jones & Sons Ltd. had become renowned for their toilet ware, not only produced in earthenware but also china. They were one of the very few manufacturers brave enough to produce china toilet ware in large quantities. After a visit to the company's showrooms in early 1904, a reporter from *The Pottery Gazette* commented:

> Buyers of high-class toilet ware ... will see a very fine collection of samples ...The range of toilet ware is very wide, from neat and inexpensive sets up to very chaste china services ... Graceful in shape, and with artistic ornamentations, these sets are most attractive.

In November 1905, George Jones & Sons Ltd. registered a design, Rd. No. 469082, for a ewer and basin. An illustration of this design is shown in Figure 628 (no. 24075).

The Army & Navy Co-operative Society Ltd. were retailers of George Jones & Sons Ltd. toilet ware. Examples of 'Crescent' ware ewers and basins were illustrated in their catalogues of the early 1900s. Figure 619 shows a ewer and basin that appeared in both the 1907 and 1908 catalogues. The composition of toilet sets available at this time is listed in the toilet ware section of Chapter 4.

In December 1913, after a visit to the warehouses of George Jones & Sons Ltd., a reporter from *The Pottery Gazette* wrote:

> as regards best china toiletware, I have certainly not seen a wider range of patterns on show anywhere than in this company's showrooms. In this china toiletware they run three shapes, which have been proven to be popular, these being known as the "Wallace", the "King", and the "Sheffield" shapes. The designs are mainly simple and chaste, as china toiletware should be, and nothing in the way of bedroom ware for the superior home could possibly look better.

An illustration of these three shapes, taken from *The Pottery Gazette*, is shown in Figure 622.

In July 1915 a reporter from *The Pottery Gazette* again sang the praises of the company's china toilet ware:

> The effects produced by George Jones & Sons, Ltd., in their china toilet ware are for the most part restrained and elegant; they are tasteful without being too ornate, handsome without being exclusive in price. This is doubtless the key to their extreme popularity. The West End stores of London know a good line when they see one, and they have invariably a good stock of ''Crescent'' china toilet ware.

The first ever advertisement featuring an example of the current design of George Jones & Sons Ltd. toilet ware appeared in *The Pottery Gazette* in 1917, and a copy of this advertisement is shown in Figure 625. This design of ewer and basin was exhibited by the company at the Board of Trade exhibition held in February 1917.

After a visit to the company's showrooms at 21 Bartlett's Buildings, Holborn Circus, London, in October 1917, a reporter from *The Pottery Gazette* stated:

> Another adjacent show-room was wholly devoted to earthen toilet ware, containing a comprehensive range of samples of pleasing shapes with artistic decorations, the best sellers just now being these with black or deep blue bands, gold borders, and floral sprays or panels.

Another of the designs for a ewer and basin, exhibited by George Jones & Sons Ltd. at the 1917 exhibition, was featured in advertisements placed in *The Pottery Gazette* in early 1918. This advertisement is shown in Figure 626. As well as this shape, another shape of ewer and basin was also advertised in *The Pottery Gazette* in 1918. This is shown in Figure 627

By 1922, the demand for china toilet ware had decreased, possibly due to their cost or bad trading conditions; however, earthenware toilet services were still in demand. The bathroom, as we know it today, was still not a feature of many homes of the early 1920s. The majority of the population used toilet services to allow them to wash in their bedrooms, as usually the only running water and sink were in the kitchen.

Commenting on toilet ware in general and George Jones & Sons Ltd. in particular, *The Pottery Gazette and Glass Trades Review* in April 1922 stated:

> a word or two should be spoken of this firm's excellent range of toilets, both in earthenware and china. In the former there is any amount of variety, which should be capable of suiting at some point every shade of preference. As for the CHINA toilets, whilst there is, naturally only a rather limited call for these at the moment, the demand is sure, sooner or later, to

be revitalised, for we can imagine nothing for the bedroom that is capable of giving more thorough and lasting satisfaction than a beautifully potted, translucent china toilet set, the production of which very few firms have had sufficient courage to tackle seriously, and none, we venture to think, with more complete success than the Crescent Potteries.

In 1923, 'Abbey' blue and white decorated wares were being advertised. The popularity of this transfer printed pattern had been fairly constant since its introduction around 1900. Examples of earthenware toilet ware of the 1920s decorated in the 'Abbey' pattern are shown in Figures 175 to 181. Examples of other toilet ware shapes and patterns available in the mid-1920s are shown in Figures 629 to 632. These illustrations are taken from a 1924 George Jones & Sons Ltd. catalogue.

By 1924, the composition of toilet services had changed. The large sets of the late nineteenth century and early twentieth century had been replaced with smaller sets comprising of five or six pieces.

A 5 piece set consisted of:

1 ewer
1 basin
1 chamber, no cover
1 covered soap dish
1 brush vase

A 6 piece set consisted of :

1 ewer
1 basin
2 chambers, no cover
1 covered soap dish
1 brush vase

As well as these two sets, other items of toilet ware could be purchased individually. These consisted of covered chamber pots, slop pails, round nappies (shallow bowls) for sponges, covered brush trays, and cuspidors (spittoons).

By late 1925, the demand for china toilet ware began to increase. In January 1926 *The Pottery Gazette and Glass Trades Review* commented:

> in regard to translucent china toilet services, George Jones & Sons, Ltd., were always renowned for this class of production, and, whilst it would be perfectly correct to say that there has been something of a lull during the last few years in regard to the call for translucent china toilet services, as distinct from the ordinary opaque earthenware, the demand during the last few months has been rather more encouraging.

By mid-1927, the market for bone china toilet ware had improved dramatically and the company, as one of the main producers of such wares, was once again in receipt of some large orders.

Patterns

By 1900, the types of patterns that were being applied to the wares of George Jones & Sons Ltd. were no longer being influenced by Horace Overton Jones. He had left the company about five years earlier and Charles Birbeck, who by 1900 had been promoted to art director, was charged with the responsibility of producing attractive and appealing patterns for the company's products. At this time, very few of Horace Overton Jones's printed patterns were being used on tableware or toilet ware, although some of the art pottery that was being produced may still have utilised some of his patterns.

The majority of the patterns designed by the art department were for application as lithographs and were printed in the company's own lithographic printing department, which was set up in the mid-1880s. The patterns of the 1900s were no longer the large all-over bold flower patterns so loved by Horace Overton Jones, but were border patterns of small flowers and swags of leaves, with centre decorations of sprays of flowers.

Border patterns were very much a feature of the dinner and tea ware of the 1900s and attractive ornate border patterns, together with centre decorations, adorned the dessert ware. Lithographic patterns incorporating flowers of all types, especially roses, were utilised to a great extent. Some lithographic patterns were hand tinted and other wares, especially dessert wares, were hand painted and signed by ceramic artists such as William Birbeck, Walter Lamonby, Charles Austin and Joseph Fenn, who later worked for Copeland.

As well as hand painted wares featuring flowers, dessert services were produced which featured birds, fishes, and landscapes. Some of these were signed by William Birbeck and Charles Austin. Americans were large purchasers of the company's hand painted dessert services. One such dessert service, of which a plate is shown in Figure 592, came from the estate of Gary Cooper, the American film actor.

In 1911 a pattern named 'Queens Coronation Carnations' was introduced and an example of this pattern is shown in Figure 550, surely designed to commemorate the Coronation of King George V and Queen Mary in 1911?

As very little advertising of wares took place before 1915, the types of decoration used until then is best shown by illustrating examples of surviving wares. Throughout this chapter, numerous pieces of tableware are shown which give a good indication of the types of decorations being produced by George Jones & Sons Ltd. during this period.

When Thomas Hammersley took over as managing director in May 1915, the policy of not advertising the company's wares was changed and a more open and forward looking policy toward advertising and exhibiting was adopted. All the very varied types of wares produced by the company were featured and reporters from *The Pottery Gazette* made many visits to their London showrooms.

In July 1915, three patterns (produced on earthenware dinner wares) were featured in an article in *The Pottery Gazette*, following a visit to the company's London showrooms. These patterns, which were three of the most popular patterns of the time, were 'York Rose', 'China Rose', and 'Durham'. These patterns are shown in Figures 573 and 574. All three patterns were underglaze lithographic printed patterns typical of the style of decorations being applied to earthenware dinner ware.

In April 1916, three more border patterns for earthenware dinner ware were advertised. They were named 'Kenneth, 'Bristol' and 'Perkins' and are shown illustrated in Figure 575 to 577. As can be seen from the illustrations, these patterns were also available on earthenware tea ware. During this time, due to the war with Germany, people could not always afford to buy luxury items, and although china ware was still produced, mainly for export, the majority of the market was for earthenware products. These earthenwares were required not only at home, but also overseas.

By 1917, pattern designs were becoming more bold and flowers of all types were very popular; once again roses featured heavily. Figure 625 shows pattern number V743, a design which was being applied to toilet ware, ornamental ware and tableware. Examples of this pattern on vases are shown in Figures 643 to 645. At this time, patterns of black stripes on a white ground with flowers were very popular. Another popular form of decoration being produced in 1917 featured ground-laid bodies of pink, green, yellow, lavender, and heliotrope, with vertical black stripping. These were especially suited for decorating coffee and tea sets.

One pattern that had been produced by the company for some time was 'Old Swansea'. After a visit to the company's London showroom, a report of the visit was published in *The Pottery Gazette* in October 1917, and a comment, with reference to this pattern, stated:

> In the history of pottery decoration there have been roses, roses, and again roses; but it is generally admitted that this flower found its most sympathetic and accurate expression at the old Swansea works, where delicate shading of the natural flower, due to the curving and translucence of the petals,

was faithfully copied. This form of achievement George Jones & Sons, Ltd., may fairly claim to emulate, for they have studiously followed the tradition of careful hand-painting which was the secret of the success of the Swansea artist.

A type of decoration on earthenware toilet ware that was popular at this time featured black, or deep blue bands, gold borders and floral sprays or panels. Figures 626 and 627 show two more styles of patterns that were used to decorate earthenware toilet ware in early 1918.

As well as lithographic patterns for earthenware, sponged and brushwork patterns were also being used to decorate earthenware tableware for export to West Africa. Commenting on the company's exhibits at the 1919 Board of Trade Exhibition, *The Pottery Gazette and Glass Trades Review* stated:

> George Jones & Sons, Ltd. of Crescent Potteries, Stoke-on-Trent, showed a full and very interesting range of their earthenware and china production. In the former they had many inexpensive patterns of refined characteristics suitable for the foreign markets ... Many of the plain printed patterns were extremely select, and the sponged ware, was more than ordinarily interesting.

In March 1920 a rare reference to the company producing nursery ware appeared in *The Pottery Gazette and Glass Trades Review*. It stated:

> Another really novel line in the present "Crescent" exhibits is a range of nursery wares, decorated in an extremely new style, which gives one the impression that the decoration is done by hand. Although this is not the case, it would be somewhat difficult for the unpractised eye to detect just where the mechanical element comes in.

The illustration that accompanied this article is shown in Figure 560.

The styles and types of decoration used on table and toilet ware during the 1920s were numerous: some were freehand painted, some were lithographic printed, others were a combination of lithographic prints and hand painting. There were underglaze transfer printed patterns and overglaze patterns; the range was enormous. Figure 562 shows china dinner and tea ware decorated in coloured grounds with gold wheat borders. More examples of these and many more types of patterns are shown in Figures 516 to 524 and are all taken from a 1924 George Jones Catalogue.

Printed patterns were used extensively on dinner ware. A list of named patterns available on George Jones & Sons Ltd. dinner ware in 1923 is shown in Appendix 3. From this list probably the most popular pattern, used on earthenware dinner ware of the 1920s, was undoubtedly the 'Abbey' blue and white pattern. It was used to decorate dinner ware, tea ware, coffee sets, toilet ware, dessert ware and ornamental ware — in fact, you name it and the 'Abbey' pattern was used to decorate it. It was by far the most well known of the underglaze transfer printed patterns and today is very much sought after by collectors. Other underglaze blue and white transfer printed patterns were also used to decorate earthenware tableware. The 'Willow' and 'Suez' patterns shown in Figure 225 were two such.

In May 1925, what was described as a successor to the 'Abbey' pattern was introduced by the company. This was the 'Cyrene' pattern, and although it had been available on dinner and tea ware in the early 1920s and had been in production for some time, it was hoped that by introducing it on all types of tableware, it would become as popular as the 'Abbey' pattern. Although examples of this pattern can be found, it was never to succeed and sales of 'Abbey' decorated wares went from strength to strength.

One feature of decorated ware, especially china ware, that tends to be overlooked, is gilding. In the late 19th century George Jones & Sons were well known for their high quality gilding. This was achieved by using trained gilders, usually women, and was still very much in evidence in the 1920s and later. The head of the gilding department in the 1920s was Miss Florence Mollart. A reference to the quality of

the company's gilding appeared in an article published in *The Pottery Gazette and Glass Trades Review,* in 1925. The article stated:

> In new china patterns, which the writer has had the privilege of inspecting, one notices chiefly the numerous neat, simple but high-toned designs which have been got out during recent months, to sell at distinctly reasonable prices. These lower prices have, if we may venture to say so, come about partially through the steady lowering that has taken place lately in the sterling price of gold. We have emphasised the fact on previous occasions that George Jones & Sons, Ltd., do not use liquid gold on china, and therefore any lowering in the price of gold as a metal finds its reflex in comparative lowering of the costs of production of those brands of pottery on which best gold is employed as an important medium of decoration.

Around 1927, a new style of decorating earthenware tableware was introduced by the company. This consisted of embossed floral decorations which were painted in underglaze colours. The embossed decoration was around the border on flat ware and on the main body of such pieces as jugs, cups, tureens, and dishes etc. An example of this style of decoration is shown in Figure 568. This particular shape was named 'Bouquet' and the embossed pattern was called 'Mayflower'. This style of decorating was to feature heavily in the late 1920s and early 1930s.

By 1927, the only ceramic artist still employed by George Jones & Sons Ltd. was William Birbeck. He had been with the company since 1881 when he commenced, at the age of fourteen, as an artist on china. In 1927, William Birbeck was producing beautiful work on all types of wares, especially dessert services which were so popular with Americans, and ornamental wares. A lot of his designs on plates comprised of hand painted centres of fruit, flowers, and landscapes. He was also producing work which incorporated fish and birds. Examples of some of his work of the mid-1920s are shown in Figures 613 and 614.

Ornamental ware

Although the major part of the production coming from the Trent Potteries was classed as 'useful ware' in the form of tableware and toilet ware, the company was also producing ornamental ware such as vases, jardinières, pedestal and pots, garden seats, and bowls etc.

During the *Art Nouveau* period of the early 1900s, some very bizarre designs were being produced. However, George Jones & Sons Ltd. chose not to pander to the eccentricities of the day, but to concentrate on the production of wares that were of a more 'restrained' style, and would appeal to the majority of the market.

Art pottery, such as 'Madras', 'Melrose', and 'Orient' ware, produced during the 1890s, continued into the early 1900s. It was at this time that 'Imperial' and 'Moorish' ware were added to the range available. An examples of early 'Imperial' ware is shown in Figure 634.

Up until 1915, when Thomas Hammersley took control of the company, few references as to the types of ornamental wares being produced by George Jones & Sons Ltd. were made in the trade magazines of the day. When advertisements did appear, they were usually limited to advertisements for tableware and toiletware. One of the first references to ornamental wares appeared in *The Pottery Gazette* in June 1915. Here, a review of the company's ornamental wares, on display at the 1915 Board of Trade Exhibition, at the Victoria and Albert Museum, states:

> In the V688 series an old pebble print has been ... revived from engravings which have been in use on [sic] the factory for over half a century, and in combination with old Lowestoft flowers in panels this makes an excellent decoration of modern vogue. Another line which this firm is doing

very well with just now is the V594 an Imperial blue pattern with painted tulips. This gives a very rich and deep toned effect at a moderate price.

This particular 'Imperial' pattern was named 'Imperial Rouge' and as well as tulips, the 'Imperial Rouge' pattern also featured iris, crocuses, azaleas, and daffodils. Another similar pattern, No. V595, was named 'Imperial Amethyst'. These patterns, it is believed, were designed by Edward Overton Jones around 1912-13. 'Imperial Rouge' and 'Imperial Amethyst' patterns adorned ornamental wares of all shapes, and were still available in the mid-1920s. Figures 647, 656, 657, 658 and 660 show various vases, jardinières, bowls etc., decorated in these two patterns. Figure 663 shows a selection of ornamental wares decorated in the 'Imperial Rouge' pattern taken from a 1924 George Jones & Sons Ltd. catalogue.

The company published the advertisement shown in Figure 642 in *The Pottery Gazette* of March 1916. This featured vases and bowls decorated with black stripes and dahlias, pattern number V713. According to the advertisement, examples of these decorated wares were purchased by Queen Mary after she visited the 1916 Board of Trade Exhibition.

In August 1916, the company, in an article placed in *The Pottery Gazette* advertising the forthcoming country wide tour by their representatives, also illustrated a new decoration applied to vases. The pattern number was V743 and a garniture of vases decorated in this pattern is shown in Figure 644. This pattern was also used to decorate toilet ware in 1917.

In the April 1917 edition of *The Pottery Gazette*, an advertisement and an article featured illustrations of some different shapes of ornamental wares available at that time. The article that accompanied the illustration, shown in Figure 645, describes the exhibits of George Jones & Sons Ltd. at the 1917 Board of Trade Exhibition. Of the ornamental wares, 'Imperial Rouge' vases decorated with iris were much in evidence, as were trinket sets and jardinières decorated in a new powder blue decoration. Floating-flower bowls were also on display, and the popularity of this type of ornamental ware was to last well into the 1920s as examples are illustrated in the 1924 George Jones & Sons Ltd. trade catalogue.

In October 1917, after a visit to the company's London showrooms, an article was published in *The Pottery Gazette*, accompanied by the illustration of ornamental ware decorated in pattern number V793, shown in Figure 646. These shapes had been available for some time and were still being manufactured in the late 1920s. This particular pattern had been introduced in 1917 and a good description appeared in this article:

Special emphasis is just now being given to a really beautiful series of decorations with panels of gay-plumaged exotic birds on a blue pebble ground, embellished with tasteful gilding. The blue is of a soft peacock hue, and the pebble ground affords a notable scope for the delicate graduation of colour produced by the "powdering" or blowing on through gauze — a type of decoration which originated in the famous K'anghsi period, in the golden age of Chinese porcelains ... The exotic birds are of the pheasant species, and gorgeous in colouring as the fabled Phoenix, the birds of Paradise, or the golden pheasant beloved of "Chanticlere". The gilding is of fine quality.

This decoration was applied to a variety of articles, including vases, jardinières, sweet trays, inkstands, match holders, ring boxes, etc., as well as dinner, tea, and toilet wares. A jardinière and a vase are decorated in this pattern and are shown in Figures 651 and 654.

In early 1920, some very bold designs were introduced and exhibited at the company's Spring exhibition. They had been designed by Edward Overton Jones, who had only just rejoined the company after serving in the war. An illustration of this decoration, which featured sailing ships, is shown in Figure 659. This design was best suited to large vases, jardinières and plaques. Commenting on these designs, an article in *The Pottery Gazette and Glass Trades Review* in March 1920 stated:

There is nothing in the trade like it, and the reason of this is, probably, that it has been conceived by an artist who has recently returned from military service, with a freshness of vision, enlarged views, and a confidence born of travel and novel experiences, such as is now seeking expression in a practical form through the medium of pottery decoration.

Some of the varied shapes of ornamental wares and types of decoration available in 1924 are shown in Figures 661 and 665. These illustrations are again taken from a 1924 George Jones & Sons Ltd. catalogue. The majority of the shapes had been in production for many years and it was a credit to the design department, headed by its art director, Charles Birbeck, that they were able to produce designs that had a lasting appeal.

Ornamental wares were produced in both earthenware and china. In the mid-1920s the popularity of the 'Abbey' blue and white pattern was at its height. Figure 215 shows some of the vases, jardinières, pedestals and pots, that were available decorated in this underglaze transfer printed pattern. These illustrations are from the 1924 catalogue.

In 1926 the company introduced a range of new patterns for ornamental ware. The theme of the patterns were richly coloured birds and they were applied to a ground of powder blue. An illustration, Figure 668, taken from *The Pottery Gazette and Glass Trades Review*, shows examples of these patterns on various shaped vases and an example of a vase featured in this illustration is shown in Figure 667. The popularity of ornamental wares reflected the economic situation at any one time, and by 1927 the country was beginning to recover from the problems of the early 1920s and sales of ornamental wares were increasing.

Figure 487. Earthenware biscuit barrel, ca. 1900. Shape name 'Sterling', pattern no. A4000, height 9". £80-100; $130-165.

Figure 488. Earthenware commemorative mug, ca. 1902. Commemorating the Coronation of King Edward VIII and Queen Alexander on June 26th 1902, height 3.25". *Courtesy of Arthur Bowden.* £40-50; $65-80.

Figure 490. Bone china sardine dish with fixed stand, ca. 1903. Pattern no. 16480, length 8". £80-100; $130-165.

Figure 489. Base of Figure 488, showing that the commemorative mug was presented by the Borough of Stoke-upon-Trent. *Courtesy of Arthur Bowden.*

Figure 491. Earthenware biscuit barrel, ca. 1905. Shape Rd. No. 269723, height 9.5". *Courtesy of Marjorie Winters.* £80-100; $130-165.

Figure 492. Bone china biscuit barrel, ca. 1905. Pattern no. 18963, height 6". *Courtesy of Derek and Shirley Weyman.* £100-120; $165-200.

Figure 494. Earthenware biscuit barrel, ca. 1905. Height 9". £80-100; $130-165.

Figure 493. Bone china salad bowl, ca. 1905. Diameter 8.5". £80-100; $130-165.

Figure 495. Bone china chamber stick, ca. 1905. Pattern no. 17887, diameter 5". £140-160; $230-265.

Figure 496. Bone china luncheon tray, ca. 1905. Pattern no. 16339, width 12.5". *Courtesy of Derek and Shirley Weyman.* £70-90; $115-150.

Figure 498. Earthenware biscuit barrel, ca. 1910. Pattern no. E1184, height 9". *Courtesy of Marjorie Winters.* £80-100; $130-165.

Figure 497. Bone china preserve pot on fixed stand, ca. 1906. Pattern no. 17837, height 6.5". £50-70; $80-115.

Figure 499. Earthenware salad bowl complete with servers, ca. 1910. Diameter 8.5". *Courtesy of Fred and Joyce Moseley.* £90-110; $150-180.

Figure 500. Earthenware biscuit barrel, ca. 1910. Height 9". £60-80; $100-130.

Figure 502. Earthenware commemorative mug, ca. 1911. Commemorating the Coronation of King George V and Queen Mary on June 22, 1911, height 3.25". *Courtesy of Derek and Shirley Weyman.* £30-40; $50-65.

Figure 503. Reverse side of figure 502 showing that the mug was presented by the Corporation of Stoke-on-Trent.

Figure 501. Bone china biscuit barrel, ca. 1910. Shape name 'Lincoln', pattern no. E2360, height 9.5". £90-110; $150-180.

Figure 504. Earthenware biscuit barrel, ca. 1915. Pattern no. E1514, height 5.5". *Courtesy of Derek and Shirley Weyman.* £80-100; $130-165.

Figure 506. Advertisement illustrating the 'Carlisle' shape tableware, from *The Pottery Gazette,* June 1917. *Courtesy of Tableware International.*

Figure 505. Earthenware mustard pot with silver plated stand, ca. 1915. Pattern no. E2458, pot height 2.75". *Courtesy of Derek and Shirley Weyman.* £50-70; $80-115.

Figure 507. Bone china condiment set in silver plated stand, ca. 1918. Salt pot height 3". *Courtesy of Fred and Joyce Moseley.* £60-80; $100-130.

190

Figure 508. Earthenware salad bowl, ca. 1918. Pattern no. E2240, diameter 7.5". *Courtesy of Marjorie Winters*. £50-70; $80-115.

Figure 510. Reverse side of figure 509 showing that the mug was presented by the Corporation of the County Borough of Stoke-on-Trent.

Figure 509. Earthenware commemorative mug, ca. 1919. Mug issued to commemorate the ending of The First World War, height 4". *Courtesy of Arthur Bowden*. £30-40; $50-65.

Figure 511. Earthenware sugar shaker, ca. 1920. Height 6.5". *Courtesy of Marjorie Winters*. £30-40; $50-65.

Figure 512. Earthenware biscuit barrel, ca. 1920. Pattern no. E2277, height 5.5". *Courtesy of Derek and Shirley Weyman.* £60-80; $100-130.

Figure 514. Earthenware condiment set with silver plated stand, ca. 1920. Salt pot height 2". *Courtesy of Derek and Shirley Weyman.* £50-70; $80-115.

Figure 513. Bone china biscuit barrel, ca. 1920. Pattern no. E2007, pattern name 'Old Swansea', height 5.75". *Courtesy of Derek and Shirley Weyman.* £100-120; $165-200.

Figure 515. Photograph of George Jones & Sons Ltd. display at the British Industries Fair held in London in 1923. *Courtesy of Tableware International.*

Figure 516. Illustration of 'Mount Vernon' shape tableware, from a 1924 George Jones & Sons Ltd. trade catalogue. *Courtesy of Hanley Reference Library.*

Figure 518. Illustration of tableware, from a 1924 George Jones & Sons Ltd. trade catalogue. *Courtesy of Hanley Reference Library.*

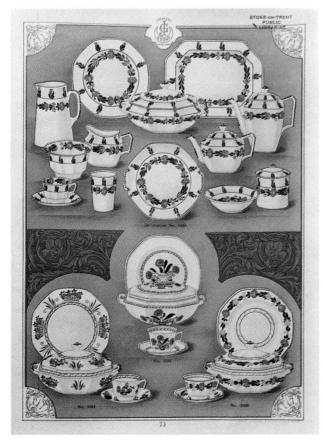

Figure 517. Illustration of 'Octagon' shape tableware, from a 1924 George Jones & Sons. Ltd. trade catalogue. *Courtesy of Hanley Reference Library.*

Figure 519. Illustration of 'Monmouth' shape tableware, from a 1924 George Jones & Sons Ltd. trade catalogue. *Courtesy of Hanley Reference Library.*

Figure 520. Illustration of tableware, from a 1924 George Jones & Sons Ltd. trade catalogue. *Courtesy of Hanley Reference Library.*

Figure 522. Illustration of tableware, from a 1924 George Jones & Sons Ltd. trade catalogue. *Courtesy of Hanley Reference Library.*

Figure 521. Illustrated here are four engraved patterns on plates. Top left 'Rhine', top right 'Cyrene', middle left 'Palestine', middle right 'Casino', from a 1924 George Jones & Sons Ltd. trade catalogue. *Courtesy of Hanley Reference Library.*

Figure 523. Illustration of tableware, from a 1924 George Jones & Sons Ltd. trade catalogue. *Courtesy of Hanley Reference Library.*

Figure 524. Illustration of 'Cardiff' shape tableware, from a 1924 George Jones & Sons Ltd. trade catalogue. *Courtesy of Hanley Reference Library.*

Figure 526. Photograph of George Jones & Sons Ltd. display at the Paris Exhibition of Decorative Arts held in 1925. *Courtesy of Tableware International.*

Figure 525. Illustration of 'The Bordeaux' pattern on 'Cardiff' shape tableware, from an advertisement in *The Pottery Gazette & Glass Trade Review* August 1924. *Courtesy of Tableware International.*

Figure 527. Earthenware fish plate, ca. 1927. Interestingly marked with both the George Jones backstamp and the 'Bisto' backstamp of Bishop and Stonier, length 18". *Courtesy of Fred and Joyce Moseley.* £60-80; $100-130.

Figure 528. Illustration of the 'Bouquet' shape tableware, from an article published in *The Pottery Gazette & Glass Trade Review*. March 1927. *Courtesy of Tableware International.*

Figure 530. Bone china tea cup and saucer, ca. 1900. Pattern no. A2046, saucer diameter 5.5". £40-60; $65-100.

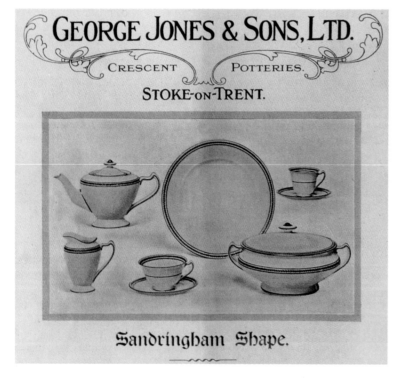

Figure 529. Illustration of the 'Sandringham' shape tableware, from an advertisement in *The Pottery Gazette & Glass Trade Review* August 1927. *Courtesy of Tableware International.*

Figure 531. Bone china breakfast cup and saucer, ca. 1900. Shape Rd. No. 269723, pattern no. 16015, saucer diameter 6.25". £50-70; $80-115.

Figure 532. Bone china tea cup and saucer, ca. 1902. Pattern no. A3481, saucer diameter 5.25". £40-60; $65-100.

Figure 533. Bone china coffee cup and saucer, ca. 1902. Pattern no. 16633, manufactured for Harrods, London, saucer diameter 4.75". £30-50; $50-80.

Figure 534. Bone china tea cup and saucer, ca. 1904. Pattern no. A143, saucer diameter 5.75". £40-60; $65-100.

Figure 535. Bone china tea cup and saucer, ca. 1904. Pattern no. 16113, saucer diameter 5.5". £40-60; $65-100.

Figure 536. Bone china two-handled cup and saucer, ca. 1904. Pattern no. 16530, saucer diameter 5.25". *Courtesy of Mike and Jenny Dunn.* £50-70; $80-115.

Figure 537. Bone china tea cup and saucer, ca. 1904. Pattern no. 17145, saucer diameter 5.5". £40-60; $65-100.

Figure 538. Bone china tea cup and saucer, ca. 1904. Saucer diameter 5.25". *Courtesy of Derek and Shirley Weyman.* £50-70; $80-115.

Figure 539. Bone china *solitaire* set, ca. 1905. Pattern no. 16339, tray diameter 10". *Courtesy of Fred and Joyce Moseley.* £225-250; $370-415.

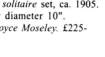

Figure 540. Bone china tea pot, ca. 1905. Pattern no. 17837, height 5.5". *Courtesy of Fred and Joyce Moseley.* £100-120; $165-200.

Figure 541. Bone china cup and saucer, ca. 1905. Pattern no. A3786, saucer diameter 5.5". £40-60; $65-100.

Figure 542. Bone china coffee can and saucer, ca. 1905. Pattern no. 16113, saucer diameter 3.875". £30-50; $50-80.

Figure 543. Bone china jug and basin, ca. 1905. Pattern no. N3361, jug height 2.5". £25-35; $40-60 each piece.

199

Figure 544. Bone china two-handled cup and saucer, ca. 1906. Pattern no. 19175, saucer diameter 5.5". £50-70; $80-115.

Figure 545. Bone china tea cup and saucer, ca. 1907. Pattern no. 16998, saucer diameter 5.5". £40-60; $65-100.

Figure 546. Bone china coffee cup and saucer, ca. 1907. Pattern no. A4675, saucer diameter 4.75". £30-50; $50-80.

Figure 547. Bone china tea cup and saucer, ca. 1908. Pattern name 'Enfield', pattern no. 20320, saucer diameter 5.375". £40-60; $65-100.

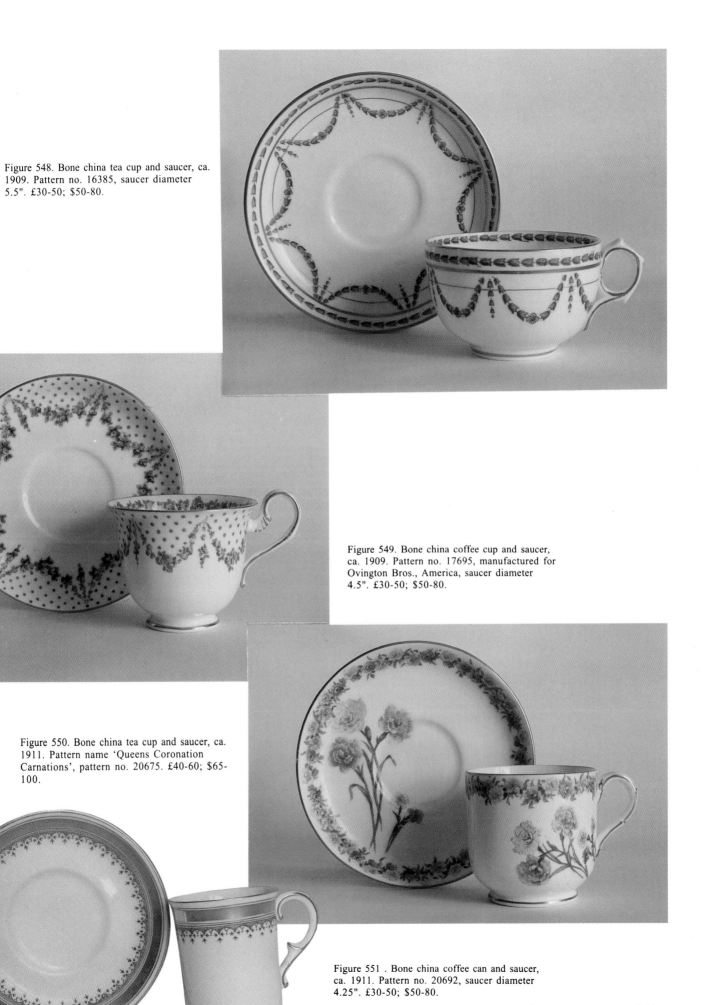

Figure 548. Bone china tea cup and saucer, ca. 1909. Pattern no. 16385, saucer diameter 5.5". £30-50; $50-80.

Figure 549. Bone china coffee cup and saucer, ca. 1909. Pattern no. 17695, manufactured for Ovington Bros., America, saucer diameter 4.5". £30-50; $50-80.

Figure 550. Bone china tea cup and saucer, ca. 1911. Pattern name 'Queens Coronation Carnations', pattern no. 20675. £40-60; $65-100.

Figure 551 . Bone china coffee can and saucer, ca. 1911. Pattern no. 20692, saucer diameter 4.25". £30-50; $50-80.

Figure 552. Bone china slop bowl, milk jug and tea pot, ca. 1912. Pattern no. 23674, tea pot height 5". £120-140; $200-230.

Figure 553. Bone china tea cup and saucer, ca. 1912. Pattern no. 23674, saucer diameter 5.5". £40-60; $65-100.

Figure 554. Bone china tea cup and saucer, ca. 1915. Pattern no. TC521, manufactured for Mappin and Webb, London, saucer diameter 5.375". £40-60; $65-100.

Figure 555. Bone china coffee cup and saucer, ca. 1915. Pattern signed W. Birbeck, saucer diameter 4.375". £50-70; $80-115.

Figure 556. Advertisement illustrating the new 'Patent Nesting Cups', from *The Pottery Gazette* November 1916. *Courtesy of Tableware International.*

Figure 557. Bone china coffee can and saucer, ca. 1917. Pattern no. V743, saucer diameter 4". £30-50; $50-80.

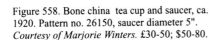

Figure 558. Bone china tea cup and saucer, ca. 1920. Pattern no. 26150, saucer diameter 5". *Courtesy of Marjorie Winters.* £30-50; $50-80.

Figure 559. Bone china coffee can and saucer, ca. 1920. Pattern no. 25655, saucer diameter 3.875". £30-50; $50-80.

203

GEORGE JONES & SONS, LTD.,: A NEW AND FREE TREATMENT IN NURSERY WARE.

[Photo. by "The Pottery Gazette."]

Figure 560. Illustration of nursery ware, from an article in *The Pottery Gazette & Glass Trade Review* March 1920. *Courtesy of Tableware International.*

Figure 562. Illustration of new decoration pattern no. 26269 on china tea ware, from an advertisement in *The Pottery Gazette & Glass Trade Review* November 1922. *Courtesy of Tableware International.*

Figure 561. Illustration of 'Monmouth' shape dinner and tea ware, from a 1924 George Jones & Sons Ltd. trade catalogue. *Courtesy of Hanley Reference Library.*

Figure 563. Bone china tea cup and saucer, ca. 1922. Pattern no. 20675, saucer diameter 5.25". £40-60; $65-100.

Figure 564. Bone china partial coffee set, ca. 1924. Shape Rd. No. 623290, coffee pot height 4". *Courtesy of Fred and Joyce Moseley.* £250-270; $415-445 complete set.

Figure 565. Bone china cup and saucer, ca. 1925. Pattern no. 30187, saucer diameter 5.5". *Courtesy of Derek and Shirley Weyman.* £50-70; $80-115.

Figure 566. Bone china tea cup and saucer, ca. 1925. Pattern no. 25083, saucer diameter 5.5". £40-60; $65-100.

Figure 567. Bone china coffee can and saucer, ca. 1925. Pattern no. 25618, saucer diameter 3.875". £30-50; $50-80.

Figure 568. Earthenware coffee cup and saucer, ca. 1927. Shape name 'Bouquet', pattern name 'Mayflower', saucer diameter 4.75". *Courtesy of Derek and Shirley Weyman.* £30-50; $50-80.

Figure 569. 'Anglo' china covered vegetable dish, ca. 1902. Pattern no. 4945, length 11". £80-100; $130-165.

Figure 570. Bone china covered vegetable dish, ca. 1905, length 10.5". *Courtesy of Fred and Joyce Moseley.* £80-100; $130-165.

Figure 571. 'Semi-Porcelaine' oval meat tray, ca. 1907. Pattern name 'Cymric', length 11". *Courtesy of Derek and Shirley Weyman.* £50-70; $80-115.

Figure 572. An elegant earthenware soup tureen with stand and ladle, ca. 1911. Pattern name 'Whitby', height 10". *Courtesy of Roger and Heather Burt.* £200-225; $330-370.

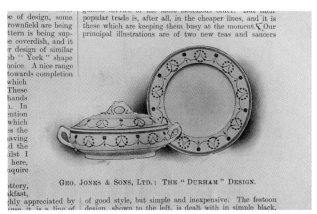

GEO. JONES & SONS, LTD.: THE "DURHAM" DESIGN.

Figure 574. Illustration of the 'Durham Rose' pattern, from *The Pottery Gazette* July 1915. *Courtesy of Tableware International.*

majority of our readers will already be well aware, manufacturers of domestic china and earthenware of every description from everyday lines upwards to the most expensive and elaborate. Their "Crescent" china is now known in all the markets of the world, for it is a brand that is popular, both on account of its price and its quality. It is sometimes difficult to give an individual line its correct classification, but not much risk is run, I think, in venturing the opinion that "Crescent" china, judging it from its average, occupies a position which may be described as in the higher middle class; that is to say, the great bulk of the goods supplied by this house are neither inordinately expensive nor excessively cheap, but the happy medium. The firm has its cheap lines, it is true, just as it also has its classical productions which have appealed more than once to the highest branches of royalty. It is difficult in reviewing this firm's samples to pick out any single branch in which they may be said to absolutely specialise, unless it be china toilet ware. The range of their productions is so far-reaching that it really covers everything needed in the home or in the institution. Truly this is a house that the dealer can approach for almost anything, and at the same time be pretty sure of getting it. I have mentioned their productions in china toilet ware on several previous occasions; on the last I observed that I had not seen a wider range of china toilet patterns anywhere than is to be found in this firm's show room, and that statement has not been challenged. The effects produced by George Jones & Sons, Ltd., in their china toilet ware are for the most part restrained and elegant; they are

and quality, just as in all departments, to produce that which shall appeal to the most luxuriously inclined. They enjoy the great advantage of making all their own lithographs, which makes it possible for them to bring out patterns which are always kept select and can never become hackneyed through being produced by a number of houses simultaneously, as was often the case in regard to the lithographs purchased from Germany and elsewhere. They have largely developed this branch of decoration, and in many cases their lithographs are painstakingly touched up with brush by hand to give an effect very near to that of hand painting. Especially is this the case with many of their neat coloured borders, and it is this which is one explanation of the extremely low prices which are asked for many of the really attractive and well-executed decorations. At the moment some of their elaborate decorations are at a discount; it is the more popular styles that the public is interested in. It is one or two of these, therefore, that we will endeavour to call attention. Our illustrations are of three of this firm's popularly selling earthenware printed dinner patterns:—(1) The "York Rose," (2) the "China Rose," and (3) the "Durham." These are typical of many other equally inviting, and all at a popular price. The principal colours are cobalt blue and myrtle green, and whilst the particular patterns illustrated are not kept in stock at the factory they can all be had fairly promptly. The trade will now have become fairly well acquainted with this firm's "Abbey" pattern, an old English all-over blue print of distinctive merit, which cannot fail to sell.

GEO. JONES & SONS, LTD.: THE "YORK ROSE" PATTERN.

GEO. JONES & SONS, LTD.: THE "CHINA ROSE" PATTERN.

Figure 573. Illustration of the 'York Rose' and 'China Rose' pattern on dinner ware, from an article in *The Pottery Gazette* July 1915. *Courtesy of Tableware International.*

April 1, 1916.   THE POTTERY GAZETTE.   341

George Jones & Sons, Ltd.
Crescent Potteries, STOKE-ON-TRENT.

TRADE MARK
GJ AND SONS
ENGLAND.

Telegrams:
"IONIA,
STOKE-ON-TRENT."

Telephones:
Works—
815 Central.
London—
3409 Central.

"KENNETH" (STOCK PATTERN).
Splendid Selling Line, Printed in Dark Blue and Myrtle Green.

London Showrooms (always open), 21, BARTLETT'S BUILDINGS, HOLBORN CIRCUS, E.C.

Figure 575. Advertisement showing the 'Kenneth' pattern, from *The Pottery Gazette* April 1916. *Courtesy of Tableware International.*

GEO. JONES & SON, LTD.: THE "BRISTOL" PATTERN,
IN DARK BLUE OR MYRTLE GREEN.

Figure 576. Illustration of the 'Bristol' pattern on dinner ware, from an article in *The Pottery Gazette* April 1916. *Courtesy of Tableware International.*

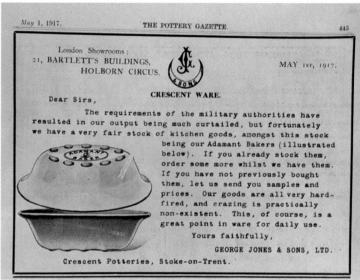

Figure 578. Advertisement showing an item from a range of 'Adamant Bakers' kitchen ware that appeared in *The Pottery Gazette* May 1917

GEO. JONES & SON, LTD.: THE "PERKINS" DESIGN, ESPECIALLY SUITABLE
FOR THE OVERSEA MARKETS.

Figure 577. Illustration of the 'Perkins' pattern on dinner ware, from an article in *The Pottery Gazette* April 1916. *Courtesy of Tableware International.*

Figure 579. Earthenware covered vegetable dish, ca. 1920. Diameter 10.5". *Courtesy of Fred and Joyce Moseley.* £50-70; $80-115.

Figure 580. Earthenware meat plate, ca. 1922. Shape name 'Octagon', hand painted pattern, length 14.5". £40-60; $65-100.

Figure 582. Illustration of earthenware dinner ware from a 1924 George Jones & Sons Ltd. trade catalogue. *Courtesy of Hanley Reference Library.*

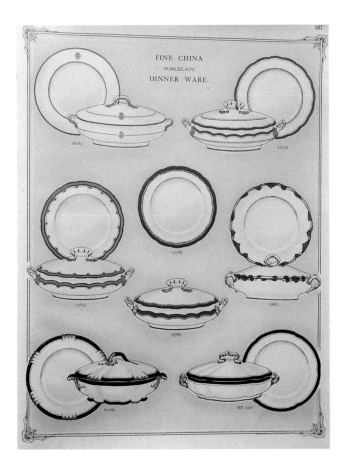

Figure 581. Illustration of china dinner ware from a 1924 George Jones & Sons Ltd. trade catalogue. *Courtesy of Hanley Reference Library.*

Figure 583. Illustration of earthenware dinner ware from a 1924 George Jones & Sons Ltd. trade catalogue. *Courtesy of Hanley Reference Library.*

209

Figure 586. Bone china dessert plate, ca. 1900. Pattern no. A3213, diameter 9". *Courtesy of Marjorie Winters.* £60-80; $100-130.

Figure 584. Advertisement showing a range of covered dishes and plates, from *The Pottery Gazette & Glass Trade Review* November 1925. *Courtesy of Tableware International.*

Figure 587. Bone china dessert plate, ca. 1900. Pattern no. A3213, diameter 9". *Courtesy of Marjorie Winters.* £60-80; $100-130.

Figure 585. Earthenware sauce tureen with stand, ca. 1927. Pattern name 'Paisley', diameter 6". *Courtesy of Derek and Shirley Weyman.* £50-70; $80-115.

Figure 588. Bone china dessert plate, ca. 1900. Pattern no. A3213, diameter 9". *Courtesy of Marjorie Winters.* £60-80; $100-130.

Figure 590. Bone china dessert plate, ca. 1901. Picture of Ptarmigan signed W. Birbeck, manufactured for Gilman Collamore & Co., New York, diameter 8.5". £130-150; $215-250.

Figure 589. Bone china dessert plate, ca. 1900. Pattern no. A1346, outside diameter 9.5". *Courtesy of Derek and Shirley Weyman.* £60-80; $100-130.

Figure 591. Bone china dessert plate, ca. 1901. Picture of Quail signed W. Birbeck, diameter 9". *Courtesy of Shirley Weyman.* £130-150; $215-250.

Figure 592. Bone china dessert plate, ca. 1902. Pattern no. D495, picture of a Partridge signed W. Birbeck, manufactured for Davis Collamore & Co. Ltd., New York. This plate is one of a set of six that came from the estate of Gary Cooper, the American film actor, diameter 9". £130-150; $215-250.

Figure 594. Bone china dessert plate, ca. 1902. Pattern no. D396, picture of Warwick Castle signed C. Austin, diameter 8.5", £130-150; $215-250.

Figure 593. Bone china dessert plate, ca. 1902. Pattern no. D398, picture of Heidelberg Castle signed C. Austin, diameter 8.5". £130-150; $215-250.

Figure 595. Bone china dessert plate, ca. 1902. Pattern no. 18128, picture of an American Partridge signed W. Birbeck, diameter 8.5". £130-150; $215-250.

Figure 596. Bone china compote, ca. 1903. Pattern no. A4343, pattern initialled H.O.J., height 4". £100-120; $165-200.

Figure 598. Bone china dessert plate, ca. 1904. Pattern no. 18050, diameter 9". *Courtesy of Marjorie Winters.* £60-80; $100-130.

Figure 597. Bone china dessert plate, ca. 1903. Pattern no. A4343, pattern initialled H.O.J., diameter 9". £80-100; $130-165.

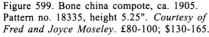

Figure 599. Bone china compote, ca. 1905. Pattern no. 18335, height 5.25". *Courtesy of Fred and Joyce Moseley.* £80-100; $130-165.

Figure 600. Bone china compote, ca. 1905. Pattern no. A3222, diameter 9". *Courtesy of Fred and Joyce Moseley.* £60-80; $100-130.

Figure 601. Bone china dessert plate, ca. 1905. Pattern no. 21137, manufactured for Alfred B. Pearce & Co., London, diameter 8.75". £60-80; $100-130.

Figure 603. Bone china dessert plate, ca. 1906. Pattern no. 18388, diameter 9". Courtesy of *Durham House Antique Centre, Stow-on-the-Wold.* £60-80; $100-130.

Figure 602. Bone china dessert plate, ca. 1905. Pattern no. TC466, signed W. Birbeck, manufactured for Ovington Bros., America, diameter 8.875". £130-150; $215-250.

214

Figure 604. Bone china dessert plate, ca. 1907. Pattern no. A4337, diameter 9". *Courtesy of Marjorie Winters*. £60-80; $100-130.

Figure 606. Bone china dessert plate, ca. 1907. Pattern no. A4988, pattern signed W. Lamonby, diameter 8.5". £130-150; $215-250.

Figure 605. Bone china dessert plate, ca. 1907. Pattern no. D539, picture of Grouse signed W. Birbeck, diameter 8.75". £130-150; $215-250.

Figure 607. Bone china dessert plate, ca. 1908. Pattern no. 21151, signed J. Fenn, manufactured for Maple & Co., London & Paris, diameter 9". £130-150; $215-250.

Figure 608. Bone china dessert plate, ca. 1909. Pattern no. 21258, manufactured for Waring & Gillow, London, diameter 8.5". £60-80; $100-130.

Figure 610. Bone china dessert plate, ca. 1912. Pattern no. 21201, signed W. Birbeck, diameter 9". *Courtesy of Derek & Shirley Weyman.* £130-150; $215-250.

Figure 609. Bone china dessert plate, ca. 1910. Pattern no. 21230, diameter 8.5". £50-70; $80-115.

Figure 611. Bone china dessert plate, ca. 1919. Pattern no. 19623, pattern name 'Old Swansea', diameter 8.75". £60-80; $100-130.

Figure 612. Earthenware dessert plate, ca. 1924. Shape name 'Pearl', pattern no. E2224, diameter 9". £30-50; $50-80.

Figure 614. Bone china dessert plate, ca. 1927. Pattern no. 26962, centre picture signed W. Birbeck, diameter 10.25". £140-160; $230-265.

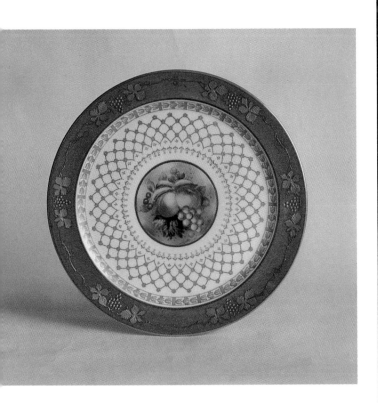

Figure 613. Bone china dessert plate, ca. 1926. Pattern no. D726, centre picture signed W. Birbeck. £130-150; $215-250.

Figure 615. Bone china ewer, ca. 1905. Pattern no. 15790, manufactured for Harrods, London, height 11.5". *Courtesy of Derek and Shirley Weyman.* £100-120; $165-200.

Figure 616. Earthenware ewer and basin, ca. 1905. Pattern no. 21864, ewer height 12". *Courtesy of Marjorie Winters.* £230-260; $380-430.

Figure 618. Earthenware chamber pot, ca. 1906. Pattern no. 15467, diameter 9". £40-60; $65-100.

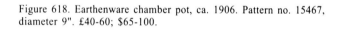

Figure 617 . Bone china ewer and basin, ca. 1906. Pattern no. 20705, manufactured for Harrods, London, ewer height 11.5". *Courtesy of Derek and Shirley Weyman.* £230-260; $380-430.

Figure 619. Stone china ewer and basin, ca. 1907. Pattern no. A4802, basin diameter 16". £250-300; $415-495.

Figure 620. Stone china slop bucket to match Figure 619, ca. 1907. Height 12". £100-120; $165-200.

The first chairman of directors in the limited company was Mr. F. R. Benham, who died in October, 1911, and whose position is now filled by Mr. G. H. Jones, the present

bedroom ware for the superior home could possibly look better. We illustrate the three shapes mentioned, without describing the decorations beyond saying that

CHOICE CHINA TOILET SETS : GEORGE JONES & SONS, LTD. [*Photo. by "The Pottery Gazette."*]

directorate consisting of Messrs. G. H. Jones, C. S. Jones, F. B. Benham, A. O. Jones, and E. G. Jones. The Crescent Potteries are quite extensive, covering about four acres of land, and employing a staff of from 800 to

they are perfectly executed, are powerfully appealing, and reflect the highest artistic talent; we will refrain from saying more, simply commending them to the notice of our readers. Much might be said about the firm's

Figure 622. Illustration of three shapes of bone china toilet ware, from an article in *The Pottery Gazette* December 1913. The shape names are, from left to right, 'Wallace', 'King', and 'Sheffield'. *Courtesy of Tableware International.*

Figure 621. Bone china soap dish, ca. 1915. Pattern no. 20599, length 5". £50-70; $80-115.

Figure 623. Earthenware ewer, ca. 1915. Pattern no. V917, height 9.5". *Courtesy of Fred and Joyce Moseley.* £70-90; $115-150.

Figure 624. Earthenware ewer, ca. 1915. Pattern no. 22101, height 11".
Courtesy of Derek and Shirley Weyman. £70-90; $115-150.

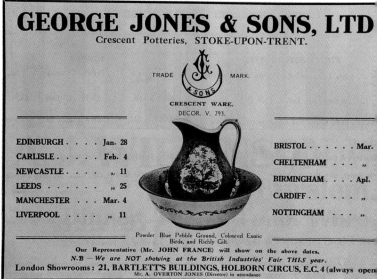

Figure 626. Advertisement featuring toilet ware decorated with pattern no. V793, from *The Pottery Gazette* February 1918. *Courtesy of Tableware International.*

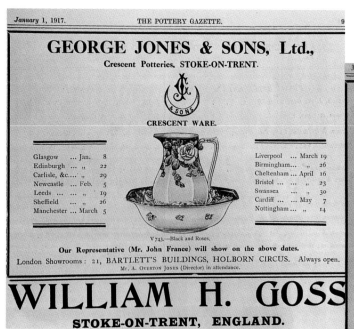

Figure 625. Advertisement featuring toilet ware decorated with pattern no. V743, from *The Pottery Gazette* January 1917. *Courtesy of Tableware International.*

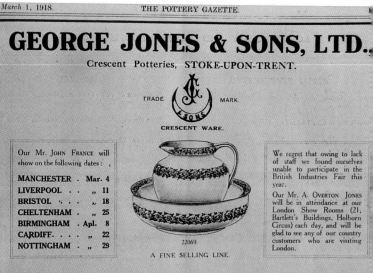

Figure 627. Advertisement featuring toilet ware decorated with pattern no. 22069, from *The Pottery Gazette* March 1918. *Courtesy of Tableware International.*

Figure 628 . Illustration of bone china toilet ware, from a 1924 George Jones & Sons Ltd. trade catalogue. *Courtesy of Hanley Reference Library.*

Figure 630. Illustration of toilet ware, from a 1924 George Jones & Sons Ltd. trade catalogue. *Courtesy of Hanley Reference Library.*

Figure 629. Illustration of toilet ware, from a 1924 George Jones & Sons Ltd. trade catalogue. *Courtesy of Hanley Reference Library*

Figure 631. Illustration of toilet ware, from a 1924 George Jones & Sons Ltd. trade catalogue. *Courtesy of Hanley Reference Library.*

Figure 632. Illustration of toilet ware, from a 1924 George Jones & Sons Ltd. trade catalogue. *Courtesy of Hanley Reference Library.*

Figure 634. Earthenware vase, ca. 1900. Pattern name 'Imperial', height 11.5" £180-200; $300-330.

Figure 633. Earthenware vase, ca. 1900. Pattern name 'Pompeian', height 10". £150-200; $250-330.

Figure 635. A pair of bone china vases, ca. 1905. Hand painted picture of climbing roses signed W. Birbeck. £350-400; $580-660 pair.

Figure 636. Earthenware jardinière, ca. 1910. Pattern no. 15844, height 11". *Courtesy of Derek and Shirley Weyman.* £200-250; $330-415.

Figure 638. Earthenware vase, ca. 1910. Height 8". £150-200; $250-330.

Figure 637. A very attractive bone china vase, ca. 1910. Pattern no. V366, height 8.5". *Courtesy of Mike & Jenny Dunn.* £250-300; $415-495.

Figure 639. Bone china vase, ca. 1910. Shape no. 341, picture of climbing roses signed W. Birbeck, height 9.5". £150-180; $250-300.

Figure 640. Bone china 'footed' vase, ca. 1915. Pattern no. V539, height 11". *Courtesy of Mike and Jenny Dunn.* £200-250; $330-415.

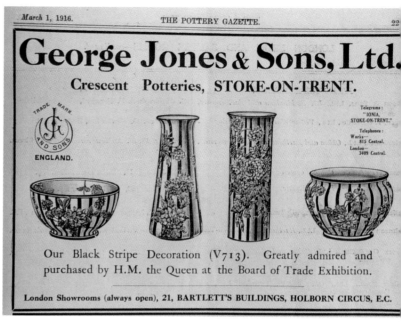

Figure 642. Advertisement featuring vases and jardinières decorated with pattern no. V713, from *The Pottery Gazette* March 1916. *Courtesy of Tableware International.*

Figure 643. Advertisement featuring vases decorated with pattern no. V743, from *The Pottery Gazette* August 1916. *Courtesy of Tableware International.*

Figure 641. Bone china jardinière, ca. 1915. Height 5". *Courtesy of Marjorie Winters.* £60-80; $100-130.

Figure 644. Garniture of vases, ca. 1916. Middle vase shape no. 440, outer vases shape no. 343, pattern no. V743, centre vase height 9". £60-80; $100-130 each.

DECORATION V 793.
A large assortment of Shapes and Articles can be had.

Figure 646. Illustration featuring vases, jardinières and an ink well all decorated with pattern no. V793, from an advertisement in *The Pottery Gazette* September 1917. *Courtesy of Tableware International.*

Figure 645. Advertisement featuring vases and jardinières decorated with pattern no. V743, from *The Pottery Gazette* April 1917. *Courtesy of Tableware International.*

Figure 647. Earthenware vase, ca. 1920. Pattern no. V412, pattern name 'Imperial Amethyst', height 13". *Courtesy of Derek and Shirley Weyman.* £120-150; $200-250.

Figure 650. Earthenware vase, ca. 1920. Shape no. 31, pattern no. V709, height 10.5". *Courtesy of Marjorie Winters.* £80-100; $130-165.

Figure 648. Earthenware vase, ca. 1920. Pattern no. V648, height 8". *Courtesy of Fred and Joyce Moseley.* £80-100; $130-165.

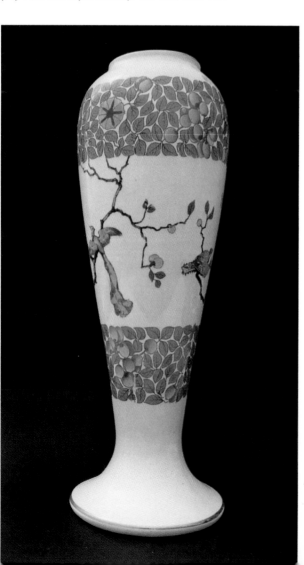

Figure 651. Earthenware jardinière, ca. 1920. Shape no. 267, pattern no. V793, height 8". £150-175; $250-290.

Figure 649. Earthenware vase, ca. 1920. Pattern no. V665, height 12". *Courtesy of Derek and Shirley Weyman.* £60-80; $100-130.

Figure 652. Earthenware jardinière, ca. 1920. Shape no. 259, pattern no. V385, height 8.5". £200-250; $330-415.

Figure 654. Earthenware vase, ca. 1920. Shape no. 328, pattern no. V793, height 8". £100-120; $165-200.

Figure 653. Earthenware vase, ca. 1920. Shape no. 371, pattern no. V595, pattern name 'Imperial Amethyst', height 18". £350-400; $580-660.

Figure 655. Three small bone china vases, ca. 1920. Pattern no. V785, largest height 4". Average £20-40; $35-65 each.

Figure 656. Earthenware vase, ca. 1920. Shape no. 413, pattern no. V594, pattern name 'Imperial Rouge', height 10.25". £150-200; $250-330.

Figure 658. Earthenware vase, ca. 1920. Shape no. 320, pattern no. V594, pattern name 'Imperial Rouge', height 9.75". £275-325; $455-535.

Figure 659. Illustration showing a new form of decoration, from *The Pottery Gazette & Glass Trade Review* March 1920. *Courtesy of Tableware International.*

Figure 657. Earthenware vase, ca. 1920. Shape no. 438, pattern no. V594, pattern name 'Imperial Rouge', height 8". £100-130; $165-215.

Figure 660. Earthenware two-handled jardinière, ca. 1920. Shape no. 201, pattern no. V594, pattern name 'Imperial Rouge', height 11". *Courtesy of Derek and Shirley Weyman.* £200-250; $330-415.

Figure 662. Illustration of vases and jardinières decorated with pattern no. V385, from a 1924 George Jones & Sons Ltd. trade catalogue. *Courtesy of Hanley Reference Library.*

Figure 661. Illustration of vases, jardinière and a garden seat decorated with pattern no. V213 (dark blue) and V392 (light blue), from a 1924 George Jones & Sons Ltd. trade catalogue. *Courtesy of Hanley Reference Library.*

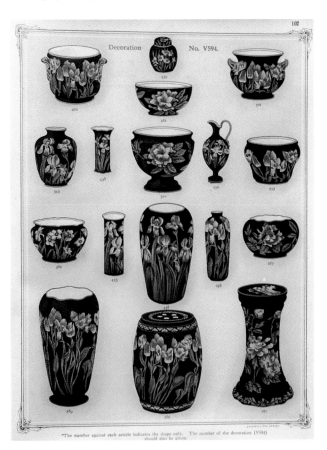

Figure 663. Illustration of vases, jardinières and a garden seat decorated with pattern no. V594, from a 1924 George Jones & Sons Ltd. trade catalogue. *Courtesy of Hanley Reference Library.*

Figure 664. Illustration of vases and jardinières decorated with pattern nos. V648 (solid black and roses), V743 (half black and roses) and V790 (half black with roses and stripes), from a 1924 George Jones & Sons Ltd. trade catalogue. *Courtesy of Hanley Reference Library.*

Figure 665. Illustration of vases, bowls and jardinières decorated with a gold print of seaweed and fishes on a cobalt ground, from a 1924 George Jones & Sons Ltd. trade catalogue. *Courtesy of Hanley Reference Library.*

Figure 666. Garniture of earthenware vases, ca. 1924. Middle vase shape no. 439, outer vases shape no. 214, height 8". £100-150; $165-250 each.

Figure 667. Earthenware vase, ca. 1926. Pattern no. V1148, height 10.5". *Courtesy of Fred and Joyce Moseley.* £100-130; $165-215.

Figure 668. Illustration featuring vases decorated with pattern no. V1148, from an article in *The Pottery Gazette & Glass Trade Review* January 1926. *Courtesy of Tableware International.*

With the death of chairman Charles Samuel Jones and the untimely retirement through ill health of Thomas Hammersley, the company was now being run by Arthur Overton Jones, deputy chairman. He had temporarily relinquished his position as manager of the company's London showrooms to take control of the management of the company until a successor to Thomas Hammersley could be found.

The design department was still under the control of Charles Birbeck and the factory was busy producing the infinite variety of wares that the company was well known for. These included table services, supper sets, fruit sets, bridge sets, water sets, ornamental and miscellaneous goods, wares suitable for hotels, cafes, ships, railways and institutions, and also complete ranges of kitchen and utility goods. The wares were produced in fine bone china and earthenware, with both white and Ivory coloured bodies; for both the home and overseas markets.

In May 1928, Walter Bakewell joined the board of directors and assumed managerial control of the company. He was a man with a wealth of experience in the pottery industry.

Although the company produced such a variety of wares, 1928 was not a good trading year, the company making a loss of £6,000. Toward the end of 1928, the management decided to engage in a process of concentration and, to this end, produced a number of special 'open stock' patterns in earthenware which could be used for every item of tableware.

In January 1929, four such patterns were introduced and were called 'Greek Key': the 'Dominion', the 'Barclay', and the 'Chester'. These four patterns covered a range of treatments from simple and dignified, to fairly ambitious and ornate.

At the same time, two new shapes were introduced, named 'Rhapsody' and 'Marlborough'. The 'Rhapsody' shape had a wide border of floral embossment and was produced in many contrasting colours. It was produced on an Ivory body and had nearly thirty different styles of presentation and became very popular, especially in America.

The 'Marlborough' embossed design, instead of being continuous around the border as on the 'Rhapsody', was broken up into panel form. It too was produced in very many different colours. Examples of both these types of wares are shown in Figures 677 and 697.

As well as these embossed patterned wares, much of the tableware being produced at this time was decorated with patterns that were a combination of lithographic prints and hand painting. Many of these patterns were designed by Cyril Shingler, who had joined George Jones & Sons Ltd. as a designer around 1929.

During 1929, the 'Abbey' blue and white underglaze transfer printed earthenware was advertised; this was still as popular as ever.

By the middle of 1931, the 'Rhapsody' and 'Marlborough' shapes were two of the leading lines in

tableware produced by the company, having been something of a revolution in design for the late 1920s period. Two more shapes for tableware were introduced in mid-1931 and were named 'Stirling' and 'Canterbury'. 'Stirling was used on earthenware and 'Canterbury' was used on bone china wares. An illustration taken from *The Pottery Gazette & Glass Trades Review* featuring both these designs is shown in Figure 699. A beautifully decorated dessert plate in the 'Stirling' shape, with a hand painted centre by William Birbeck, is shown in Figure 704.

In the early 1930s, earthenware pieces decorated with underglaze patterns in black and white became popular. Once again the company turned to their stock of old William Adams copper plate engravings for patterns to be applied to modern shaped pieces. Three patterns are illustrated. The first to be illustrated, shown in Figures 681 and 697, is the 'Cyrene' pattern shown on two 'Marlborough' shaped plates and a 'Marlborough' shaped cup and saucer. The second pattern, illustrated in Figure 709, is shown on a small dessert bowl and has a backstamp incorporating the name 'Genoa'. This was another William Adams pattern bought by George Jones in 1861. This pattern may have been produced in underglaze blue and white, but as yet, no examples have been seen by the author. The third pattern, shown in Figure 705, is on a small 'Stirling' shaped plate. This plate does not show a backstamp incorporating a pattern name, but the subject matter looks as though it may have been produced from some old copper plate engravings — could this be another William Adams pattern?

These designs must have been some of the last to come from the art department while it was still under the control of Charles Birbeck because in September 1931 he was forced to retire due to ill health. Charles Birbeck had spent all his working life at George Jones & Sons Ltd. For over thirty years Birbeck had been the company's art director, responsible for the beautiful and very varied designs of patterns and shapes for which the company was well known. His place as art director was taken by Leon Grice. He had joined the company as a designer after Cyril Shingler left around 1930.

With Walter Bakewell in control of the company, both from a financial and managerial position, it now operated differently. Advertisements in the early 1930s were not as prolific as they once were when Thomas Hammersley was in control.

The last of the reports made by *The Pottery Gazette and Glass Trades Review* about the company's factory and showrooms appeared in the magazine in June 1932. The whole of this report is reproduced below as it says much about what was happening in the early 1930s, not only with regard to the Crescent Potteries but also to world trade.

It was with much pleasure that we recently had an opportunity of traversing once again the workshops, warehouse, and showrooms of the well-known "Crescent" Potteries at Stoke-upon-Trent, which are to be counted amongst our oldest and best known pottery manufacturing concerns.

Our readers on the distributing side of the trade will be well aware, of course, that the "Crescent" Potteries are now operating under a changed administration, Mr. Walter Bakewell having assumed some few years ago the controlling interest. It is Mr. Bakewell's present task - and no small one, it must be admitted - so to remodel the general productions of the concern that they will just as effectively cater for a world trade in times of financial stringency as they were capable of doing when money was freer and tastes correspondingly more elaborate. But, as Mr. Bakewell's whole life has been spent in association with pottery manufacture, he can be trusted to assess, with courage and vision, what the dealers require at the present time and to cater correspondingly, yet with due regard to the traditional quality of the productions which have always emanated from the "Crescent" Potteries.

The majority of our readers will not need reminding that the "Crescent" Potteries make both china and earthenware, and that it has always been the aim of those in command to cater for the requirements of the upper- and middle-class trades. The variety of their creations is practically illimitable, every household need being accommodated, from white or underglaze printed wares upwards. So far as plain prints are concerned, such patterns as "Abbey" have earned worldwide appreciation, and live on from generation to generation by virtue of their intrinsic merit and the universality of their appeal. In the same way there are distinctive patterns in enamelled earthenware and bone china which dealers would have some difficulty in associating with any other name than "Crescent". Of such patterns dealers unhesitatingly renew their stocks from time to time as they become depleted, simply because experience has taught them that this is the reasonable and logical thing to do.

In spite of this, however, the "Crescent" Potteries, in common with all other manufacturing concerns, are finding it necessary in these present days to meet a new set of conditions, and in order to ensure a maintenance of their turnover they are obviously striving to give the best possible value in many additional ways. This is tending to alter very perceptibly the general character of the ruling patterns. Undoubtedly there is a spirit of real freshness about the newer patterns in general.

Dealing first of all with the earthenware one observes many new printed-and-filled-in patterns which aim at presenting the effect of hand painting. Floral designs, simply rendered, are seen in many new services in tableware, and very pretty these are. Again, one notices that whilst in former days quite the majority of the "Crescent" tableware patterns were coloured underglaze, on-glaze treatments have largely been substituted in the latest patterns with a view to the presentation of brighter and livelier colouring.

A new coverdish has been modelled with a slightly scalloped edge. This has been christened the "Balmoral". Having a plain edge, there is a similar shape which takes the name of "Montrose". Applied to these new shapes there are some new and appealing designs, consisting of bands of various colours - several bands on one and the same piece. Some of the colour contrasts and harmonies are very effective. We recall such renderings as green, orange and black; ivory, brown and orange; and black, grey and orange.

A new line, printed, filled-in and gilt, conveys the impression of "Derby." This is something altogether different from what has hitherto been encountered with the "Crescent" productions.

A pattern which we are assured has sold exceedingly well is the No. 30394, which has a rim treatment of colour bands in quiet shades and, executed in correspondingly quiet tints, a spray centre not altogether unlike the old Leeds ware. The general effect is impressive and dignified.

Another pattern in special demand at the present time is the No. 30587. This has a strongly coloured decoration applied to an ivory glaze. A pattern somewhat similar in spirit but more restrained is the No. 30599.

On the bone china one's attention is arrested by many patterns which strike an altogether new note. Of these there

are several with bands or spottings of on-glaze colour in conjunction with platinum and gold. A very modern style of treatment is seen in the No. 30146, which is offered in a series of different colourings. Another noteworthy pattern, which reveals a new decorative outlook in gold printing associated with colour to form a border effect, is the No. 30246, which is available in a variety of colour schemes, of which green, maroon, and turquoise appear to be best favoured.

A neat black and gold design, embodying a slight touch of coral, is seen in the No. 30185, and similar in style is No. 30189, which is a combination of gold, platinum and coral. Such patterns are very appealing, and they are noteworthy in that they are altogether different from the designs which one has traditionally associated with the name of "Crescent".

One could write at length concerning the range of "Crescent" patterns of the higher-priced variety in bone china, such patterns as those which, in more normal times, appeal with special force to the well-to-do classes both at home and abroad, and especially in the United States. For the time being, however, such decorations are more or less in abeyance. That the call for these will be revived in due course is unquestionable, and when this happens George Jones & Sons, Ltd., will be fully prepared to cater, as they have for many generations shown themselves capable of doing, for a world-wide demand in higher priced lines.

It only remains to be said that the full range of "Crescent" samples can be inspected at any time under very favourable conditions either at the works or at the London showrooms, 47, Holborn-viaduct, EC1, in charge of Mr. J. Leather.

Two of the patterns that accompanied this article are reproduced in Figure 702.

At the end of 1932, Walter Bakewell was forced to retire due to ill health and he sold George Jones & Sons Ltd. to Harrison & Son (Hanley) Ltd. This was the start of many changes that were to take place at the "Crescent" Potteries, which greatly affected in particular, the production of George Jones & Sons Ltd. marked wares. At the same time as Walter Bakewell sold George Jones & Sons Ltd. to Harrison & Son (Hanley) Ltd., the Shelton pottery manufacturing company Bishop & Stonier was also bought by Harrisons and this company's (Bishop & Stonier's) production moved to the "Crescent" Potteries. At this time, Harrisons also bought Charles Allerton & Sons and Goss China Co. Ltd. These two companies also moved to the "Crescent" Potteries. Thus, with all these companies operating under their own name within the "Crescent" Potteries, space for the production of George Jones & Sons Ltd. wares was greatly reduced. As a result, the amount of "Crescent" ware produced over the next few years was greatly diminished. Any advertisements that were placed in the trade papers merely advertised "Crescent" ware and did not show any new products.

One former employee who began work at the "Crescent" Potteries in 1930 at the age of fourteen, remembers that in the mid-1930s, high quality china was being produced by George Jones & Sons Ltd. for Heals, the London department store. She commented that one particular pattern was only painted by one lady, as all painters painted flowers, etc., slightly differently and the work for Heals had to be very special. She also remembered the company producing wares for the P.& O. shipping company which bore the shipping company's emblem.

In 1936, Coalport, which included Cauldon and was also owned by Harrison & Son (Hanley) Ltd., moved from their Shelton factory to the "Crescent" Potteries site. They brought with them their own workers, some of whom had been with the company for over forty years. This further diminished the production of George Jones wares. A former employee commented that from 1936 until the outbreak of the Second World War, the majority of wares produced at the "Crescent" Potteries bore the Coalport backstamp. Some of the wares produced at this time were decorated with the same pattern, but sometimes they would have the Coalport backstamp and sometimes the George Jones backstamp. One such pattern was 'Junetime', which was a very popular pattern and can still be found in great abundance. This pattern was designed by D. Capey.

In 1937, advertisements for George Jones & Sons Ltd. began to appear again in *The Pottery Gazette and Glass Trades Review*. The advertisements, Figure 724, featured dessert plates with hand painted centres of bird and flowers etc., and stated that the designs illustrated could be supplied in service plates, tea, and dinner ware for the home and export markets. Some of these plates could have been painted by William Birbeck — although by this time he was seventy years old, he was still working at the "Crescent" Potteries and was also producing hand painted wares for Bishop & Stonier.

By 1938, the depression of the early 1930s was fading into history and the world was looking forward to more prosperous times. The fortunes of George Jones & Sons Ltd., which now incorporated many more companies, began to improve and wares bearing the George Jones backstamp were once again being advertised. The first of these advertisements appeared in *The Pottery Gazette and Glass Trades Review* in January 1938. This advertisement, illustrated in Figure 726, was for an existing earthen tableware shape named 'Whieldon', decorated in a new pattern named 'Chrysanda'. In February 1938, the company advertised the same pattern on china tableware, see Figure 727, but this time the pattern was called 'Chrysola'. The shape of the ware featured in this advertisement was the 'King' shape; a shape originally introduced in the early 1900s, which had been very popular for over thirty years. Examples of this shape are illustrated in Figures 695, 701 and 731. In April 1938, the 'Stirling' shape that was originally introduced in 1931, was again featured in an advertisement in *The Pottery Gazette and Glass Trades Review*, see Figure 728.

In early 1939, a new decoration called 'Chintz' was introduced. This pattern, illustrated in Figure 733, appears on 'King' shaped china tea ware and 'Cardiff' shaped earthen dinner ware.

Along with other manufacturers, lustre ware was produced by George Jones & Sons Ltd., with some pieces signed by Lucien Boullemier, the well-known designer of Maling ware. A plate signed by him and bearing the George Jones backstamp is shown in Figure 729. Whether he worked for George Jones & Sons Ltd. on a full time basis, or whether he produced a few designs on a freelance basis is not known. In the September 1939 issue of *The Pottery Gazette and Glass Trades Review*, the company featured a lustre decorated ashtray and two cigarette boxes. These pieces are shown in Figure 734.

The Second World War broke out in September 1939 and for a while things in the pottery industry remained as they had been for the past few years. In January 1940, George Jones & Sons Ltd. placed the two advertisements, shown in Figures 737 and 738, in *The Pottery Gazette and Glass Trades Review*. One featured the 'Lichfield' shape for tableware and the second featured a new shape for tableware called 'Trentham'. Both these designs incorporated embossing and were produced plain or with decoration. At the same time, the pattern 'Old Swansea' was revived, first introduced in about 1915.

In 1941, the Government was forced to make decisions to save valuable fuel and release much needed manpower and factory space for the war effort. The pottery industry was one of the industries heavily affected. In September 1941, the Board of Trade published a list of pottery manufacturers to whom nucleus certificates had been issued, authorising them to produce undecorated wares for the home market and allowing them to produce decorated wares for export. George Jones & Sons Ltd. was not on this list, as a decision had not been made by the Board of Trade as to their future.

Although only undecorated earthenware was allowed to be sold on the home market, coloured wares of both earthenware and fine bone china was still being produced for export, to help generate much needed foreign currency to pay for the war effort.

In October 1941, the advertisement shown in Figure 741 was placed in *The Pottery Gazette and Glass Trades Review*, featuring a new range of wares designed especially for the North American market. The article that accompanied the illustration gives a fair description of the types of wares the "Crescent" Potteries were producing under the George Jones trade name. It stated:

Producers of good class china and earthenware, both in dinner, tea and coffee services, the high standard and durability of "Crescent" wares carries one's mind back to such famous patterns as the old English Blue Abbey - patterns which for well over a hundred years have enjoyed worldwide appreciation and which, by virtue of their intrinsic merit and universal appeal, have lived on with undiminished popularity right through to the present day. Similarly too, there are to be found in the firm's wide range of enamelled earthenware and china patterns, many equally distinctive decorations which dealers would have difficulty in associating with any other name than "Crescent" and to this range, new designs, planned to appeal with special force to the U.S.A. are constantly being added.

Indicative of the high order and dignity of these, we illustrate here, on the "King" shape, decoration No. 33197 ... Samples of these new patterns may be seen at any time either at the works or in the showrooms of the firm's agents in New York or Toronto.

By November 1941, the company was still awaiting a decision by the Board of Trade as to their future. In the meantime, they continued to produce all types of wares in both decorated and undecorated earthenware and bone china, although with a much depleted workforce.

It was not until September 1942 that the company was informed that it had been licensed to produce undecorated domestic earthenware for the home market. This was to be sold at a maximum price set by the Board of Trade, having regard to the cost of production. George Jones & Sons Ltd. was placed in group II and all the wares had to be marked with the letter B. Reproduced below are the types of bodies and description of wares that were allowed to be manufactured under the *Domestic Pottery (Manufacture and Supply) Order 1942*.

The manufacturer of undecorated domestic pottery is restricted to the following articles made:
a) from a white or light ivory body, glazed with a colourless or white glaze
b) from stoneware made in the natural colour of the clay and glazed with a colourless or brown glaze, or with a brown glaze on the outside and a white or colourless glaze on the inside; or
c) from a natural clay body with a brown glaze or colourless glaze inside and outside, or with a brown glaze on the outside and either a white glaze or a colourless glaze on the inside, that is to say:
cups
egg cups
mugs
beakers
plates
saucers
teapots
coffee pots
jugs
meat dishes and vegetable dishes
sauce boats
cooking ware including pie dishes
bowls
ewers
basins
chambers

hot water bottles and stoppers
rolling pins

In September 1942, wares produced by the Swansea China Co. Ltd., which was part of the Coalport Group that had moved to the Crescent Potteries with Coalport in 1936, were featured in an advertisement in *The Pottery Gazette and Glass Trades Review*. Interestingly, the centre decoration on the wares was designed by William Birbeck. Shortly after this, William Birbeck left the Crescent Potteries and went to work for one of his ex-apprentices, Harold Holdway, who by then was art director at the Copeland-Spode factory.

Although only undecorated earthenware was available on the home market, the Crescent Potteries still continued to produce decorated wares and advertisements were still placed in trade magazines, emphasising that these products were available for the export market.

In September 1943, an advertisement in *The Pottery Gazette and Glass Trades Review* for George Jones & Sons Ltd. featured an all over flower design by Donald Simmill. This advertisement is shown in Figure 743. At this time, Donald Simmill was the decorating manager for the combined group of companies.

In August 1944, another advertisement (figure 744) appeared in *The Pottery Gazette and Glass Trades Review* and featured more designs by Donald Simmill. Accompanying this advert was a article which stated:

> Examples from a set of twelve assorted multi-coloured floral sprays (designer D. Simmill) applied only to dessert plates and to teas and saucers and coffees and saucers on a cream ground. The shape reserved for the tea and coffee ware is "'Leeds," the "Gainsborough" shape being used for the dessert plates. The pastel solid rim-width border may be in any of six different tints.

An example of one of these designs on a "Gainsborough" dessert plate is shown in Figure 736.

In June 1945, George Jones & Sons Ltd. was licensed, by the Board of Trade, to produce fancies for the home market. These had been forbidden to be produced since 1942. The range of articles that were permitted to be produced were figures, vases (not flower jugs), animals, and wall ornaments (including plaques, lamp bases, brooches and ornamental flowers). From this list, it is thought that the company probably produced vases and wall ornaments.

Even though the Second World War had finished, production of pottery was still very restricted and production of pottery for the home market was still controlled by the Board of Trade. In October 1945 the *Domestic Pottery (Manufacturer and Supply) Order 1945* was published and under this order George Jones & Sons Ltd. was licensed to manufacture undecorated domestic earthenware for the home market. This new order superseded the 1942 order but the types of wares permitted to be produced by this order remained the same as the 1942 order. As before, the wares produced by the company had to be marked with a letter B. This order was to remain in force until 1952, when the Government decided to allow some decorated pottery to be sold on the home market.

The last advertisement featuring wares manufactured bearing the George Jones & Sons Ltd. backstamp appeared in August 1944. The majority of advertisements placed in *The Pottery Gazette and Glass Trades Review* from then until 1951, when the trade name ceased to be used, merely stated that three main companies operated from the Crescent Potteries, namely George Jones & Sons Ltd., The Coalport China Co. Ltd., and Cauldon Potteries Ltd. No mention was made of the type of wares that were being produced for export, even though they were producing fine bone china for the markets of the world.

After the Second World War, George Jones & Sons Ltd. bone china was marketed under the name 'Swansea Bone China' and an example of teaware manufactured in 1948 is shown in Figure 746. This example is decorated in a lithographic print. Other patterns produced with the George Jones/Swansea Bone China backstamp, included 'Fragrance' designed by P. Granet and 'Thistle' designed by T. Hall.

Many of the late 1940s and early 1950s patterns used on George Jones & Sons Ltd. bone china were numbered in the range R1006 - R1503 and were mostly lithographic patterns. Most of the George Jones wares produced during the period after the Second World War until 1951 were similar in shape to the Cauldon and Coalport wares produced at the same time.

After the George Jones & Sons trade name ceased to be used in 1951, the Crescent Potteries continued to produce the same shaped bone china but marked with a Swansea China Co. Ltd. backstamp.

So ended ninety years of producing fine pots which, because they did not bear a glamorous name, have gone largely unrecognised. The family and the makers are dispersed, but many of their products survive, scattered around the world, a permanent testimony to the quality which came from George Jones and Sons, Stoke-upon-Trent!

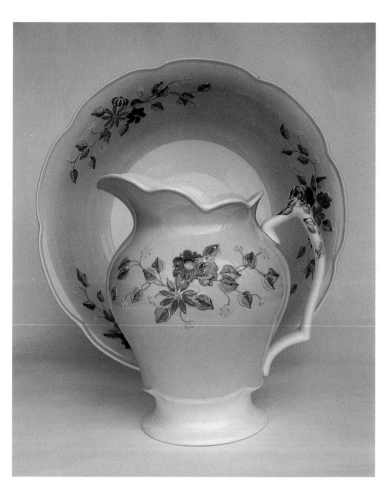

Figure 669. Earthenware ewer and basin, ca. 1928. Shape name 'Bouquet', pattern name 'Mayflower', basin 15.5". *Courtesy of Fred and Joyce Moseley.* £200-250; $330-415.

Figure 670. Earthenware slop pail, soap dish and sponge bowl, ca. 1928. Shape name 'Bouquet', pattern name 'Mayflower', height 11.5". *Courtesy of Fred and Joyce Moseley.* £250-300; $415-495 as a set with Figure 669.

Figure 672. Bone china dessert plate, ca. 1928. Pattern no. 26820, diameter 9". £60-80; $100-130.

Figure 671. Bone china dessert plate, ca. 1928. Centre signed W. Birbeck, manufactured for Phillip's Ltd., London, diameter 8.5". £130-150; $215-250.

Figure 673. Earthenware dessert plate, ca. 1928. Shape name 'Rhapsody', pattern name 'Killarney', 8.5" square. £30-50; $50-80.

Figure 674. Bone china dessert plate, ca. 1928. Pattern no. 27956, centre signed W. Birbeck, diameter 8.75". £130-150; $215-250.

Figure 676. Bone china tea cup and saucer, ca. 1928. Pattern no. 27370, saucer diameter 5.5". £30-50; $50-80.

Figure 675. Bone china jug and coffee can with saucer, ca. 1928. Pattern no. 29249, jug height 3.75". £30-50; $50-80 each piece.

GEORGE JONES & SONS, LTD.

Figure 677. Illustration of various pieces of earthenware tableware produced with the 'Rhapsody' embossed pattern, from an article in *The Pottery Gazette & Glass Trade Review* January 1929. *Courtesy of Tableware International.*

Figure 678. Bone china cup and saucer, ca. 1929. Pattern no. 28735, saucer diameter 5.5". *Courtesy of Marjorie Winters.* £30-50; $50-80.

Figure 680. Earthenware tea plate with enamelled decoration, ca. 1929, pattern no. F706, diameter 8". £20-40; $35-65.

Figure 679. Bone china coffee can and saucer, ca. 1929. Pattern no. 27434, saucer diameter 4.25". £30-50; $50-80.

Figure 681. Earthenware dessert plate, ca. 1929. Shape name 'Marlborough', pattern name 'Cyrene', 8.75" square. £40-60; $65-100.

237

Figure 682. Earthenware tea cup and saucer, ca. 1929. Shape name 'Rhapsody', pattern no. 27427, saucer diameter 5.75". £20-30; $35-50.

Figure 683. Bone china coffee can in solid silver holder with saucer, ca. 1929. Saucer diameter 4.25". £70-90; $115-150.

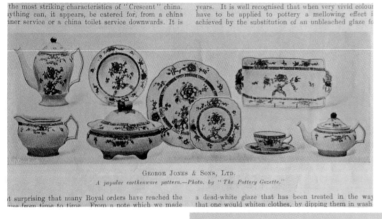

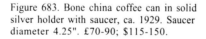

Figure 684. Illustration of various pieces of earthenware tableware decorated in a pattern that was popular in the early 1930s, from an article in *The Pottery Gazette and Glass Trade Review* June 1930. *Courtesy of Tableware International.*

Figure 685. Bone china coffee set, ca, 1930. Pattern no. 30155, coffee pot height 6.5". *Courtesy of Durham House Antique Centre, Stow-on-the-Wold.* £200-250; $330-415 complete with six cups.

Figure 686. Earthenware coffee set, ca. 1930. Shape name 'Rhapsody', U.S. patent no. 77844, coffee pot height 7". *Courtesy of Fred and Joyce Moseley.* £200-250; $330-415 complete with six cups.

Figure 687. Earthenware tea pot, ca. 1930. Shape name 'Rhapsody', height 4". *Courtesy of Derek and Shirley Weyman.* £50-70; $80-115.

Figure 688. Earthenware tea pot, jug and basin, ca. 1930. Pattern name 'Golden Dawn', U.S. patent no. 77844, teapot height 5.5". *Courtesy of Fred and Joyce Moseley.* £100-130; $165-215 set.

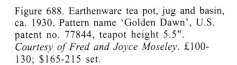

Figure 689. Bone china tea pot with stand, ca. 1930. Pattern no. 27222, height 5". *Courtesy of Derek and Shirley Weyman.* £70-90; $115-150.

Figure 690. Earthenware coffee pot, ca. 1930. Shape name 'Marlborough', height 8". *Courtesy of Derek and Shirley Weyman.* £70-90; $115-150.

Figure 692. Bone china dessert plate, ca. 1930. Centre signed W. Birbeck, diameter 8.25". £130-150; $215-250.

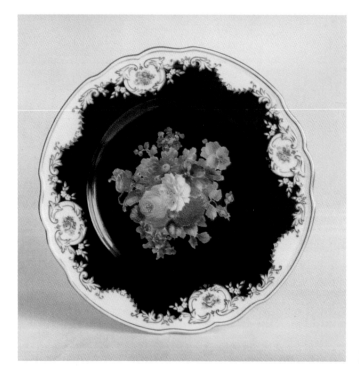

Figure 691. Bone china dessert plate, ca. 1930. Pattern no. D752, centre signed W. Birbeck, diameter 8.75". £130-150; $215-250.

Figure 693. Bone china dinner plate, ca. 1930. Pattern no. 28634, centre signed W. Birbeck, diameter 10.25" £130-150; $215-250.

Figure 694. Earthenware one pint and half pint beer mugs, ca. 1930. One pint mug height 4.75". £20-40; $35-65 each.

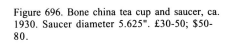

Figure 695. Bone china coffee cup and saucer, ca. 1930. Shape name 'King', saucer diameter 4.75". £30-50; $50-80.

Figure 696. Bone china tea cup and saucer, ca. 1930. Saucer diameter 5.625". £30-50; $50-80.

Figure 697. Earthenware tea cup and saucer, ca. 1930. Shape name 'Marlborough', pattern name 'Cyrene', saucer diameter 5.75". £20-40; $35-65.

241

Figure 698. Earthenware ewer and basin, ca. 1930. Pattern no. 26666, basin diameter 15.5". £150-170; $250-280.

Figure 700. Earthenware coffee pot, tea cup and saucer, and basin, ca. 1931. Shape name 'Marlborough', coffee pot height 7.5". *Courtesy of Fred and Joyce Moseley.* Coffee pot £50-70; $80-115, cup and saucer £30-50; $50-80, basin £10-20; $15-35.

Figure 699. Illustration of table ware, the outer pieces are 'Stirling' shaped earthenware, while the tureen and square plate are bone china in the 'Canterbury' shape, from an article in *The Pottery Gazette & Glass Trade Review* July 1931. *Courtesy of Tableware International.*

Figure 701. Bone china tea cup and saucer, ca. 1931. Shape name 'King', pattern no. D746, saucer diameter 5.5". £30-50; $50-80.

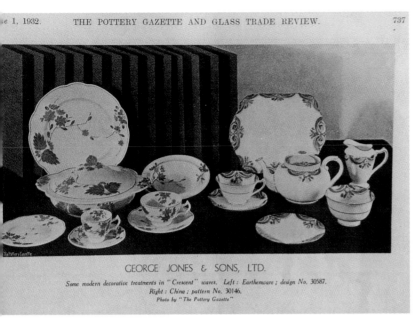

GEORGE JONES & SONS, LTD.

Some modern decorative treatments in "Crescent" wares. Left: Earthenware; design No. 30587.
Right: China; pattern No. 30146.
Photo by "The Pottery Gazette"

Figure 702. Illustration showing the types of decoration and styles of ware available in the early 1930s. On the left, earthenware tableware is decorated with pattern no. 30587 and on the right, bone china tea ware is decorated with pattern no. 30146, from *The Pottery Gazette & Glass Trade Review* June 1932. *Courtesy of Tableware International.*

Figure 704. Bone china dessert plate, ca. 1932. Shape name 'Stirling', centre signed W. Birbeck, diameter 8.875". £130-150; $215-250.

Figure 703. Earthenware dessert plate, ca. 1932. Pattern no. 29857, diameter 8.75". *Courtesy of Derek and Shirley Weyman.* £40-60; $65-100.

Figure 705. Earthenware tea plate, ca. 1932. Shape name 'Stirling', diameter 6". £20-30; $35-50.

Figure 706. Earthenware sauce tureen with stand, ca. 1932. Pattern no. 27580, manufactured for Alfred B. Pearce & Co., London, height 4.25". £30-50; $50-80.

Figure 707. Bone china tea cup and saucer, ca. 1932. Pattern no. TC521, signed W. Birbeck, saucer diameter 5.25". £50-70; $80-115.

Figure 708. Earthenware dessert plate, ca. 1933. Pattern no. 30638, diameter 9". *Courtesy of Fred and Joyce Moseley.* £40-60; $65-100.

Figure 709. Earthenware bowl, ca. 1933. Shape name 'Marlborough', pattern name 'Genoa', diameter 5.625". £20-30; $35-50.

Figure 710. Bone china meat plate, ca. 1934. Pattern Rd. No. 790003, pattern name 'Birbeck Rose', pattern signed W. Birbeck, length 18". £100-120; $165-200.

Figure 711. Bone china tea cup and saucer, ca. 1934. Pattern no. 29856, pattern name 'Old Swansea', saucer diameter 5.375". £30-50; $50-80.

Figure 712. Bone china coffee set, ca. 1934. Pattern no. 27361, pattern name 'Uni', coffee pot height 6.75". £150-175; $250-290 complete with six cups.

Figure 713. Bone china dinner plate, ca. 1935. Diameter 10.5". *Courtesy of Durham House Antique Centre, Stow-on-the-Wold*. £40-60; $65-100.

Figure 714. Bone china dessert plate, ca. 1935. Pattern no. 31468, diameter 9". *Courtesy of Marjorie Winters.* £40-60; $65-100.

Figure 717. Bone china coffee cup in a solid silver holder with a saucer, ca. 1935. Pattern no. 28708, saucer diameter 4.265". £80-100; $130-165.

Figure 715. Earthenware commemorative mug, ca. 1935. To commemorate the Silver Jubilee of King George V and Queen Mary, height. 3.25". £30-50; $50-80.

Figure 716. Reverse side of Figure 715, the earthenware commemorative mug.

Figure 718. Earthenware covered broth bowl with saucer, ca. 1935, saucer diameter 5.875". £30-40; $50-65.

Figure 720. Earthenware jug with tube-lined decoration, ca. 1936. Shape no. 605, height 8.5". *Courtesy of Fred and Joyce Moseley.* £60-80; $100-130.

Figure 719. Earthenware lustre vase, ca. 1935. Shape no. 933, height 8". *Courtesy of Fred and Joyce Moseley.* £60-80; $100-130.

Figure 721. Earthenware tea pot stand, ca. 1936. Width 6.25". *Courtesy of Derek and Shirley Weyman.* £20-40; $35-65.

Figure 722. Earthenware soup plate, ca. 1936. Pattern name 'Pheasant', diameter 10". £30-50; $50-80.

Figure 724. Advertisement illustrating a series of designs available on dinner and tea services, from *The Pottery Gazette & Glass Trade Review* April 1937. This advertisement continued for quite a few years. *Courtesy of Tableware International.*

Figure 723. Earthenware lustre vase, ca. 1936. Pattern no. 973, height 9". £70-90; $115-150.

Figure 725. Bone china dinner plate, ca. 1937. Pattern no. 19690, pattern name 'Enfield', diameter 10". £30-50; $50-80.

Figure 726. Illustration featuring the 'Whieldon' shape of earthenware tableware decorated with the 'Chrysanda' pattern, from *The Pottery Gazette & Glass Trade Review* January 1938. *Courtesy of Tableware International.*

Figure 728. Illustration featuring the 'Stirling' shape of earthenware dinner and tea ware, from *The Pottery Gazette & Glass Trade Review* 1 April 1938. *Courtesy of Tableware International.*

Figure 727. Illustration featuring the 'King' shape of bone china tea ware decorated with the 'Chrysola' pattern, from *The Pottery Gazette & Glass Trade Review* February 1938. *Courtesy of Tableware International.*

Figure 729. Earthenware plate, ca. 1938. Pattern impressed L. Boullemier, (Lucien Boullemier), diameter 11.25". *Courtesy of Derek and Shirley Weyman.* £130-150; $215-250.

Figure 730. Bone china coffee cup and saucer, ca. 1938. Pattern no. 29280, saucer diameter 4.625". £30-50; $50-80.

Figure 731. Bone china coffee pot, ca. 1938. Shape name 'King', pattern name 'Junetime', coffee pot height 7". £80-100; $130-165.

Figure 732. Bone china *tête á tête*, ca. 1938. Pattern name 'Junetime', tea pot height 5". £120-150; $200-250.

Figure 733. Advertisement featuring the 'Cardiff' shape of earthenware dinner ware and the 'King' shape of bone china tea ware decorated with the 'Chintz' pattern, from *The Pottery Gazette & Glass Trade Review* February 1939. *Courtesy of Tableware International.*

Figure 734. Illustration featuring lustre decorated cigarette boxes and ash tray, from *The Pottery Gazette & Glass Trade Review* September 1939. *Courtesy of Tableware International.*

Figure 736. Bone china dessert plate, ca. 1939. Shape name 'Gainsborough', pattern no. 32926, pattern signed D. Simmill, diameter 8.5". £80-100; $130-165.

Figure 735. Earthenware tea plate, ca. 1939. Shape name 'Rhapsody', U.S. patent no. 77844, 8" square. *Courtesy of Marjorie Winters.* £20-30; $35-50.

George Jones & Sons Ltd.

Lichfield Shape

has a delightful ricocco Edge Embossmen which we are confident will appeal to both Home & Overseas buyers.

With its rich Ivory glaze it has a li

Figure 737. Illustration featuring the 'Lichfield' shape of earthenware tableware produced with an Ivory glaze, from *The Pottery Gazette & Glass Trade Review* January 1940. *Courtesy of Tableware International.*

251

George Jones & Sons Ltd.

Figure 740. Bone china cup and saucer, ca. 1940. Pattern no. 32993, saucer diameter 5.25". *Courtesy of Marjorie Winters.* £30-50; $50-80.

Figure 738. Illustration featuring the 'Trentham' shape of earthenware tableware produced with an Ivory glaze, from *The Pottery Gazette & Glass Trade Review* January 1940. *Courtesy of Tableware International.*

Figure 741. Advertisement published in the Buyers Notes section of *The Pottery Gazette & Glass Trade Review* of October 1941, featuring 'King' shape bone china tea ware decorated in pattern no. 33197. *Courtesy of Tableware International.*

Figure 739. Advertisement featuring the 'Old Swansea' pattern of tableware, from *The Pottery Gazette & Glass Trade Review* March 1940. *Courtesy of Tableware International.*

Figure 742. Photograph of the canteen built in 1943 at the Crescent Potteries. It shows, from right to left, Mr. A. Langford, art director of the Coalport China Co., Mrs. Farmer, a flower painter with Goss, Mr. D. Simmill, decorating manager for the combine, Mr. P. Simpson, the company's fish and game painter and Mrs. Brooke, the hand painting mistress, from *The Pottery Gazette & Glass Trade Review* June 1943. *Courtesy of Tableware International.*

Figure 743. Advertisement featuring 'King' shape bone china tea ware with a floral pattern designed by D. Simmill, from *The Pottery Gazette & Glass Trade Review* September 1943. *Courtesy of Tableware International.*

Figure 745. Earthenware tea cup and saucer, ca. 1948. Saucer diameter 5.375". £20-30; $35-50.

Figure 744. Illustration featuring the 'Leeds' shape earthenware tea and coffee ware and the 'Gainsborough' shape of earthenware dessert plates, decorated with a floral pattern designed by D. Simmill, from *The Pottery Gazette & Glass Trade Review* August 1944. *Courtesy of Tableware International.*

Figure 746. Bone china tea cup and saucer, George Jones backmark 'Swansea Bone China', saucer diameter 5.375", £20-30; $35-50.

Appendix 1 - Biographies

List of Biographies

Charles Austin, 1864-fl. 1907 Artist

Charles Austin was born in Hanley in August 1864. He was the fifth son of Joseph and May Austin. His father was a bricklayer who later formed his own building company.

After completion of a formal education, Charles went to work for a pottery manufacturer in the decorating department. By 1879, he was attending the Hanley School of Art and he successfully passed, at second grade level[1], the freehand drawing examinations in 1880. In 1881, at the age of 17, Charles was employed as a potters' flower painter.[2]

In the years 1884, 1885 and 1886, Charles again attended the Hanley School of Art. One of his fellow students was Charles J. Birbeck. Charles Austin won many prizes in the yearly National Art Competitions including a free one-year scholarship to the Hanley School of Art. He completed his art studies in mid-1887.

In August 1888, Charles Austin married a Hanley girl, Annie Marie Nicholls. She was the daughter of a draper. At the time of his marriage, Charles was employed as a potters' artist. Their first home was at Boughey Terrace, Hanley.

Whether Charles Austin trained at George Jones & Sons is not known, but signed pieces, dated 1893 and 1902, bearing the George Jones & Sons backstamp exist. By 1907, Charles Austin was living at Beresford Street, Shelton and was still employed as a potters' artist, but whether this was with George Jones & Sons Ltd. is not known.

Walter Bakewell 1875-1941, Proprietor

Walter Bakewell was born in Burslem in January 1875, the son of William and Sarah Bakewell. His father was a hollow ware presser in the potteries. Walter Bakewell began his career in the pottery industry at the age of eleven years with George L. Ashworth & Bros. From a very junior position, he rose by way of commercial representative to acquire a proprietorial interest in the concern and when Mr. John S. Goddard, the then head of George Ashworth & Bros., retired, Walter Bakewell and J. Vivian Goddard remained partners. George L. Ashworth & Bros. Ltd. was later to merge into the Cauldon Potteries combine and Walter Bakewell became a director.

Late 1924, he retired from the board of Cauldon Potteries Ltd. and took his wife and two sons on an eight month trip to America. During this time, he and his sons toured practically the whole of the pottery manufacturing districts of the U.S.A., where they gathered many useful ideas from the trend of events regarding the demands of the overseas markets; information which served them later in good stead. On their return to England, both sons, Wilfred Marshall and John Kenneth Bakewell, commenced in business together as proprietors of Bakewell Bros., Britannic Potteries, High Street, Hanley.[3]

In May 1928, Walter Bakewell was invited to join the board of George Jones & Sons Ltd.[4] and in May 1929 he purchased the majority of the company shares from the Jones family. At this time, Walter Bakewell was living at Yeovil House, Regent Street, Stoke.

In January 1933, Walter Bakewell was forced to retire due to ill-health. He sold his shares in George Jones & Sons Ltd. to Harrison & Son (Hanley) Ltd. Although he had retired from George Jones & Sons Ltd., he still controlled the firm of Arthur Winkle & Co. Ltd., sanitary potters, where Walter Bakewell remained chairman and managing director until his death in February 1941.

In addition to the above mentioned interests, Walter Bakewell was a director of Shaws Glazed Brick Co. Ltd. of Darwin, Lancashire, and was, at one time, director of Beck & Moss Ltd., Hanley (surfacers of engraved copper plates and rollers for pottery transfer printing). He was also a former proprietor of Adams & Co. of Hanley, who were sanitary ware manufacturers, and a past president of the North Staffordshire branch of the Coal Trades Benevolent Fund.[5]

George Benham Benham 1870-1943, Director

George Benham Benham was born in Stoke in 1870, the eldest son of Frank Ralph and Emily Benham Jones. Like his father, George Benham was of an artistic disposition and painted many pictures. In 1893, George accompanied his father to Chicago, when Frank Jones was appointed British judge at the International Pottery Exhibition.[6]

When William Candland retired as company cashier for George Jones & Sons Ltd., around 1904, George Benham took his place and by 1914, had become a director of the company.[7] Following a personality problem, around 1916 George Benham was asked to leave the company and he moved from his home at Stone to London. George Benham died at Hornsea, Middlesex in January 1943, aged seventy-three. He left two sons.

Keith Benham Benham 1879-1942, Non-executive Director

Keith Benham Benham was born in 1879 at Stafford, the second son of Frank Ralph and Emily Benham Jones. Keith Benham was educated at University College, London, where he graduated with a BSc. degree in chemistry, after which he specialised in the application of chemistry to ceramics. Keith Benham's researches in this direction secured for him the honour of a Fellowship of The Institute of Chemistry.

In 1907, together with his brother-in-law, Mr. E. K. Phillips, Keith Benham formed The Scientific Colour Company, Stafford, supplying materials for the pottery industry; however, in 1912, Mr. Phillips was killed in a tragic accident whilst repairing a mixing machine at their works. Shortly afterwards, Keith Benham closed down the Scientific Colour Co. and joined the Universal Grinding Wheel Co., Stafford. This was a company for whom Keith Benham had done work for in the past, chemically analysing competitors' grinding wheels.

During the period 1914 - 15 George Jones & Sons Ltd. went through a difficult time commercially and Keith Benham was invited to join the company. He declined, saying he wished to stay at the Universal Grinding Wheel Co. but if things didn't work out he would consider the offer again. He was never to join George Jones but as one of the family shareholders he took a keen interest in its affairs and attended the company's annual dinners in the early 1920s.[8]

By 1916, he had become a director of the Universal Grinding Wheel Co., and under his guidance, the company became one of the largest manufacturers of grinding wheels in Europe.

Keith Benham died in October 1942, aged seventy-one. He left a wife and one son.

Charles James Birbeck 1860-1933, Art Director

Charles James Birbeck was born in March 1860 at Liverpool Road, Stoke, and was the second son of William and Elizabeth Birbeck. At the time of his birth, his father was a writing clerk (accountant) and his mother was a straw bonnet maker. Charles's father was later to become a china and earthenware merchant operating from premises in Liverpool Road / High Street, Stoke. In 1863, Charles's mother died and his father married Ellen Eardley.

Charles was the grandson of William Birbeck, a ceramic artist who was born at Worcester in 1799. William Birbeck worked for many of the Stoke pottery manufacturers, including Copeland and Mintons. William Scarratt wrote in his book, *Old Times in the Potteries*: 'William Birbeck was admired for his heraldic devices and excelled in crests and monograms etc. on china dinner ware'. Charles Birbeck joined George Jones & Sons in 1877 and, by 1881, had become an artist on china.[9] Some of his work is initialled C.J.B.

From 1878 to 1887, Charles was a very successful student at the Hanley School of Art where he was awarded many prizes in the National Art Competition.[10] In 1882, Charles became a member of the first sketching club in Hanley. In the National Art Competition in 1883, Charles won a gold medal in the art section for a powerful drawing of a gracefully-posed figure from life. The work was considered so exceptional that it was suggested at the time that it might be purchased by the Government.[11]

In the mid-1880s, Charles was a part-time assistant master at the Hanley School of Art.[12]

Charles married Alice Salmon at Hanley in June 1889. At the time of his marriage he was still employed as a painter, but by the time his second child was born in 1891, he had become a potters' designer and a leading figure in the decorating department of George Jones & Sons, working alongside the art director, Horace Overton Jones.

In 1895, Charles Birbeck was appointed art director of the company, replacing Horace Overton Jones, who had decided to cease working for the company on a full-time basis to devote more time to his love of painting. Charles held the position of art director until September 1931, when he was forced to retire through ill-health. He had been with the company for fifty-four years.

Charles lived at many addresses in Stoke, but by 1904, he was living at 22, James Street, Stoke. This was to be his home until he retired. Harold Holdway, an apprentice at George Jones & Sons Ltd. in 1928, (who eventually became art director at Copeland-Spode) said of Charles Birbeck: 'although by then an old man, he was an excellent artist and designer'. Charles Birbeck died in January 1933 at the age of seventy-three.

William Albert Ernest Birbeck 1866-1952, Potter's Artist

William Albert Ernest Birbeck was born in July 1866 at Brooke Street, Stoke-upon-Trent, the son of William Henry and Ellen Birbeck and the half brother of Charles James Birbeck. By 1881, William Birbeck had joined George Jones & Sons and was employed as an artist on china.[13] William must have been a very talented boy to have been painting on china at such an early age. According to William Scarratt in his book *Old Times in the Potteries:* 'William Birbeck trained under his brother, Charles, and was esteemed a good all-round painter and decorator in gold and colour, chiefly flowers and butterflies'. Much of his work is signed W. Birbeck. During his training, William attended the Hanley School of Art.[14]

In the late 1920s, William Birbeck was the only artist employed by George Jones & Sons Ltd. Harold Holdway, who was an apprentice at George Jones's in the late 1920s, recalled: 'William Birbeck was an excellent artist and taught me well, he painted fish, fruit, flowers and landscapes, all the designs being his own. He was one of the last of the old Victorian artists, a tall and gentle man'. Harold Holdway also remembers William Birbeck recalling days when he worked with foreign artists (names unknown) at George Jones and that some of them lived with him at his home in Stockton Brook. It was common in those days for many foreign artists to stay with fellow workers until they could afford the rent for their own home.

In 1934, George Jones & Sons Ltd. registered a design, patent number 790003, called 'Birbeck Rose', a single rose with rose buds around it, signed W. Birbeck; William was renowned for his roses. An example of this pattern is shown in Figure 710.

In the late 1930s, William produced work for some of the other companies operating from the Crescent Potteries. A reference was made in *The Pottery Gazette* of April 1937 that Bishop & Stonier produced wares with hand painted flower centres by Birbeck. In 1942 William Birbeck designed multicoloured centres for the Swansea China Co. Ltd., another of the companies belonging to George Jones & Sons Ltd. and operating from the Crescent Potteries.

William Birbeck eventually left George Jones & Sons Ltd. around 1943 and worked for a short period for Harold Holdway, who was by then, art director at Copeland-Spode. William Birbeck died in early 1952, aged eighty-five.

Henry Brunt 1852-1915, Potter's Manager

Henry Brunt was born in Penkhull near Stoke-upon-Trent in January 1852. He served his apprenticeship with George Jones & Co. but left, one or two years after his apprenticeship ended, to work for Mintons. Henry returned to George Jones & Sons in the mid-1870s as foreman of the Trent Potteries, but in 1879, he left again to assume the management of the Florence China Works, Longton.[15]

In 1881, Henry Brunt emigrated to America and initially worked at The Eagle Pottery, Trenton, New Jersey. He left these works after two years and joined Alpaugh & Magowan at the Empire Works.[16] While at these works, Henry was responsible for the introduction of the manufacture of bone china, no doubt using his experience gained at George Jones when they commenced manufacturing bone china in 1875-76.

In 1886 Henry was appointed practical manager at the Chesapeake pottery where he introduced the manufacture of opaque porcelain.[17]

On the formation of the Edwin Bennett Pottery Co. in 1890, Henry Brunt was appointed managing director. W.P. Jervis states in his *Dictionary of Pottery Terms* that:

> at the Edwin Bennett Pottery, Brunt converted a rude manufacturer of Rockingham ware into one which favourably compares with other American production.

Henry Brunt died at Baltimore in 1915, aged sixty-three years.

William Candland 1828 - 1910, Chief Cashier

William Candland was born in Penkhull, near Stoke-upon-Trent in 1828. He was the only son of Edward and Anne Candland. His father was a local inn-keeper.

It is unclear exactly when William Candland joined George Jones, but W.P. Jervis stated in 1902 in his *Encyclopaedia of Ceramics:* 'Mr W. Candland has been with the firm, we think from its inception and is now a partner in the concern'. In the 1851 census, William Candland's occupation was given as a china salesman and was living with his widowed mother in Penkhull.

From this, William probably joined George Jones around 1850, when George was establishing his business in Liverpool Road, Stoke as a commission agent and earthenware broker.

It would appear that William Candland became quite a wealthy man, since, in 1859, he owned 20, Stoke Villas, one of the large houses built by the Stoke Villas Building Society. He did not live there, however, but let the house until his marriage.

In Kelly's 1860 *P.O. Directory for Staffordshire*, William Candland was listed as being a commission agent. From that, we can surmise that he was either working in Glebe Street or Wharf Street, Stoke, for George Jones. In 1861, William's occupation was given as clerk to a glass and china merchant. Interestingly, from the same records, his sister, Martha's occupation was stated to be a glass and china dealer.[18]

William Candland married Marianne Harper in February 1862 at Lichfield. Marianne had been, up to the time of her marriage, employed as a governess to the George Jones family at 12, Stoke Villas. After their marriage, William and Marianne moved to William's house at 20 Stoke Villas. This was to be their home for the next twenty five years.

In January 1863, when their first child, a son, was born William Candland was a china agent and book keeper, but by 1865, he had left the retailing side of George Jones's business and was employed as a potters' manager, probably running the financial side of George Jones's manufacturing company. In 1877, William Candland's salary was £60 per month[19] — a substantial amount in those days. From various records, up to 1891, William's job description ranged from clerk to managing clerk (what we might now call commercial manager) to cashier for the company.

By 1891, William Candland and his family had moved from Stoke Villas to The Avenue, Alsager, Cheshire, although he still owned 20, Stoke Villas. Two of his sons were employed in the pottery industry, possibly at George Jones & Sons Ltd. Edward, aged twenty-four, was a clerk and Colin, aged sixteen, was an apprentice.

By the end of 1902, William Candland had retired from George Jones & Sons Ltd. and his position as cashier had been taken by George Benham. William Candland died at Alsager in February 1910, aged eighty-two. His will shows that he left almost £10,000.

Thomas Hammersley 1866-1931, Managing Director

Thomas Hammersley was born in Ashford Street, Hanley, in 1866. He was the eldest son of Thomas and Caroline Hammersley. His father was employed as a potters' clerk at George Jones & Co., eventually serving the company for sixty-one years.

Thomas Hammersley joined George Jones & Sons, in 1881, at the age of fifteen years as a junior clerk in the commercial department. After being employed in various capacities he was, in 1895, appointed a commercial traveller. He held this position - representing the company in many parts of the country - until April 1915, when he was given a seat on the board of directors of George Jones & Sons Ltd.[20] He was appointed managing director and was the first non-family member to be given a board position. An article in *The Pottery Gazette* of May 1915 stated: 'It is entirely creditable to the firm that they recognised his worth.'

Thomas Hammersley remained managing director until his health failed him in April 1927, cutting short his career. He died in April 1931, aged sixty-five.

Thomas Hammersley had four sons. Two of them, Vincent and Gerald, were for a time, in the 1920s, commercial travellers for George Jones & Sons Ltd.

Thomas Stanley Harrison 1899-1960, Proprietor

Thomas Stanley Harrison was born in December 1899, the son of Sydney Thomas Harrison. Until 1936, Stanley had worked for the family business — Harrison & Son (Hanley) Ltd., colour manufacturers — a firm that had been founded by Stanley's great grandfather W.R. Harrison.

In 1932, Harrison & Son (Hanley) Ltd. bought the majority of the shares in George Jones & Sons Ltd. from Walter Bakewell.[21] In October 1936, Stanley was appointed chairman and managing director of George Jones & Sons Ltd. on behalf of Harrison & Son Ltd.[22]

In 1947, the Harrison company became disassociated from George Jones & Sons Ltd., and Stanley, together with his father, Sydney T. Harrison, became sole proprietors of the Jones group (Coalport, Cauldon and George Jones). In 1951, when George Jones & Sons Ltd. ceased trading, Stanley Harrison continued as chairman and managing director of Coalport and Cauldon, who were still operating on the Crescent Potteries site.

In mid-1958, Coalport was purchased by E. Brain & Co. Ltd. and moved to nearby Fenton. Stanley Harrison continued as chairman and managing director of Cauldon, until his death in February 1960, aged sixty.

Henry Beecroft Jackson 1810-1884, Financier

Henry Beecroft Jackson was born in Etruria, Staffordshire, in 1810. He was the eldest child of Ralph and Ester Jackson. When Henry was only thirteen, his father died. Henry left school at the age of fourteen, after an ordinary education and went to work for his uncle, Jonathan Jackson of Messrs. Jonathan Jackson & Co., calico and cambric manufacturers of Cannon Street, Manchester and dyers and calenderers of Ardwick Island, Ancoats. It was there that Henry Jackson acquired the practical knowledge of goods for both the home and foreign markets which characterised his subsequent commercial career.[23]

Henry Jackson left his uncle's employment in about 1836, and joined William Crossley of York Street, Manchester, who was a shipping merchant trading to all parts of the world. Upon William Crossley's death, Henry Jackson became sole proprietor of the business and within a short space of time, became a very successful and wealthy merchant and commission agent, operating from premises in Cannon Street, Manchester.[24]

In 1855, when George Jones decided to expand his commission agency, it was to Henry Jackson, his brother-in-law, that he turned for financial assistance, and a partnership was formed between them. This enabled George Jones to move to new and larger premises in Stoke and to finance the opening of a branch in London. This partnership continued until January 1858, when it expired 'with the effluxion of time'.[25]

In 1861, when George Jones decided to open his own pottery manufacturing business, he again turned to Henry Jackson, for financial assistance for the venture.

Henry Jackson married Jemima Mander in Wolverhampton in 1839. They had five daughters and one son. In his private life Henry was a generous man, who subscribed to many causes to help the under-privileged. He was particularly involved in helping young people to further their education and in the 1870s donated funds to enable evening classes to be provided at a local college in Manchester.

Henry Beecroft Jackson died at Whalley Range, Manchester, in December 1884, aged seventy-three. His will shows he left over £187,000.

Arthur Overton Jones 1873-1958, Deputy Chairman

Arthur Overton Jones was born in James Street, Stoke, in 1873. He was the eldest son of George Henry and Elizabeth Jones. By 1891, at the age of seventeen years, Arthur was employed as an apprentice at George Jones & Sons.

When Henry Giller, manager of the George Jones & Sons Ltd. showrooms in London, died in December 1896, Arthur was appointed manager of these important showrooms, a position he held until his retirement in 1931.

By 1913, Arthur was one of the directors of George Jones & Sons Ltd.[26] and eventually became deputy chairman.[27] As well as being deputy chairman and also manager of the London showrooms, Arthur Overton Jones was very much involved with the Pottery & Glass Benevolent Institution, and in 1921 was made its chairman.

In 1900, Arthur married Violet, the only daughter of James Maddock of John Maddock & Sons, pottery manufacturers of Burslem. They had one daughter.

Arthur Overton Jones was a modest and retiring man who was very well-thought-of throughout the pottery industry. He died in Surbiton, Surrey, in October 1958, aged eighty-five.

Charles Samuel Jones 1855-1927, Chairman

Charles Samuel Jones was born in March 1855 in Stoke Villas, Stoke-upon-Trent. He was the fourth son of George and Frances Jones. Charles Jones joined his father's business in June 1871 at the age of fifteen.[28] By 1883, Charles had become a partner in George Jones & Sons. He spent over fifty years controlling the potting methods at the manufactory.[29] In October 1916, after the death of his brother George Henry Jones, Charles was appointed chairman of George Jones & Sons Ltd., a position he held until his death in 1927.

Charles Jones, like his father, was very interested in public life and was, for many years, a member of the Stoke Borough Council. He was also a Justice of the Peace for Stoke and a church warden at Boothen Church, Stoke. Charles was keenly interested in the welfare of his employees and took an earnest interest in the Pottery and Glass Trades Benevolent Institution.

Charles Jones married Ann Spilsbury in Stafford in March 1878. For many years, Charles and his family lived at various addresses in Stoke Villas (formerly The Villas), Stoke, eventually moving to 12 Stoke Villas, the house in which he was born. In 1899 the family moved to Lancaster Road, Newcastle-under-Lyme. In the mid-1920s, Charles was forced to retire from the day-to-day running of the company through blindness and moved to St. George's Avenue, Rhos-on-Sea, where he died in October 1927, aged seventy-two.

Charles had three sons and two daughters; two of his sons were involved with the pottery industry. Eric George Jones was a potter and director of George Jones & Sons Ltd., and Alfred Gordon Jones worked for Keeling & Walker, colour manufacturers of Stoke. His eldest daughter, Margaret, married Richard Varcoe, a member of the Varcoe family, who owned extensive china clay pits in Cornwall. His daughter, Ethel, married Lionel Knocker, a son of Sir Mollaston Knocker, a member of the British aristocracy. They lived most of their married life at Cowichan Station, Vancouver Island, Canada.

Edward Overton Jones 1889-1963, Designer

Edward Overton Jones was born in 1889 in Stoke Villas, Stoke-on-Trent. He was the eldest child of Horace and Constance Overton Jones. Edward was educated at Stoke Grammar School and in 1903, went to Rhos College, Rhos-on-Sea, to continue his education until 1905.

Edward then seems to have pursued some art training at Stoke and in early 1906, for a short period, at the studios of the artist Calderon. In 1910, Edward went to Paris for a period of training at the Julien Academy.

Edward commenced working for George Jones & Sons Ltd. around 1912 as an artist/designer, as his father before him. In 1913, Edward was awarded a silver medal in the pottery examination at the Stoke Art School. He worked for the company until the outbreak of the First World War, when he left to join the Artists' Rifles. He later joined the Coldstream Guards Special Reserve where he gained the rank of Lieutenant. In 1918, he was decorated in connection with military operations in France and Flanders.

In June 1919, Edward was demobilised from the armed forces and rejoined George Jones & Sons Ltd. in his previous capacity. In January 1922, he left the company and joined Copelands for a short period, after which he left Copelands to join Wedgwood.

In the mid-1920s, Edward visited America for a holiday, and during his stay he paid a courtesy call on Mr. Kennard Wedgwood, head of Wedgwoods' New York office. At this meeting Edward was offered the post as Wedgwood's representative for the Southern States of America, a position Edward readily accepted. By mid-1928, Edward had emigrated to America and commenced his employment with Wedgwood.

In 1932, Edward was loaned by Wedgwood for a month to assist in the excavations that were taking place at the Governor's Palace, Williamsburg, Virginia. These excavations were to look for shards of the original Wedgwood 'Queensware' dinner service used in the 18th century. From the shards found and with Edward's assistance, Wedgwood were able to reproduce a replica of the original dinner service.

As well as being 'on the road' selling, Edward also designed patterns specifically for the American market. One of his most popular patterns was 'Prairie Flowers', which became very popular with the Texan brides of the 1930s. It included the 'Bluebonnet', the Texan State flower. Other patterns designed by him were 'Meadow Sweet', 'Richborough' (1939) and 'Laurentia' (1939) which is said to have been inspired by the brocade worn by Martha Washington. All these patterns were designed for bone china ware.

Edward remained with the New York office as a designer and Southern States' representative and, in 1954, was made a vice president of the company.

Edward Overton Jones was married to Catherine in 1939 and they had one daughter, Judith. He died in 1963 in Darien, Connecticut, aged seventy-four.

Frank Ralph Jones (Benham) 1846-1911, Chairman

Frank Ralph Jones was born in May 1846 in Mount Pleasant, Hanley, Staffordshire. He was the first child of George and Frances Jones.

Before joining his father's business, Frank gained considerable experience at the Royal Porcelain Works, Sèvres, France.[30] Frank probably started working for his father when the company moved to the new Trent Potteries in 1865, and it was here that he found a congenial sphere for his artistic and business talents.

In June 1869, Frank Jones married Emily Benham, in Westbury-on-Trym, Gloucestershire. Emily was the daughter of William Benham, a Bristol doctor. After their marriage, their first home was at 3 Stoke Villas, Stoke, but in 1874 they moved to Deans Hill, Stafford. This was to be their home for the rest of their lives.

Toward the end of 1873 a partnership was formed and the company was renamed George Jones & Sons. The original partners were Frank Ralph Jones, his younger brother George Henry Jones and their father George Jones.

Frank Jones was for a short period, in 1891, chairman of The Staffordshire Potteries Manufacturers' Association.[31]

In 1893, Frank Jones was honoured by being appointed British judge of pottery at the Chicago International Exhibition,[32] to which he was accompanied by his eldest son, George Benham Jones.

When George Jones & Sons became a limited liability company in April 1894, Frank was appointed chairman,[33] a position he held until his death in 1911.

On the 4 March 1897, Frank Jones changed his surname, by deed poll,[34] to Benham (his wife's maiden name). Why he did this is not known, but it is thought that his wife may have had something to do with the decision.

In his spare time, Frank was an accomplished painter and exhibited twice, in 1890, at the Royal Birmingham Society of Artists' spring and autumn exhibitions. He loved painting and his house was filled with pictures painted by himself, his brother Horace and his uncle Frederick William Hulme. Frank occasionally went on painting trips, and on one such trip in 1898 with his brother, they visited Norway.

In 1902, W.P. Jervis wrote in his book *The Encyclopaedia of Ceramics*: 'Frank Jones Benham is now regarded as perhaps the best potter in Staffordshire'.

On the death of Edward Asbury, chairman of E. Asbury & Co. Ltd., china manufacturers, of Hanley, Frank Benham, who was one of the executors of Edward Asbury's will, was appointed acting chairman of E. Asbury & Co. Ltd., a position he also held until his death in October 1911, aged sixty-five.

Frank had three sons and one daughter. One son, George Benham Benham, was for a time cashier and a director of George Jones & Sons Ltd.

Frederick Arthur Jones 1851-1922, Potter's Manager

Frederick Arthur Jones was born in December 1851 in Penkhull near Stoke-on-Trent. He was the third son of George and Frances Jones.

In the census taken in April 1871, Frederick Jones's occupation was stated to be potters' manager, possibly working for his father at the Trent Potteries. In December 1871, Frederick went to Germany to work as a commercial traveller for H.C. Nolting, a commission agent in Hamburg. He remained in Germany until July 1873, when he returned to England, probably to work for his father again.

Between 1876 and 1879, Frederick lived at Deans Hill House, Stafford,[35] (later to become Newport House) and during this time worked for George Jones & Sons, where he was paid £25 per month.[36]

In March 1879, Frederick returned to Hamburg to recommence working for H.C. Nolting.[37] On the 31 May 1881, Frederick married Elisabeth Charlotte Bertha Nolting, his employer's daughter. They were to have six children (five sons and one daughter).

On the 30 April 1884, Frederick Jones was appointed a partner in the firm of H.C. Nolting[4], who were the German agents for George Jones & Sons. This partnership continued until January 1912, when the firm was taken over by H.C. Nolting & Co. Frederick joined this company as a merchant and one of the directors. He remained with the company throughout the First World War until, in May 1919, at the age of sixty-seven, he retired and returned to England.

Whilst on a visit to see his brother, Horace Overton Jones, at Little Haywood, Staffordshire, in August 1922, Frederick suffered a heart attack and died. He was seventy years old.

George Jones 1823-1893, Proprietor

George Jones was born on the 27 June 1823 in Beam Street, Nantwich, Cheshire. He was the youngest of nine children born to Samuel and Betty Jones. George's father's occupation was that of a maltster which he carried on in premises at the rear of his home in Beam Street.

When George was only fifteen months old, his mother died. He was raised by his family in Nantwich until his father died in April 1834, aged fifty-four years. One month later, George's eldest brother William died, aged twenty-five. William was the third of George's brothers to have died within three years.

In December 1834, at Nantwich Parish Church, George's sister, Elizabeth, married James William Pankhurst. He was a widower who lived in Hanley and worked as a commercial traveller for Charles Meigh, pottery manufacturer, of The Old Hall Pottery, Hanley. After James Pankhurst's marriage to Elizabeth Jones, the couple, together with George and George's sister Martha, moved to Bucknall Road, Hanley.

In 1837, after completing his formal education, George Jones began a seven year apprenticeship at Mintons in Stoke-upon-Trent. During his apprenticeship, George continued to live with Elizabeth and James Pankhurst at Hanley.[39]

Following the completion of his pottery apprenticeship, in mid-1844, George Jones continued to work for Mintons for a short time until, in October 1844, he joined Wedgwood of Etruria as a commercial traveller.[40]

Being a commercial traveller meant George was away from home for long periods, but he still found time to court a young Hanley girl, and on the 2 July 1845, George Jones married Frances Jackson at Hanley Chapel, Hanley. Frances, or Fanny as she was christened, was the youngest child of Ralph and Ester Jackson of Hanley. Ralph Jackson had been a wharfinger and agent for Henshall & Co. at Etruria Wharf, Staffordshire, but had died in 1824 leaving a widow and seven young children, two sons and five daughters.

George and Frances's first home was at Mount Pleasant, Hanley, and there, on the 7 May 1846, their first child, Frank Ralph, was born. George at this time was still employed as a commercial traveller, but for another company, having left Wedgwood in February 1846.

By April 1848, when George and Frances's second child, George Henry, was born, not only had the family moved from Hanley to Liverpool Road, Stoke-upon-Trent, but George had changed his occupation to that of a clerk.

They lived in Liverpool Road for only a short period. By early 1849, the family had moved from the centre of Stoke to Brisley Hill, Penkhull, on the outskirts of Stoke, where they lived in a rented house with a garden of one eighth of an acre.

In March 1850, their third child, Elizabeth, was born, but sadly, she died in May 1851 aged fourteen months (at this time approximately 60% of all infants died within two years of birth). By the time Elizabeth was born, George had already established his merchandising business in Liverpool Road, Stoke-upon-Trent.

His business grew rapidly and by mid-1850, George had become a leading figure in the Stoke business community. He was one of the original committee members of the Stokeville Building Society (formed on the 14 June 1850).[41] The society was formed to purchase land and to build houses to be occupied by prominent people of Stoke. The land was purchased from the Rev. Thomas Minton and was situated off the London Road, Stoke, below Brisley Hill where George Jones lived. A proposal was made to build twenty-four houses of three different classes of varying rentals. The houses were designed in the style of Italian villas by the architect, Charles Lynam, the son of a well known local architect, George Lynam.

Lots were drawn by interested parties for the various dwellings. George Jones drew a medium-sized house, but subsequently exchanged with someone who had drawn a large house. This house became 12 Stoke Villas (named Rosemount) and was the largest of the twenty-four houses built. It consisted of a drawing room, dining room, breakfast room, library, butler's pantry, large lavatory, eight bedrooms and a dressing room with toilet. The house was occupied by George Jones and his family in early 1853 and was to be their home for the next twenty-five years.

One of George Jones's neighbours was Leon Arnoux, the art director of Mintons, the man who created the majolica glazes for Mintons in the late 1840s.

By the end of 1853, George and Frances had had two more children, a son Frederick Arthur, born in December 1851 and a daughter, Frances Louise, born in August 1853. (Frances Louise married Henry Twigg, a wealthy Staffordshire landowner and lived at Weeping Cross, Stafford.)

Although busy building up his own business, George still found time for leisure pursuits. Between 1849-54, he flourished as an artist, exhibiting twice at the Birmingham Society of Artists with paintings of local views. William Scarratt noted in his book, *Old Times in the Potteries,* that: 'Mr George Jones an artist of taste and also a collector of articles of virtu.'

George, by now, had a thriving merchandising business and was becoming more affluent. In November 1855, he applied to the Stokeville Building Society for permission to erect a stable and coach house at his residence. As well as buying 12 Stoke Villas, George also rented land adjoining this property. One field (called 'Far Hunters Croft') of five acres was used for arable purposes and the other, part of Boothen Wood Field of approximately four acres, was a meadow for his horses and cows. An advertisement in *The Staffordshire Advertiser* of December 1855 stated: 'wanted, a woman as general servant who understands cooking and can take the management of milk from two cows, of good character, apply Mrs George Jones, 12 Stoke Villas'.

By the mid-1850s, two more sons had been born, Charles Samuel in March 1855 and Horace Overton in July 1856. Both were to become involved in the family business. George and Frances were to have four more children: Alfred Howell born in 1860, and Edgar William born in 1867, both of whom joined the legal profession; but Edward Clement born in 1858 and Annie Gertrude born in 1861 both died before their second birthday.

In the early 1860s, although pre-occupied with establishing his new pottery manufacturing business, George had also become involved in public life. In 1862, he became an Improvement Commissioner for Stoke-upon-Trent, serving on the Rates Committee. He also served as a guardian on the Board of Guardians for the poor of the parish of Stoke, a post he held until 1871.

The years 1864-65 were monumental years for George Jones. As well as having his new manufactory built on land at the rear of Mintons, he was, in June 1864, elected Chief Bailiff of Stoke-upon-Trent[42] — a great honour for him.

As well as being very involved in public life, George Jones was also keenly interested in horticulture and had stovehouses (hothouses) and greenhouses erected at his home. He was a frequent exhibitor at the local floral and horticultural society shows and won many prizes for his stove and greenhouse plants. George was also a generous man and often donated articles manufactured at his factory to be sold at bazaars in aid of school charities.

George handed over the day-to-day running of his factory to his two sons, Frank Ralph and George Henry Jones in 1873. By mid-1873, he had moved from his home in Stoke Villas to a rented property, Milford House, in Milford near Stafford. At the same time, he bought a small residence in James Street, Stoke,[43] which he used on his frequent visits to Stoke on company and other business.

Although George had moved to Milford, he was still very much involved in the public life of Stoke. At the beginning of 1874, George was appointed returning officer for the first elections for the new Borough of Stoke-upon-Trent, which were held on the 3rd March 1874. At a council meeting held on the 11th March 1874, a motion of thanks was given to George for the efficient way he had organised 'these first and very important elections'.[44]

For the next ten years, very little is known about George's activities, apart from his visits to Stoke on company business.

In June 1884, he moved home from Milford to Newport House, Newport Road, Stafford. This was a large house, situated just outside the then town boundary, which George had bought for £1620 in 1876 from its builders, Messrs. Joseph & William Cooke.

The house was originally known as Deanshill House, but when George moved in, he renamed it Newport House. It contained a large entrance hall, three lofty reception rooms, billiard room, housekeepers' room, domestic offices (servants quarters), principal and secondary staircases, eleven bed and dressing rooms, a large attic, kitchens, a dairy, pantries and a cellar, etc. Deanshill House had originally been occupied by George's son, Frederick Arthur Jones, but in late 1879 Frederick left to live in Hamburg, Germany.

Before moving to Newport House, George signed a lease on three acres of land at the rear of the house, land owned by Lord Stafford. The lease was signed on the 21 May 1883 and George used the land as paddock and grazing for his horses and cattle. He also had a coach house built and erected stove and greenhouses in the garden. George Jones's grandson, Edward Overton Jones, remembered that when he lived there in the 1890s, the gardens were beautifully laid-out.

George Jones lived at Newport House until, on the 3 December 1893, he died shortly after suffering a stroke. He was seventy years old and was buried in the churchyard at Baswich Parish Church, Stafford, where his gravestone can still be seen.

By his will George Jones left approximately £25,000. His widow, Frances, continued to live at Newport House until her death in April 1904.

George Henry Jones 1848-1916, Chairman

George Henry Jones was born in April 1848 in Liverpool Road, Stoke-upon-Trent.

He was the second son of George and Frances Jones. George H. joined his father's pottery business in about 1866.

In June 1871, George H. married Elizabeth Burgess. Although Elizabeth came from Penkhull, Stoke, where her late father had been a partner in the firm of Burgess & Kent, seedsmen & market gardeners, the couple were married at the home of her uncle, James Booth, in Paterson, New York, U.S.A. At the time of his marriage, George H. was employed as a potter's manager at his fathers manufactory.[45]

Toward the end of 1873 a partnership was formed and the company was renamed George Jones & Sons. The original partners were George Henry Jones, his eldest brother Frank Ralph Jones and their father George Jones.

According to W.P. Jervis in his book *The Encyclopaedia of Ceramics,* George H. was involved with the financial and sales side of the business. George H. studied at the Potters Mechanics Institute in Stoke where, in 1873, he passed his chemistry examination with a grade two.[46]

In his early married life, George H. lived at 'Sunnyside', a house he had had built in Howard's Place, James Street, Stoke, but in 1885 he moved to Park Lodge, Lichfield Road, Stone, Staffordshire, where he lived until his death in 1916.

When in 1894, George Jones & Sons became a limited liability company, George H. was appointed company secretary and a director of George Jones & Sons Ltd.

He held this position until late 1911 when, upon the death of his brother, Frank Ralph Benham, George H. was appointed chairman of George Jones & Sons Ltd., a post he held until his death in October 1916 at the age of sixty-eight.

George H. Jones was a man of quiet and reserved temperament who, unlike his father, took no part in public life. He had three sons and two daughters, although only one son, Arthur Overton Jones, was employed in the family business, as manager of the London showrooms and eventually deputy chairman.

Horace Overton Jones 1856-1928, Art Director

Horace Overton Jones was born in July 1856 at Rosemount, 12 Stoke Villas, Stoke-upon-Trent. He was the fifth son of George and Frances Jones.

In his early life, Horace studied at the National Art Training School, South Kensington. In the National Competition in 1877, whilst still at Kensington, Horace won two prizes (a silver medal and a book) in the category 'painting flowers from nature'.[47]

At the end of his formal training, his father sent him on a world tour ending in America, where, in August 1880, he visited Trenton, the home of the American pottery industry. He made a tour of the many factories in the area and, according to a report in the *Crockery & Glass Journal* of September 1880, Horace: 'expressed much satisfaction with what he had seen'.

By the end of 1880, Horace had joined the family business as an artist/designer.

When he joined the company, Horace was living with his parents at Milford near Stafford; however, by 1881 he had moved to The Nursery House, Penkhull and by late 1884, he had moved to 18 Stoke Villas, Stoke. In August 1887, Horace married Constance May Beckett; he was thirty-one years old and she was just eighteen. They were married at Tixall Parish Church, a village about one mile from Milford. Their first home together was at 18 Stoke Villas.

By March 1889, Horace had become the fourth son to be appointed a partner in the family business. He was, by then, art director of the company and had been responsible for a large proportion of the patterns produced in the 1880s. Much of his work bears his initials H.O.J. Horace's and Constance's first child, Edward Overton Jones, was born in 1890. They were to have two more sons but only Edward was to be involved in George Jones & Sons Ltd.

In 1892, Horace moved to 'Westover', a house he had had built in Sandon Road, Stone, Staffordshire.

When George Jones & Sons became a limited liability company in April 1894, Horace Overton Jones was not appointed to the board of directors. Why this was is not known, but at the beginning of 1895, he relinquished his position as art director and ceased to work for the company on a full-time basis, having decided to spend more time as an artist.

In April 1895, Horace sold his house in Stone and went to live with his widowed mother at Newport House, Newport Road, Stafford. In Constance's diary of that year she wrote: 'it was with great sadness that we left Stone'.

As an artist, Horace first began to exhibit his work in the spring of 1894 at The Royal Society of Artists, Birmingham. This was to be the first of many such exhibitions at which he exhibited, both in Birmingham and also at the Walker Art Gallery, Liverpool, until 1922.

Constance Overton Jones's diaries are a great source of information and they tell of Horace going on long painting trips, with Constance and sometimes other artists, in a horse-drawn caravan and later in a motor car.

In June 1898, Horace held his first one-man exhibition at the Swan Hotel, Stafford.[48] Horace obviously made a reasonable living as an artist because in December 1899 he purchased Ivy House, Little Haywood, Staffordshire. This was to be, for most of the time, the family home for the next twenty-five years.

Horace Overton Jones held another exhibition in July 1900, this time at the Crown Hotel, Stone.[49] In the year 1900, Horace sold paintings to the value of £133-5s-0d (the average price for one of his paintings was between ten and fifteen guineas).

By the middle of 1904, Horace had let Ivy House and the family had moved to Chorleywood, Hertfordshire, there to pursue his career as an artist.

In October 1910, Horace and Constance sailed to New Zealand to visit Constance's father, who had emigrated in the early 1880s. Whist there Horace spent a lot of time painting and, in March 1911, he held an exhibition of his works at Waimate, in the South Island, where Constance's father lived. They returned to England in June 1911 and went back to live at Chorleywood until mid-1912, when they moved back to Little Haywood.

In July 1913, Horace held another exhibition of his paintings. Horace held this exhibition with another local artist, John Murdoch, and it was staged at the Swan Hotel, Stafford.[50]

In 1916, Horace had the honour of having one of his pictures accepted for the Royal Academy Exhibition in London; the picture was called 'Showery Weather'.

Most of Horace's paintings were of flowers and landscapes, but in 1918, he produced a series of sketches of local Staffordshire buildings and views which were reproduced as postcards and sold in local shops.

Horace Overton Jones continued to live at Little Haywood and pursued his career as an artist until 1925, when he and Constance emigrated to New Zealand to be with their second son, Raymund, who had emigrated with his family in 1922. Whilst living in Wellington, Horace went on frequent painting trips and held regular exhibitions of his work. Three of his works were exhibited at the New Zealand Academy of Fine Arts in Wellington in 1928.

Horace died in Wellington in July 1928, aged seventy-two. After his death, Constance returned to England. She died in Scotland in 1943.

Walter Lamonby 1884-1952, Potter's Artist

Walter Lamonby was born in 1884. After a formal education he joined George Jones & Sons Ltd., in 1898, as an apprentice pottery painter.[51] During his apprenticeship he attended the Stoke School of Art, where he was said to be an outstanding pupil.

Walter Lamonby was still working for George Jones & Sons Ltd. in late 1907. When he left is not known, but between leaving George Jones & Sons Ltd. and joining S. Fielding & Co. Ltd., Devon Pottery, Stoke, in about 1912, he had spent some time working for John Aynsley & Sons Ltd., Longton. He joined S. Fielding & Co. Ltd. as head artist, a position he held for forty years until his death in June 1952, aged sixty-eight.

During his time at Crown Devon, Walter Lamonby produced work not only under his own name but also under the names of Coleman, Hinton, Cox, and Marsh. Quite why this was is unclear.

James William Pankhurst 1807-1889, Pottery Manufacturer

James William Pankhurst was born in Clerkenwell, London, in May 1807. His family eventually moved to Walgherton, Cheshire, where his father, Francis James Pankhurst, had obtained the position as headmaster of the Delves Church School, which had been erected in 1822.

In January 1830, James Pankhurst married Lydia Brownfield of Hanley. At the time of his marriage, James was living at Hough, Cheshire, and was employed as a schoolmaster. His wife, Lydia, was a grand-daughter of Job Meigh I and a niece of Charles Meigh, pottery manufacturer at The Old Hall Pottery, Hanley. Sadly the marriage was to last only eight months as on the 19 August 1830 Lydia died. At the time of her death James was still employed as a schoolmaster and living at Wybunbury, Cheshire, but by the time of his second marriage in December 1834, James was living in Hanley and working for Charles Meigh as a commercial traveller. His second marriage was to Elizabeth Jones in Nantwich, Cheshire. Elizabeth was a sister of George Jones.

James Pankhurst's younger brother Alfred married Ann, another of George Jones's sisters. Both Alfred and Ann died in 1838, leaving one daughter. She was adopted by James and Elizabeth Pankhurst and was to be their only child.

By 1841 James Pankhurst was employed as a general overlooker (manager) at the works of Charles Meigh. In 1849, he was made a partner in the company of Charles Meigh & Son. The company was renamed Charles Meigh, Son & Pankhurst. This partnership was short-lived and was dissolved in July 1850.[52]

James Pankhurst then went into business on his own account and he took over the pottery manufacturing business of W. Ridgway, which was situated in Charles Street/Old Hall Street, Hanley. The company was named J.W. Pankhurst and initially produced white granite ware for the American market.

In 1852, James Pankhurst went into partnership with John Dimmock and the company was renamed J.W. Pankhurst & Co. This partnership ceased in 1858[53] and James then went into partnership with a James Meakin until 1883, when business was so bad that the company had only one customer for its granite ware. The partnership was dissolved[54] and James Pankhurst sold the pottery to two brothers called Johnson (Johnson & Co, later to become Johnson Bros. (Hanley) Ltd.).

According to his obituary,[55] James Pankhurst took no part in municipal affairs; however, in the first election of Councillors for the Municipal Borough of Hanley in August 1857 he was successfully elected a Councillor for the East Ward.[56] In January 1867, James Pankhurst was placed on the Commission of the Peace for the borough of Hanley and remained a Justice of the Peace until his retirement in 1883.

After retiring from the pottery business, James and his wife moved from Barlaston, Staffordshire, where they had lived since 1872, to Southsea, Hampshire, to enjoy the benefit of the more healthy climate of the south coast. James's wife, Elizabeth, died in 1887 and James then moved to Torquay, Devon, where, in April 1889, he died at the age of eighty-one. His will shows that he left over £21,000.

Harold Taylor Robinson 1877-1953, Sales Manager

Harold Taylor Robinson was born in 1877. He commenced his business career in 1899 at the age of twenty-three when he was appointed a traveller with the firm of Wiltshaw Robinson & Co., Stoke-upon-Trent. In 1903, he commenced business as a china manufacturer on his own account under the name of Arkinstall & Son, manufacturing novelties and souvenirs under the trade name 'Arcadian'. Later he became a partner in the firm Wiltshaw & Robinson.

From 1903 until 1920, Harold Robinson was interested, alone or jointly, in the acquisition of a number of china and earthenware manufacturing concerns, either for resale or for the formation of companies to take them over and run them. In 1920, he acquired Cauldon Ltd., more correctly Cauldon (Brown-Westhead, Moore & Co.) Ltd. At this time, he had an interest in the business of J.A. Robinson & Sons Ltd., F.R. Pratt & Co. Ltd., Ford & Pointon, and Henry Alcock Pottery Co. Ltd. These businesses were amalgamated into Cauldon Pottery Ltd.

In 1927, Harold Robinson took the controlling interest in Royal Crown Derby Porcelain Co. Ltd., his family retaining control of the firm until his son, Philip Robinson, resigned as chairman in 1961.

Harold Robinson later gained control of Ridgways (Bedford Works) Ltd., Shelton, Bishop & Stonier, Hanley, and The Worcester Royal Porcelain Co. Ltd. Other firms purchased by Harold Robinson were W.H. Goss and Hewitt Bros. These were absorbed into the Cauldon Group as W.H. Goss Ltd. (1930) and Willow Potteries (1925). After other purchases of manufacturers of sanitary wares

and suppliers of clay and fuel, Harold Robinson suffered financial losses and was declared bankrupt in 1932.[57]

In January 1933, he was appointed sales organiser of the new company formed when George Jones & Sons Ltd., which was by now owned by Harrison & Son (Hanley), bought Bishop & Stonier.[58] He remained with George Jones & Sons Ltd. until 1936 when, due to ill-health, he was forced to resign.[59]

Harold Robinson died in 1953, aged seventy-six.

Frederick Emil Eberhard Schenck 1849-1908, Free Lance Modeller

Frederick Emil Eberhard Schenck was born in August 1849 in Edinburgh. He was the second son of E. E. F. T. Schenck and Jane (nee Vedder).

Frederick's father was a lithographer, writer and Professor of German, who, by 1850, had become one of Scotland's foremost lithographers, having achieved considerable distinction for his brilliant colour lithography.

After a formal education, Frederick is believed to have spent around two years working in his father's lithographic business before entering the Edinburgh School of Art. Whilst at art school, Frederick was awarded a bronze medal in the National Art Competition of 1872.

In mid-1872, Frederick moved from Edinburgh to Stoke-upon-Trent where, on the 3 August, he began his employment with Wedgwoods at their potteries in Etruria. He was employed as a modeller, creating new models and modifying existing models where necessary, for which he was paid five shillings a day.[60] Whilst at Wedgwoods, Frederick attended the Hanley School of Art and attained 'satisfactory work'[61] in the advanced section of the National Art competition of 1873. He also secured an Armstrong scholarship to the National Art Training School, South Kensington. After completion in 1875, Frederick returned to Edinburgh, where he trained for three years in the life class of the Royal Scottish Academy. During this time, he exhibited a number of busts.

In 1878-79, Frederick returned to Stoke to work as a modeller in the pottery industry. At the same time, he also took up a part-time appointment as modelling master at the Hanley School of Art.

Frederick Schenck married Mary Ann Goodall in August 1879 in Birmingham. Their first home was in Boothenwood Terrace, Stoke.

At what point in time Frederick Schenck began working for George Jones & Sons is unclear; however, a jardinière with the patent registration date 31 October 1877 has two pâte-sur-pâte panels signed F. Schenck.

As well as producing work for George Jones & Sons, Frederick Schenck also produced very similar designs for Brown-Westhead, Moore & Co., which would suggest he was employed on a freelance basis.

In 1881, Frederick's occupation was that of artist/figure modeller and he was still living at Boothenwood Terrace, but, by 1884, he had moved to Bedford Street, Basford, Stoke, although still employed as a modeller. At the end of the school year in mid-1886, Frederick relinquished his position as an assistant master in charge of the modelling classes at the Hanley School of Art owing to pressures from his other duties.[62]

In an 1887 trade directory for Stoke, Frederick's name appears in the commercial section as a modeller. With the demise of pâte-sur-pâte wares and encouraged by the response to a low-relief panel which he had exhibited at the Royal Academy, London, he decided to change both his residence and the direction of his career and, in 1888, he moved to London.

From that time onward, he was engaged almost exclusively in architectural sculpture, working with equal facility in stone, plaster and terracotta. He exhibited numerous architectural panels and played an important part in the movement to encourage closer co-operation between sculptor and architect.

At the Paris Universal Exhibition held in 1889, Brown-Westhead, Moore & Co. was awarded a Grand Prix for a four-foot high china trophy designed by Frederick Schenck.

Frederick Schenck died in London in February 1908, aged fifty-eight.

Cyril Shingler 1902- , Designer

Cyril Shingler was born in Stoke-on-Trent in January 1902. He was the son of Philip and May Shingler. His father was employed as a clerk with the North Staffordshire Railway & Canal Co. Cyril was educated at Newcastle High School and later won a scholarship to Christ College, London.

After completion of his formal education, his father secured a job for Cyril, working for the North Staffordshire Railway Co., but after a very short time, Cyril decided that this was not for him. He left and joined the Doulton pottery. Although Cyril received no formal training in the pottery industry, he had artistic abilities. By 1929 Cyril, after leaving Doulton and after spending a short time working in the United States, had returned to England and was working as a designer for George Jones & Sons Ltd.[63]

In October 1930, Cyril married Margaret Beardmore. She was a niece of the well known author Arnold Bennett.

Cyril Shingler left George Jones & Sons Ltd. around 1931 and went to work for Grindleys and for Doulton again. During the Second World War, he was in the Intelligence Corps. After the war, Cyril went to work for Worcester Royal Porcelain and later became curator of the Dyson Perrins Museum. At the time of writing he was living in Malvern, Worcestershire.

[1]The Staffordshire Advertiser 24 July 1880, 7
[2]Census 1881
[3]The Pottery Gazette & Glass Trades Review, February 1941, 156
[4]The Pottery Gazette & Glass Trades Review, June 1928, 970
[5]The Pottery Gazette & Glass Trades Review, February 1941, 156
[6]The Pottery Gazette December 1911, 1367
[7]The Pottery Gazette December 1913, 1379
[8]The Pottery Gazette & Glass Trades Review, March 1921, 466
[9]Census 1881
[10]The Staffordshire Advertiser, 1878-1887, passim
[11]The Staffordshire Advertiser, 11 August 1883, 2
[12]The Staffordshire Advertiser, 6 November 1886, 3
[13]Census 1881
[14]The Staffordshire Advertiser 20 August 1881, 5
[15]W.P. Jervis, Encyclopaedia of Ceramics, 1902, 95
[16]W.P. Jervis, Encyclopaedia of Ceramics, 1902, 95
[17]W.P. Jervis, Encyclopaedia of Ceramics, 1902, 95
[18]Census 1861
[19]National Westminster Bank Archives, Current Account Ledger, Ref. B11138
[20]The Pottery Gazette, May 1915, 551
[21]Hanley Reference Library, Ref. 738.94246 OS: E. Living 'Story of Royal Cauldon'
[22]The Pottery Gazette & Glass Trades Review, February 1937, 282
[23]Manchester Guardian, 22 December 1884
[24]Manchester Guardian, 22 December 1884
[25]London Gazette, 25 January 1858, 451
[26]The Pottery Gazette, December 1913, 1379
[27]The Pottery Gazette & Glass Trades Review, March 1920, 382
[28]The Pottery Gazette & Glass Trades Review, March 1920, 382
[29]The Pottery Gazette & Glass Trades Review, November 1927, 1791
[30]The Pottery Gazette, December 1911, 1367
[31]The Pottery Gazette, December 1911, 1367
[32]The Pottery Gazette, December 1911, 1367
[33]National Westminster Bank Archives, Information Book, Ref. B11139
[34]National Westminster Bank Archives, Letter Book, District Bank, Stafford
[35]Register of Electors
[36]National Westminster Bank Archives, Current Account Ledger, Ref. B11138
[37]State Archives, Hamburg
[38]State Archives, Hamburg
[39]Census 1841
[40]Wedgwood Archives, Ref. Hiring Book 1837-92
[41]Hanley Reference Library, The Stokeville Building Society
[42]Stoke-upon-Trent Commissioners Minute Book, 1855-64
[43]Stoke-upon-Trent Rating Book
[44]Stoke-upon-Trent Council Minute Book, 1874-81
[45]Census 1871
[46]The Staffordshire Advertiser, 12 July 1873
[47]Science & Arts Department, 25th Report 1878, page 405
[48]The Staffordshire Advertiser, 25 June 1898, 4
[49]The Staffordshire Advertiser, 30 June 1900, 1
[50]The Staffordshire Advertiser, 19 July 1913, 1
[51]The Pottery Gazette & Glass Trades Review, July 1952, 1110
[52]The Staffordshire Advertiser, 13 July 1850, 1
[53]London Gazette, 1 January 1858
[54]The Staffordshire Advertiser, 4 August 1883, 8
[55]The Staffordshire Advertiser, 4 May 1889
[56]The Staffordshire Advertiser, 22 August 1857, 1
[57]The Pottery Gazette & Glass Trades Review, July 1932, 899
[58]The Pottery Gazette & Glass Trades Review, January 1933, 93
[59]The Pottery Gazette & Glass Trades Review, February 1937, 282
[60]Wedgwood Archives, Ref. W/M 1812
[61]The Staffordshire Advertiser 19 July 1873
[62]The Staffordshire Advertiser 6 November 1886, 3
[63]Letters of Arnold Bennett page 560

Walter Bakewell. *Courtesy of Tableware International.*

Keith Benham. *Courtesy of Christopher Phillips.*

Charles James Birbeck. *Courtesy of Tableware International.*

MR. THOS. HAMMERSLEY
(Geo. Jones & Sons, Ltd.)

[Photo. by "The Pottery Gazette."
MR. ARTHUR OVERTON JONES.

Thomas Hammersley. *Courtesy of Tableware International.*

Arthur Overton Jones. *Courtesy of Tableware International.*

Thomas Stanley Harrison. *Courtesy of Tableware International.*

[Photo. by R. Brown.
THE LATE MR. CHARLES S. JONES.

Charles Samuel Jones. *Courtesy of Tableware International.*

Framed wax bust of Henry Beecroft Jackson. *Courtesy of Kenneth and Ingrid Phillips.*

Edward Overton Jones. *Courtesy of Robin and Leslie Swinton.*

Frederick Arthur and Elisabeth Jones. *Courtesy of Frank and Hazel Stevens.*

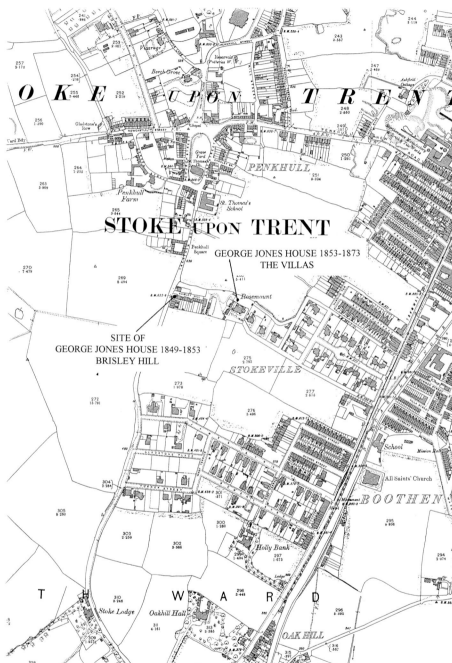

Map showing sites of George Jones's homes in Stoke-upon-Trent. Reproduced from the 1900 Ordnance Survey map.

Francis Ralph Jones (Benham). *Courtesy of Christopher Phillips.*

Milford House, Milford, Stafford, ca. 1900. *Courtesy of A. Middlefell.*

Horace Overton Jones, ca. 1884. *Courtesy of Robin and Leslie Swinton.*

Newport House, Newport Road, Stafford, ca. 1991. *Courtesy of Robert Hitchinor.*

Frederick Emil Eberhard Schenck. This is the only known surviving photograph of Frederick Schenck and is taken from his obituary in the *Edinburgh Evening News* of 24 February 1908. *Courtesy of David and Mavis Schenck. Photograph by Keith Wakeley Studios Wimbledon.*

Appendix 2 - George Jones Shape Names

Table	Tea	Dessert	Coffee	Jug	Toilet
Albany	Adelaide	Acme	Doric	Agra	Athens
Bow	Albion	Albany	Hamilton	Barrel	Banbury
Bouquet	Ashworth	Barclay	Kings	Burton	Bruce
Burns	Aspeu	Belmont	Camden	Camden	Cain
Bute	Athens	Blenheim	Nelson	Churn	Camden
Cambridge	Boston	Chelsea	Sandringham	Girton	Clifton
Canterbury	Bouquet	Devon		Grecian	Corea
Cardiff	Bow	Duchess		Hooped Tankard	Doric
Carlisle	Brooklyn	Empire		Pear	Durban
Chester	Bute	Gains-borough		Regal	Egyptian
China	Cardiff	Georgian		Roman	Empress
Clevaland	Carlisle	Gothic		Silver	Girton
Clyde	Chad	Grafton		Sirdar	Gothic
Crescent	Churchill	Lorne			Grecian
Crown	Cleveland	Lotus			Guelph
Cuba	Connaught	Osbourne			Hampton
Douglas	Corea	Pompon			Haywood
Douro	Doric	Premier			Helmet
Dover	Elgin	Queens			Ionic
Duchess	Empress	Salisbury			Imperial
Edna	Eton	Sevres			Italian
Enid	Exeter	Sheffield			Kew
Exhibition	Garnet	Shield			Lichfield
Gothic	Georgian	Silver			Limoge
Granada	Girton	Stirling			Medway
Grinton	Globe	Stoke			Milton
H/A	Gothic				Monarch
Hereford	Kew				Norman
Hopton	Kings				Olympic
Jewel	Leeds				Oxford
Kings	Lichfield				Percy
Laurel	Limoge				Prah
Leeds	Lorne				Raymond

Table	Tea	Toilet
Limoge	Marine	Regent
London	Marlborough	Ronar
Lorne	May	Royal
Madrid	Milford	Rustic
Marine	Monmouth	Sandon
Marlborough	Mount	Sandring-ham
	Vernon	
Monmouth	M/S	Saxon
Mount	Octagon	Stuart
Vernon		
Nairn	Ornate	Sydney
Naples	Pear	Trent
Nelson	Pearl	Tudor
Norman	Premier	Wallace
Octagon	Preston	Wheat
Pearl	Princess	
Premier	Queens	
President	Rhapsody	
Princess	Richmond	
Queens	Royal	
Regal	Sandon	
Riga	Sandringham	
Round	Silver	
Rhapsody	Sirdar	
Royal	Stanton	
Safety Oval	Star	
Senator	Stirling	
Sheffield	Sydney	
Stirling	Talbot	
Sweden	Trentham	
Trentham	Tulip	
Truro	Warwick	
Venice	Weston	
Wheat	Wheat	
Wheildon	Wheildon	
Willow	Worcester	
York	York	

Pattern Name

Abbey	Chelmsford	Fragrance
Aberdeen	Chilian	Golden Dawn
Adansi	China Rose	Gourd
Agra	Chinese Flowers	Grecian
Albion	Choco	H.O.J. Familiar Flowers
Alhambra, The	Chrysanthemum	Hawthorn
Almonds	Coburg Chain	Howard
Anemone	Colony	Imperial
Annette	Congo	Imperial Amethyst
Azalea	Cornflower	Imperial Rouge
Belfast	Country Wreath	Ionia
Birbeck Rose	Crete	Ivy Bower
Birds And Blooms	Cuba	Jersey
Blantyre	Cymric	Junetime
Blooms	Cyprus	Kenneth
Bon Bon	Cyrene	Kent
Bordeaux	Damascus	Kio
Bourbon	Denmark	Lasso
Bow	Devon	Laurel
Briar	Dorothy	Lilium
Brighton	Douglas	Lily
Bristol	Dragon	Lotus
Broselely	Dual	Malta
Cairo	Durham	Marlborough
Caius	Eden	Mayflower
Canada	Empire	Mead
Casino	Enfield	Medici
Charm	English Oak	Nebo
Chatsworth	Entwine	Negato
	Farm	Old English
	Flower Basket	Old Swansea

Old Nankin
Our Roses
Overton
Paisley
Paradise
Pastoral
Peach Blow
Perkins
Persian
Perth
Pheasant
Plevna
Pompeian
Primrose
Queens Coronation Carnation
Regent

Ruby
Russell
Salonika
Shandon
Sing An
Sistova
Spanish Festivities
Spring
Stafford
Stratford
Strawberry
Stuart
Suez
Summer
Sunbury
Swedish Sprays

Thistle
Tom Tit
Toro
Trentville
Truro
Truscan
Tulip
Virginia
Warwick
Wave
Westbourne
Whitby
Willow
Woodland
York Rose

George Jones Registered Design Pattern Names

Name	Date registered	Patent No.
Country Wreath	28 October 1863	167715
Ionia	10 May 1864	174455
Stratford	10 May 1864	174457
Persian	10 May 1864	174458
Coburg Chain	4 October 1864	179445
Laurel	31 December 1864	182699
Grecian	11 February 1869	227277
Crete	9 March 1869	227744
Lotus	1 December 1869	236756
Cuba	13 October 1873	277148
Stafford	13 October 1873	277149
Kent	3 March 1874	280907
Adansi	21 April 1874	281899
Plevna	7 June 1878	322309
Briar	16 September 1881	370093
Ivy Bower	29 September 1881	370636
Overton	19 July 1883	400994

Name	Date registered	Registered Design No.
Blantyre	25 June 1884	8851
Chrysanthemum	3 February 1885	21391
Cornflower	8 December 1885	39348
Birds And Blooms	13 September 1886	56152
Primrose	24 February 1887	68515
Charm	7 July 1887	76274
Chatsworth	21 October 1887	84746
Azalea	12 May 1888	100000
Bon Bon	8 June 1888	101485
Westbourne	4 October 1888	111984
Dual	14 February 1891	166458
Birbeck Rose	1934	790003

List of pattern names available on printed dinner ware in 1923

Pattern name	
Abbey	Flower Basket
Aberdeen	Howard
Albion	Jersey
Almonds	Kenneth
Bourbon	Malta
Bow	Mead
Briar	Negato
Bristol	Paisley
Canada	Perkins
Casino Border	Perth
Charm or Chinese Flowers	Pheasant
Chelmsford	Regent
China Rose	Ruby
Chrysanthemum	Russell
Coburg	Salonika
Colony	Stuart
Cymric	Suez
Cyprus	Trentville
Denmark	Truro
Dorothy	Truscan
Douglas	Warwick
Dragon	Wave
Durham	Whitby
English Oak	Willow
Empire	York Rose

George Jones majolica pattern numbers

In her pioneering book *Majolica,* Victoria Bergesen gives a list of George Jones majolica pattern numbers compiled from the shape books now held in the Wedgwood Archives, which she described as "unfortunately incomplete and quite late."

The additions to that list which follow are taken from pieces actually seen and include further details of some items already given in the existing George Jones list.

It becomes clear that some marked numbers can be misleading. Occasionally the same item will reappear with the pattern number wrongly painted, e.g. 2251 strawberry dish marked as 2521. The pattern numbers are generally painted by hand in small black figures on an unglazed patch on the underside, familiarly finished in a mottled green and brown tortoiseshell glaze. Sometimes the glaze has run over the patch in firing, thus partially obscuring the painted number. Sometimes no patch has been left and the number is so cursorily painted that reading it is not easy, or it may be read in several different ways. With most of the numbers given here we have been able to double check on further examples.

Particular designs were registered at the Patent Office in London, to establish copyright, all be it for only three years. In some cases, however, the same registration lozenge mark with the date code and parcel number, may appear on widely differing pattern numbered pieces, e.g. 2515, 2521, 2593, 2725 and 3219 all bear the lozenge mark for 22 December 1869.

The pattern numbers are frequently combined with letters, other numbers or cyphers. A and B indicate ground colour variations. Sometimes pieces of a set, perhaps a tea pot, jug and basin, have the same number with added I, II or III. Various cyphers and squiggles appear, impressed letters and numerals and large, clearly-painted numbers, confusingly with or without a recognised pattern number. These may be painters' marks, though their haphazard appearance is a mystery.

Unidentified

number	Description
1	Square cachepot with ferns, acanthus leaves and bamboo. Height 9 in.
2	Straight-sided cachepot, apple blossom on bark. Impressed lozenge mark for 31 March 1875.
5	Cheese bell with apple blossom and fence pattern. (Certainly pattern number 3240)
11	As preceding pattern number.
30	Nut dish with squirrel holding nut. Impressed lozenge mark for 9 March 1869.
40	Ashtray with fox-head on rim, tail below.
111	Plate with large maple leaf and small ferns.

Note: It is reasonably certain that the numbers above are not pattern numbers, although in each case they appear clearly painted in the usual unglazed patch, with no other numbers.

Pattern

number	Description
184	Salt as boy in clam shell on dolphin. No factory mark. Height 7 in.
242	Nut dish. Two large and two small pans, squirrel on all-fours in centre. Marks: GJ monogram in circle, impressed letter B. Impressed lozenge mark for 29 May 1872. Painted letter N below pattern number. This is identical to 2521 but with later lozenge mark.
259	Dish as inverted helmet supported by pair of doves with swags. No factory mark. Pattern number only.
337	Jug, all-over bark ground with branches of small apple blossom rising from base back and front. Marks: GJ monogram in circle. Impressed A2.
344	Table centre as column of coral supporting shell with elaborate arrangement of coral, shells and putti resting on dolphins at base. Marks: GJ monogram in circle. Painted letter A below pattern number and large painted ampersand. Height 11.5 in., length 13.25 in.
954	Fish pâté dish as oval basket and under-plate with three fish on lid. Marks: dish has only four vertical strokes, under-plate has pattern number with three vertical strokes below, impressed GJ monogram in circle, D and 12. Length 9.25 in.
1249	Table centre as three large, heavily veined leaves as dishes with three smaller leaf-dishes between. Centre turned back fern leaves with tall trumpet-shaped lily, white and pink. Marks: the pattern number is on an applied paper label
1304	Plate with large chestnut leaf on folded napkin. Marks: GJ monogram in circle with letter B painted below.
1464	Dish as three large scallop shells on foot made as smaller scallop shells. Handle as three dolphins. Marks: blue-grey applied tablet, with GJ monogram and Stoke-on-Trent, number painted on tablet.
1758	Game dish with fern decoration and dead partridge as knop. Mark: tablet applied as previous item.
1777	Vase as hand holding lily, decorated with lace and beads. No factory mark, pattern number painted on to white patch painted over tortoiseshell base. Height 8.75 in.
1785	Game dish with dead partridge. Number evidently painted incorrectly for 1758.
1806	Jug, cobalt ground with long green leaves, ears of wheat and inverted acanthus leaves round top rim. Marks: pattern number painted on base, covered all over with pink glaze. Also painted cross-shaped symbol resembling Minton year mark for 1873. Given in Bergesen as Foliage jug, pink ground.
1856	Cake platter, flowers, berries and thorn branches. Double chevron mark painted below pattern number. No factory mark. Diameter 12.75 in.
1875	Large cachepot, cobalt with groups of white and yellow chrysanthemums. Marks: GJ monogram/crescent and 8J impressed. Height 12.75 in. This reappears as pattern number 5281.
2200	Stilton dish, half size, pink ground, cow finial. Same number given in George Jones pattern book for dish with goat finial.
2222	Butter dish on oval plate, plank and bamboo design. dish marked four large impressed Figures 4571. Plate

marked GJ monogram/crescent and impressed 5 1 + F with curlicue painted below number. Plate length 7 in., dish length 5.25 in.

2243 Strawberry dish, cream and sugar fitting open rings either end of oval shape with napkin design. No factory mark. Letter G painted below pattern number. Length 14.5 in.

2271 Oval tray with handles. Fern on bark ground. No factory mark. Length 16 in.

2297 Double vase, turquoise ground with two large swans.

2423 Strawberry dish as plank box, crossed branch handles either end supporting blue tits. Cream and sugar as wooden tubs. Marks: GJ monogram in circle. Impressed lozenge mark for 23 October 1869. Length 15.25 in.

2472 Sweetmeat dish, holly on cobalt ground, bird with spread wings. Underside plain green painted over pattern number. Impressed lozenge mark for 19 October 1870.

2514 Dog bowl with three feet. Acanthus leaves on cobalt, turquoise interior. Number on applied pad with GJ monogram and Stoke-on-Trent.

2515 Nut dish, lobed shape, large leaf and hazel on turquoise ground. Handle as squirrel holding hazel nut. Impressed lozenge mark for 22 December 1869. Width 10.25 in.

2521 Nut dish, two large and two small pans, squirrel on all-fours in centre. Marks: pattern number on blue-grey pad with GJ monogram and Stoke-on-Trent. Impressed lozenge mark for 22 December 1869 (same date as preceding). This is identical to 242 but with different registration number.

2544 Biscuit barrel with fixed plate. Yellow stephanotis on cobalt. Lid with moss and ivy in centre and robin as knop. No factory mark. Lozenge mark for 19 October 1870. Height 7.5 in.

2553 Vase with ivy and insects on turquoise ground with three frogs supporting.

2554 Strawberry dish, ferns and strawberry on turquoise ground. Lobed oval shape with two bird's nest recesses on one side for cream and sugar, with thrush between. Large serving spoon and two ladles match this piece. No factory mark, but impressed lozenge mark for 8 March 1870. This has also been seen with lozenge mark for 19 October 1870. Both have painted X below pattern number. The same number appears on a variation with open rings in place of the bird's nest dishes, with removable jug and basin. The same number is also used on 8 in. matching plates which are additionally marked with the GJ monogram in circle.

2556 Strawberry dish, oval bracket shape with leaves and blossom on turquoise ground. Handle as pile of twigs with thrush. Mark: GJ monogram/circle. Painted letter H below pattern number. Width 10 in.

2584 Plate, large maple leaf with ferns round. White background has inverted 4 painted below pattern number; turquoise background has 3. Both colour versions have impressed GJ monogram.

2588 Sweetmeat dish, holly on turquoise ground. Similar to 2472 but has two birds with spread wings. Same lozenge mark for 19 October 1870. No factory mark. Width 12.75 in.

2593 Nut dish, large maple leaf with smaller leaves and flowers. Bacchanalian putto with leopard skin, grapes, vine leaves and wine cup, on cushion with

lion's head. No factory mark. Lozenge mark for 22 December 1869. Width 10.25 in.

2716 Game dish with liner, tortoiseshell ground. Lid has dead hare on bed of ferns with twig handle over. Two vertical strokes (11 or II) painted below pattern number on dish and inside lid.

2725 Double dish with two small compartments between. All-over pattern of leaves and ferns with semi-recumbent goat finial. No factory mark. Lozenge mark for 22 December 1869.

2735 Nautilus-shell spoon-warmer (listed as turquoise) as seaweed on cobalt with turquoise interior, on rock base. Painted curlicue below number. Length 6.25 in.

2763 Salmon dish. Marked Rd. No. 30. Length 23 in. Marked Rd. No. 24. Length 19 in. Both with lozenge mark for 29 August 1871.

2764 Mackerel dish, listed in pattern book as No. 126. No factory mark. Lozenge mark for 23 December 1871. Length 15 in.

2779 Jug with bearded head below lip, handle as twigs of holly and mistletoe. Head in full colour on cobalt or mottled green/brown. Three sizes, sometimes with impressed monogram in circle.

2797 Given in list as Cornucopias Centre. Has two large swans.

3203 Tea Pot as cockerel, beak as spout, tail as handle. No factory mark. Painted 5 below pattern number. Length 11.25 in.

3205 Compote as dish supported by tree, dog below stalking quail.

3206 Given in list as Asia Centrepiece. Dish on tree support with camel on base. height 10.25 in.

3217 Strawberry dish, oval with cream and sugar fitting into circular holes either end. Has impressed lozenge mark for 16 February 1872. Length 14.75 in.

3219 Fruit or nut dish with pattern of cherries, blossom and leaves. Handle as blackbird on pile of twigs. Marks: GJ monogram/circle. Painted A below pattern number. Lozenge mark for 22 December 1869. Width 10.25 in.

3221 Given in pattern list as America Centrepiece. Dish on tree support with pair of bison on base.

3222 Plate, turquoise centre with yellow ochre basket-weave rim. Bamboo on rim. No factory mark. Painted 6 below pattern number, (may be associated with a particular dish or platter). Diameter 10 in.

3223 Jug with panels back and front, dog and quail and fox and rabbit. Pewter mounted lid with fox and handle as riding crop. No factory mark. Lozenge mark for 27 May 1872. Figure 5 painted below pattern number. Although the pattern number is very clearly painted, it is probably a mistake for 3228, listed as Hunting Claret or Beer Jug). Height 11.5 in.

3227 Listed as Giraffe Centre, tall compote with deer and giraffe. This has been seen with the giraffe, with the remains of a giraffe (hooves) and with no sign of a giraffe ever having been there. It is a delicate piece and may have been produced in two versions. Height 14 in.

3252 Long serving dish as overlapping marrow leaves scattered with yellow flowers, handle one end as baby marrow. Impressed GJ monogram in circle, painted cypher below pattern number. Width 9.25 in., length 17 in.

3259   Large cachepot. Given in pattern list, variations here. Humming birds and Stephanotis on turquoise ground, white ribbing above and below. No factory mark. Impressed letters A M G. Height 11.25 in., diameter 11 in.

3262   Centrepiece as man half-seated on dolphin, carrying large shell on his back. Man has moustache but not the customary Neptune beard. (Listed in pattern book as Neptune Shell Centre). Outside of shell turquoise or green/brown tortoiseshell, inside pink in both cases. No factory mark. Painted X below pattern number. Pattern book gives 3262A as White Shell Tinted. There is also a matching female Figure, number not noted. (Given as 3320 in Pattern Book, qv).

3263   Compote as cobalt dish with rim and handles as twigs, on stem as oak tree, leaves and acorns spreading at top. Mark: GJ monogram in circle. Height 5.5 in., width 9.5 in. This is possibly incorrectly marked. The following item with the same number is given in the pattern list.

3263   Given as Rose Basket. Triple shallow bowl as gathered fabric with tall loop handles as bamboo. Various colour schemes. Pattern list gives A B C colour variations and three sizes are noted. Marked with GJ monogram in circle. Various painted symbols below pattern numbers.

3264   Given in pattern list as Hunter's Scroll Game Pie Dish, Sportsman Lid. Outside of dish has three cartouches of swirling leaves framing dog, deer and Cupid carrying arrow and blowing horn, in full colour on cobalt. Lid has ground of fern, grasses and bracken, Figure of kneeling huntsman with broad-brimmed hat and shotgun, small dog in front. No factory mark. Painted crescent below pattern number. Diameter 10.75 in.

3268   Game dish. Same as preceding item, but with fawn deer on lid instead of huntsman and dog. Pattern list also gives 3268A as colour variation with turquoise ground.

3279   Stilton cheese stand as beehive. Lozenge mark for 18 March 1872.

3290   Oval cachepot, humming birds and Stephanotis, same pattern as 3259 without ribbing. Given in pattern list as 3290A. No factory mark. Has painted 80 below pattern number. Length 15.75 in. Height 8.5 in. and 7.25 in.

3294   Small cachepot, oblong shape. Pale green bamboo on cobalt, making curved handles. No factory mark. Height 6.5 in. This number is given in pattern book as Pine with Parakeet variation.

3299   Muffin dish and cover. Apple blossom pattern on turquoise. No factory mark. Lozenge mark for 29 April 1873.

3300   Strawberry dish with loop handle, two large and two small compartments. Flowers and leaves, turquoise ground with 5 painted and white ground with X painted below pattern number. Both have lozenge mark for 29 April 1873.

3302 and 3302A Further items in the Humming bird/Stephanotis series. Small round pots cobalt and turquoise grounds. Height 7 in.

3320B   Tea Pot in form of Chinese junk, with junkmaster standing at top, forming handle of lid. This number is given in the George Jones archives, but may not be correct. 3320 is the number for the mermaid Figure with shell. See 3520.

3327   Footed bowl as ribbed circular shell on stem of coral and seaweed. No factory mark. Height 5 in., diameter 9 in. Pattern book list gives 3327A as Shell Dessert Set, plates and two comports.

3340   Cachepot in form of tower, with under-tray fitted with rim to raise the pot, with drainage hole, away from tray. Marks: pot has GJ monogram/circle and painted 5 below pattern number. Tray has only painted P. Both pieces have lozenge mark for 25 August 1873. Matches Stilton dish 3341.

3349   Strawberry dish with bullfinch either end of oval shape. Example and impressed lozenge mark under glaze without letters or figures and lozenge mark printed on the unglazed patch for 3 November 1873. Length 15.5 in.

3368   Small bowl, bark pattern with small pink flowers and green leaves on three twig feet. No factory mark. Number with curlicue on one foot. Diameter 3.75 in. Probably part of tea or dessert service.

3374   Jug, large, possibly one of set. Bark ground with branches, palmate leaves and pink flowers in high relief. Two sides very different. No factory mark. Painted T below number.

3376   Cachepot, round with straight sides. Papyrus leaves and flowers. No factory Mark. Painted 5. Height 7 in.

3380   Given in pattern list as Indian Garden Seat. Has pattern of birds and flowers on turquoise ground.

3383   Sardine box, fish and coral sides, lid with grebe, sometimes with fish in beak. Mark: GJ monogram/circle. Embossed lozenge mark for 28 March 1874.

3385?   Vase menu holder as weaver bird with nest made of bulrushes on mossy mound with leaves and blossom. This has not been seen with a legible number, but has a lozenge mark for 28 March 1874. This is the same registration date as 3384 Wren Menu Holder in the George Jones pattern list. The menu holders are both 5.5 in. high. There is also a taller version 9.5 in. high, without the slot for the menu. The Wren holder is given again in the list as 3397 and the registration number also appears on 3383 sardine box.

3395   Sweetmeat bowl on foot as water lily leaves and flowers. Stem as reeds and bulrushes. Mark: GJ monogram/circle. Painted number 34. Height 5.5 in.

3406   Preserve dish with under-plate, basket pattern with blackberry leaves, flowers and fruit. Blackberry knop. Marks: GJ monogram/circle on dish and plate and impressed A 4M on dish. Painted 80 on dish, plate and lid.

3412   Stilton cheese dish, water lilies, dragonflies and bulrushes on pink ground. Large closed water lily flower as knop. Marks: GJ monogram/circle and lozenge mark for 19 February 1876. Height 9.75 in. Given in George Jones pattern list as Cattail and Bird Stilton Cheese Stand, with dark blue ground. This one has no birds.

3416   Game dish. Border of rabbits to dish and leaf pattern lid with quail as knop. Two sizes, length 10 in. and 8 in.

3423   Strawberry serving dish, as rustic planks with leaves, flowers and fruit. Handle as two X pieces with connecting bar and two blue tits. Either end, half-round pots for sugar and cream. Marks: GJ monogram/circle, impressed A 5 and small symbol. Applied lozenge mark for 9 February 1875. Length 15.25 in.

3441	Sardine box, oblong shape with chamfered corners. Fish and water plants on box, leaves on separate under-plate. Lid has flying pelicans, with swimming pelican as knop. Marks: GJ monogram/circle on box and plate. Box has painted 58, plate painted 40. Lozenge mark on base for 12 March 1875 and on plate for 26 June 1875. (Under-plate added as afterthought?) Box length 6 in. Plate length 8.25 in.
3454	Strawberry plate, circular with ten lobes, flowers and leaves. Marks: painted 30, impressed 9A. Diameter 8.5 in.
3457	Given as rustic Jug in Pattern list, in four sizes. Bark background with large leaves and pendulous flower clusters. Flared foot with four small frogs. Branch handle. Marks: painted 30. Embossed GJ monogram applied in reverse. Impressed 12. Lozenge mark for 26 June 1875.
3468	Punch bowl, as Mr. Punch lying on back supporting bowl. Mark: painted X. Cobalt ground, two sizes. Jones pattern list gives 3468B as turquoise ground.
3475	Lobed circular dish with fixed marmalade pot in centre as orange on base of leaves, lid with twig and leaf knop. Cut-out for spoon in lid. Marks: GJ monogram/circle impressed with A 9. Painted II and printed lozenge mark for 5 November 1875.
3476	Tray, oblong with shaped corners and two handles. Wheat and insects, including butterfly, on turquoise. Marks: GJ monogram/cresecent impressed. Painted X.
3481	Shallow dish, eight-lobed shape. Strawberry leaves and blossom on tortoiseshell and cobalt. Marks: painted XX. Impressed GJ monogram/crescent. Diameter 7 in.
3484	Given in pattern list as Lotus. Is Stilton dish in two versions.
3499	Jardiniere, with finches, dragonflies, white flowers and three 'coral' feet, on turquoise ground. Marks: GJ monogram/crescent and lozenge mark for 30 March 1876 on all three feet. Pattern number and painted 2A on one foot. Height 20 in.
3501	Strawberry dish, three-lobed shape, large green leaf with strawberry leaves and blossom. Two large white cup-shaped flowers with yellow stamens, as cream and sugar holders. Three colour versions. Marks: turquoise ground - painted!! Impressed WBV. Cobalt ground - painted 30. Yellow ochre ground - painted 3. All versions have GJ monogram/circle and lozenge mark for 19 February 1876.
3502	Jardiniere with finches, perched and flying, among orchids. Strong leaves to orchid plants coming down to three flattened corm feet. Marks: GJ monogram/circle under one foot with impressed 8 C. All three feet have lozenge mark for 30 March 1876.
3504	Fish pâté dish as oval basket on basket tray, both with open handles. Lid as crowded pile of fish. Length 8.5 in.
3507	Given in pattern list as Humming Bird Hanging Basket. Actually is wall pocket, pointed oval shape with flat back, humming bird in relief with white trumpet-shaped flowers and pointed leaves. Edged with bamboo, forming hanging handle at top. Turquoise ground. Cobalt variation has painted H below pattern number. Both versions have impressed lozenge mark for 30 March 1876.
3517 & 3518	These two numbers are listed as Fish Game Pie Dish and Lobster Game Pie Dish. They are in fact pâté dishes with lids and under-plates with handles. The dishes and plates have a basket-work and seaweed pattern with rope edging and handles. The lids have seaweed with a large and small fish on the one, and a lobster on the other. Bowls and plates are marked with GJ monogram/circle and lozenge mark for 12 September 1876. Fish: painted 30. Lobster: painted P. Overall length 9.5 in.
3519	Small coffee cup (demi-tasse), briar rose flowers and leaves on bark ground, twig handle. Marks: GJ monogram/crescent, impressed 7 on cup. Pattern number only on saucer with painted J. Cup height 2.25 in., saucer diameter 5 in.
3520	Tea Pot as Chinese junk laden with tea-chests, with junkmaster standing on top, forming knop to lid. The number given for this piece in the Jones pattern list, 3320B, is almost certainly wrong. It has a lozenge mark for 30 March 1876, the same as 3507. There is a painted 30 below the pattern number. The pattern list gives 3520 B as Gondolier, which may increase the confusion.
3539	Cachepot, turquoise with brown fence pattern to upper part. Bamboo round foot and up sides to form handles at top. No factory mark. Height 7.25 in., width 9.5 in.
3547	Sardine box on trug-shaped dish, three sardines on lid.
3550	Vase, triple shape as bulrushes and irises, with mossy base. This number, clearly painted on the example, does not correspond with the Jones pattern list. Height 6.5 in.
3565	Tea-kettle, briar roses on bark with branch handle. Marks: GJ monogram/crescent, impressed F, painted IIII and lozenge mark for 31 October 1877.
5132	Cachepot, water lily flowers and arrow-shaped leaves, two colours of green on cobalt. Painted X below number. Height 8.5 in.
5204	Cheese bell with wood-railing fence, daisies, wheat, bramble fruit and flowers on turquoise ground. Deep plate. No factory mark, painted J. Height 10 in.
5236	Cachepot, cobalt ground with white lilies, some with yellow centres; large arrow-shaped leaves. Large egg-shaped beading to rim. No factory mark. Painted X below pattern number. This is associated with a tall stand to make a multiple centrepiece for conservatory. Height 9 in.
5253	Cheese dish, half Stilton, basket-weave and apple blossom on turquoise. Knop as three stout twigs. Marks: GJ/crescent. Painted 30. Diameter 10.25 in. A matching butter-dish has the same number.
5258	Given in pattern list as Stag Wall Bracket. The same number appears on a wall bracket as a garlanded donkey's head.
5273	Large lobed shape cachepot, marsh marigolds with band of basket-weave top and bottom. No factory mark. Painted XX. Height 10.75 in.
5281	Large cachepot, three-handled, chrysanthemums on cobalt. This is identical to 1875. The reason for renumbering is not known.

This list is to date, mid-1997. More will undoubtedly be found.

The dating of George Jones wares has been compiled by myself from observations I have made of marked pieces. No charts of marks or years survive (and probably never existed) and I have drawn up this suggested dating from marked pieces in my possession and other marked pieces I have seen and noted in the course of my research.

From 1862 to 1912 the date code used on certain types of wares, especially plates, saucers, bowls, toilet sets etc. consisted of a number, indicating month, followed by a letter, indicating year of manufacture, impressed into the unfired wares.

From 1862 to 1874 the year letter used was a large capital approx. 5 mm high starting with the letter N in 1862.

From 1875 to 1882 the year letter used was a small capital approx. 3 mm high starting with the letter A in 1875 and finishing with the letter H in 1882.

From 1883 to 1912 the letter stamped reverted to a large capital approx. 5mm high starting with the letter I in 1883.

Example: 10 L = October 1886 and 9 A = September 1875.

During 1912 the year letter was replaced by a number: Example 6/12 = June 1912.

List of year letter codes: 1862 - 1912

Letter	Large Capital	Small Capital Capital &	Large
England			
A		1875	1901
B		1876	1902
C		1877	1903
D		1878	1904
E		1879	1905
F		1880	1906
G		1881	1907
H		1882	1908
I	1883		1909
J	1884		1910
K	1885		1911
L	1886		1912
M	1887		
N	1862 or1888		
O	1863 or1889		
P	1864 or1890		
Q	1865		1891
R	1866		1892
S	1867		1893
T	1868		1894
U	1869		1895
V	1870		1896
W	1871		1897
X	1872		1898
Y	1873		1899
Z	1874		1900

A further guide to dating: in 1891 'ENGLAND' was added to the printed backstamp to comply with the American McKinley Act, which required all imported goods to be marked with the country of origin.

An explanation as to why George Jones began his year numbering system at the letter 'N' could be that he started his year numbering from when he first commenced in business, as a merchant, in 1849. In 1862, when he became a pottery manufacturer, he had been in business for 14 years, consequently he then used the fourteenth letter of the alphabet, which is 'N'.

Dating of George Jones Pattern numbers

Pattern Numbered	Approximate period when designed
1-9999	1862-1890
15000-20999	1890-1910
21000-23999	1910-1920
24000-29999	1920-1930
30000-33000-	1930-1940s
A1-A5300	1890-1900
D100-D753	1898-
E1000-E3000	1910-1920s
F100-F1300	1920s-1930s
R1-R1503	1933-
TC series	1900-
V1-V1728	1890-

Patent Office Registration Marks

In 1842, to enable manufacturers to protect their designs from piracy, the Patent Office in London introduced a system whereby articles would be marked with a diamond-shaped device. The purpose of the device was to indicate that a design had been registered at the Patent Office and was protected from being copied for an initial period of three years.

Although one column in the 1862-83 registered design list shows patent numbers, these numbers were not patent numbers in the true sense of the word as these designs were only protected for three years whereas true patents were protected, at that time, for fourteen years.

Usually, if the diamond mark is impressed or moulded into the article then it is the shape that was registered. If the diamond mark is a transfer, then it relates to the decoration. This form of registration continued until the end of 1883 when a new form of marking registered designs was adopted.

From 1842 to 1867 the diamond mark was as presented as below:

Index to year letters from 1842-1867

letter	year
X	1842
H	1843
C	1844
A	1845
I	1846
F	1847
U	1848
S	1849
V	1850
P	1851
D	1852
Y	1853
J	1854
E	1855
L	1856
K	1857
B	1858
M	1859
Z	1860
R	1861
O	1862
G	1863
N	1864
W	1865
Q	1866
T	1867

From 1868 to 1883 the diamond mark was as below:
Index to year letters from 1868-1883

letter	year		letter	year
X	1868		V	1876
H	1869		P	1877
C	1870		D	1878
A	1871		Y	1879
I	1872		J	1880
F	1873		E	1881
U	1874		L	1882
S	1875		K	1883

The month code was the same for both periods

letter	month
C	January
G	February
W	March
H	April
E	May
M	June
I	July
R	August
D	September
B	October
K	November
A	December

Notes:
(i) In 1857 the letter R was used 1-19 September.
(ii) In 1860 the letter K was used for December.

From 1884 onward, this method of marking registered designs was abandoned. A new method was implemented whereby all designs were numbered consecutively starting with Rd. No.1 in January 1884. It is not possible to date accurately when a design was registered without looking in the Register of Designs, held at the Public Record Office, Kew. Here the date of registration is indicated for every design.

The dates of the George Jones registered designs, from 1884, have been obtained from this register. The description of the designs were obtained from the Representation of Designs also held at Kew. These usually show either a drawing or photograph of the pattern or shape that was registered.

George Jones Registered Designs 1862-1883

Date of Registration	Parcel No.	Patent No.	Description of Design
14 May 1862	3	151672	Design of pattern
14 May 1862	3	151673	Design of pattern

Date		Number	Description
18 December 1862	3	158498	Design of border pattern
28 October 1863	8	167715	Design of pattern named 'Country Wreath'
6 November 1863	1	168234	Design of pattern
6 November 1863	1	168235	Design of pattern
15 April 1864	4	173659	Design of border pattern
10 May 1864	5	174455	Design of pattern named 'Ionia'
10 May 1864	5	174456	Design of pattern
10 May 1864	5	174457	Design of pattern named 'Stratford'
10 May 1864	5	174458	Design of pattern named 'Persian'
20 August 1864	10	177912	Design of tureen shape named 'Laurel'
4 October 1864	2	179445	Design of border pattern named 'Coburg Chain'
10 November 1864	10	181286	Design of embossed border pattern named 'York'
31 December 1864	6	182699	Design of border pattern named 'Laurel'
14 January 1865	4	183331	Design of embossed decoration
25 July 1866	3	199295	Design of table service tureen
12 July 1867	5	209530	Design of table service tureen
14 October 1868	8	222736	Design of embossed ornamentation on toilet ware
1 January 1869	8	226051	Design of dinner service shape name 'Grecian'
11 February 1869	10	227277	Design of pattern named 'Grecian'
9 March 1869	1	227743	Design of embossed decoration named 'Lotus'
9 March 1869	1	227744	Design of pattern named 'Crete'
9 March 1869	3	227746	Design of tray
15 October 1869	6	234486	Design of mince pie and cake dish
23 October 1869	4	235012	Design of cigar ash tray
1 December 1869	3	236756	Design of pattern named 'Lotus'
22 December 1869	7	237500	Design of nut tray with squirrel
3 January 1870	4	237742	Design of embossed pattern named 'Erica'
8 March 1870	1	239424	Design of bird trinket tray
8 March 1870	1	239425	Design of leaf on expandia wings trinket tray
8 March 1870	1	239426	Design of bird strawberry set
10 March 1870	1	239474	Design of a rope handle for ewer with basin & chamber set
30 May 1870	15	242077	Design of dinner service tureen
27 June 1870	1	242715	Design of pineapple tea pot
23 August 1870	6	244173	Design of Cupid grape tray
19 October 1870	2	245985	Design of bird tray
19 October 1870	2	245986	Design of bird biscuit box
22 November 1870	3	247944	Design of fruit shape dinner service
10 January 1871	7	249439	Design of box
29 August 1871	2	255274	Design of fish basket & cover
1 December 1871	6	258095	Design of ornamental tray
23 December 1871	3	258956	Design of fruit centre piece
23 December 1871	3	258957	Design of camel fruit & flower holder
20 January 1872	6	259854	Design of fruit compotier
3 February 1872	4	260255	Design of camel fruit centre piece
3 February 1872	4	260256	Design of flower stand named 'Louise'
16 February 1872	7	260504	Design of strawberry dish with cream and sugar
16 February 1872	7	260505	Design of fruit centre piece named 'Africa'
16 February 1872	7	260506	Design of elevated fruit stand
4 March 1872	3	260868	Design of elephant vase
27 May 1872	1	262951	Design of jug and cover
29 May 1872	2	262990	Design of match box
20 July 1872	3	264306	Design of bamboo flower holder
20 July 1872	3	264307	Design of lily leaf tray
18 October 1872	5	267317	Design of jug
18 October 1872	5	267318	Design of basket
18 October 1872	5	267319	Design of butter pot, honey pot and Stilton cheese
10 January 1873	1	269585	Design of dinner service
25 February 1873	6	270700	Design of wicker and apple blossom jug
26 March 1873	6	271561	Design of dinner service tureen
26 March 1873	6	271562	Design of dessert service
29 April 1873	3	272384	Design of strawberry set
29 April 1873	3	272385	Design of apple blossom tea and breakfast set
25 August 1873	1	275514	Design of tortoise spittoon
25 August 1873	1	275515	Design of 'Tower' Stilton dish
13 October 1873	3	277148	Design of pattern named 'Cuba'
13 October 1873	3	277149	Design of border pattern named 'Stafford'
3 November 1873	4	277845	Design of tray
3 November 1873	4	277846	Design of tray
3 November 1873	4	277847	Design of jam pot
10 December 1873	12	279180	Design of tray with bird
27 December 1873	7	279437	Design of game pie dish
19 February 1874	1	280609	Design of lizard handle jug
25 February 1874	7	280786	Design of cruet set
3 March 1874	4	280907	Design of pattern named 'Kent'
28 March 1874	3	281429	Design of sardine box
28 March 1874	3	281430	Design of flower and card holder
21 April 1874	8	281899	Design of pattern named 'Adansi'
25 April 1874	2	281984	Design of ewer
9 May 1874	3	282218	Design of flower stand
9 May 1874	3	282219	Design of garden seat or pedestal
23 May 1874	4	282567	Design of flower stand
23 May 1874	4	282568	Design of flower wall bracket
28 August 1874	4	284699	Design of flower pot
28 August 1874	4	284700	Design of tray
15 September 1874	2	285281	Design of oyster plate
21 October 1874	8	286424	Design of napkin and menu holder

Date		Reg. No.	Description
10 November 1874	3	286794	Design of flower vase
8 December 1874	2	287699	Design of jug
12 December 1874	3	287776	Design of Stilton cheese stand
18 December 1874	6	287982	Design of an eight piece toilet set
21 January 1875	2	288682	Design of dinner service tureen
9 February 1875	2	289173	Design of 'Marie' strawberry set
23 February 1875	6	289504	Design of spill case
12 March 1875	5	289874	Design of jug
12 March 1875	5	289875	Design of sardine box and stand
12 March 1875	5	289876	Design of jug
7 May 1875	7	291109	Design of jewel or trinket stand
31 May 1875	8	291568	Design of flower pot and stand
26 June 1875	2	292367	Design of 'Monkey' tea and jug service
26 June 1875	2	292368	Design of leaf shape dessert service
26 June 1875	2	292369	Design of 'Wilopose' flower holder
26 June 1875	2	292370	Design of 'Park' jug shape
13 September 1875	2	294434	Design of 'Mr Punch' bowl
13 September 1875	2	294435	Design of jug
18 September 1875	2	294571	Design of flower holder
18 September 1875	2	294572	Design of flower stand
5 November 1875	3	295551	Design of orange tray
5 November 1875	3	295552	Design of tray
5 November 1875	3	295553	Design of bread tray
12 November 1875	1	295908	Design of flower vase
3 December 1875	4	296531	Design of fruit tray
22 January 1876	6	297809	Design of ash tray (with dog)
22 January 1876	6	297810	Design of ash tray (with cat)
22 January 1876	6	297811	Design of meat plate with gravy well
19 February 1876	5	298458	Design of strawberry dish
30 March 1876	4	299497	Design of flower pot
30 March 1876	4	299498	Design of tea pot
30 March 1876	4	299499	Design of wall bracket
10 May 1876	3	300463	Design of ash or trinket tray
29 May 1876	8	300809	Design of tea service
29 May 1876	8	300810	Design of tea service
26 July 1876	3	302125	Design of 'Duke of Edinburgh' flower holder
12 September 1876	6	303522	Design of covered dish on stand
12 September 1876	6	303523	Design of covered dish on stand
9 October 1876	1	304149	Design of sardine box and stand
9 October 1876	1	304150	Design of egg basket and flower basket
8 November 1876	3	305080	Design of bedroom service
25 January 1877	7	307237	Design of hanging basket
25 January 1877	7	307238	Design of handled basket
25 January 1877	7	307239	Design of tea service
10 March 1877	7	308357	Design of strawberry and fruit basket
2 May 1877	2	309818	Design of caviar set
2 May 1877	2	309819	Design of 'Moth' flower trough
2 May 1877	2	309820	Design of flower bracket
2 May 1877	2	309821	Design of flower suspender
15 October 1877	2	315271	Design of flower pot
15 October 1877	2	315272	Design of flower pot
31 October 1877	6	315765	Design of flower pot
30 January 1878	3	318158	Design of jug
30 January 1878	3	318159	Design of vase
1 February 1878	4	318239	Design of flower pot
7 June 1878	1	322309	Design of pattern named 'Plevna'
8 June 1880	1	350477	Design of moulded jug
16 September 1881	10	370093	Design of dinner service tureen
29 September 1881	3	370636	Design of pattern named 'Ivy Bower'
11 April 1882	6	379434	Design of strawberry dish
13 May 1882	6	380789	Design of dessert plate
14 July 1882	3	383436	Design of vase
14 July 1882	3	383437	Design of flower basket
22 July 1882	8	383802	Design of jug
21 February 1883	3	394452	Design of dessert plate
19 July 1883	21	400994	Design of pattern named 'Overton'
1 August 1883	4	401624	Design of jug with lid

George Jones Registered Designs 1884-1899

Date of Registration	Registered Design No.	Description of design
25 January 1884	826	Design of pattern for table set
15 March 1884	3657	Design of dinner service tureen
2 April 1884	4591	Design of pattern
25 June 1884	8851	Design of pattern named 'Blantyre'
12 July 1884	9725	Design of dressing table set
14 October 1884	14976	Design of embossed pattern on jardinière
14 October 1884	14977	Design of toilet set
3 February 1885	21391	Design of pattern named 'Chrysanthemum'
25 February 1885	22566	Design of cheese bell, honey and jam pots
8 December 1885	39348	Design of pattern named 'Cornflower'
30 January 1886	42306	Design of tableware
13 September 1886	56151	Design of pattern
13 September 1886	56152	Design of pattern
22 October 1886	59451	Design of dinnerware
24 February 1887	68515	Design of pattern named 'Primrose'
2 May 1887	73024	Design of dinnerware
7 July 1887	76274	Design of pattern named 'Charm'
21 October 1887	84746	Design of pattern named 'Chatsworth'
6 January 1888	90805	Design of dressing table set
6 January 1888	91237	Design of dinnerware
25 January 1888	92160	Design of toilet set
1 February 1888	92673	Design of teaware
20 March 1888	96154	Design of teaware
23 March 1888	96411	Design of a moulding for securing pot lids
12 May 1888	100000	Design of pattern named 'Azalea'
8 June 1888	101485	Design of pattern named 'Bon Bon'
4 October 1888	109822	Design of teaware
8 November 1888	113169	Design of hot water jug
5 February 1889	119035	Design of tableware
19 February 1889	119984	Design of pattern named 'Westbourne'
28 March 1889	122292	Design of pattern
28 March 1889	122293	Design of pattern
25 April 1889	124120	Design of dessertware
29 April 1889	124321	Design of embossed pattern
20 September 1889	133641	Design of toilet set
27 September 1889	134138	Design of pattern
7 November 1889	137548	Design of teaware
30 January 1890	143137	Design of dinnerware
30 January 1890	143138	Design of embossed pattern
1 February 1890	143264	Design of pattern
26 March 1890	146574	Design of toilet set
21 January 1891	165075	Design of teaware
14 February 1891	166458	Design of pattern named 'Dual'
3 June 1891	172273	Design of toilet set
19 August 1891	176769	Design of sardine box
19 August 1891	176781	Design of lidded bowl
8 January 1892	186000	Design of pattern
18 February 1892	187959	Design of menu slate
29 October 1892	201593	Design of teaware
2 December 1892	203571	Design of tableware
25 May 1893	212635	Design of toilet set
5 January 1894	225065	Design of tableware
7 September 1894	239437	Design of toilet set
4 December 1894	245408	Design of tableware
29 May 1895	255552	Design of dinnerware
23 January 1896	269723	Design of teaware
11 February 1896	270717	Design of dessert dishes
12 November 1896	288114	Design of two section vegetable dish with cover
21 December 1897	311150	Design of tableware
17 March 1899	335404	Design of a vase

This list is complete up to 1900, but the registration of designs continued after this date. All registered designs are held at the Public Record Office, Kew.

Appendix 7

Major stores and china dealers supplied by George Jones & Sons, having their names incorporated into George Jones backstamps.

Name	Address
America	
Bailey, Banks & Biddle Co., The.	Philadelphia.
Ball & Co.	Cleveland.
Bedell & Co., D. B.	New York.
Bowman & Co., G. H.	Cleveland, Ohio.
Burley & Co.	Chicago.
Caldwell & Co., J. E.	Philadelphia.
Cowell & Hubbard Co., The	Cleveland.
Creange - Walter Inc.	17 East North St. New York.
Davis Collamore & Co. Ltd.	Fifth Avenue & 37th St., New York.
Davis Collamore & Co. Ltd.	Broadway & 21st. Street, New York.
Dickinson & Co., T. & E.	Buffalo.
Dublin & Martin Co.	Washington D.C.
Freeman & Co., J.J.	Toledo, Ohio.
French & Co., A.	Boston.
Gallaher, P.	New York.
Gilman Collamore & Co.	Fifth Avenue, New York.
Hansel Sloan & Co.	Hartford, Conn.
Higgins & Seiter.	New York.
Holmes & Co. D.	New Orleans.
Hudson & Son.	Minneapolis.
Jones McDuffee & Stratton Co., The	.Boston.
Kinney & Levan Co.	Cleveland.
Lynde, Charles R.	Boston.
Mannheim Bros.,	St Pauls.
Marshall Field & Co.	Chicago.
Nathen Dohrmann Co.	San Francisco, California.
Ovington Bros.	
Parmelee Dohrmann Co.	Los Angeles, California.
Pitkin & Brookes.	Chicago.
Reizenstein & Sons. C.	Pittsburg.
Richard Briggs & Co., The.	Boston.
Sellers & Co. M.	
Selzer C.A.	Cleveland.
Shreve Crump & Low Co.	Boston.
Shreve & Co.,	San Francisco.
Simmon Hardware Co.	St Louis.
Stone, Theodore B.	New York.
Stowell & Co.,	Boston.
Tiffany & Co.	New York.
Van Heussen Charles C., The.	Albany.
Vollmer Jantzen & Co.	Los Angeles.
Wattles & Sons. W.W.	Pittsburg.
Wisner Co., Henry C.	Rochester.
Wright Kay & Co.	Detroit & Paris.
Canada	
Ellis Bros. Ltd.	Toronto.
Follett & Cox Ltd.	Toronto.
Morgan & Co., H.	Montreal.
Ryrie Bros.	Toronto.
England	
Abrahams, J.	Pembroke House, 138 Oxford St. London W.

Name	Address
Abrahams J.	Canterbury.
Aldis, Frederick.	Belgravia, London.
Apsley Pelatt & Co.	21 Northumberland Ave., London.
Awmack, J.H.	8 New Briggate, Leeds.
Baker & Co. Ltd., F.P.	London.
Barker Bros.	Birmingham.
Breward.	Chester.
Cullum & Sharpes.	3 Cockspur St., Pall Mall, London.
Defries & Sons.	147 Houndsditch, London.
Friend.	Birmingham.
Fox & Sons, Geo.	Leicester.
Goode & Co., T.	London.
Greene & Sons, H.	153 & 155 Cannon St. London.
Harrods Ltd.	Brompton Rd., London S.W.
Hawkins, J.	Henley on Thames.
Heal & Son.	London W.
James Green & Nephew.	London.
Lumley, W.	25 St Mary St., Weymouth.
Maple & Co.	London & Paris.
Mappin & Webb Ltd.	
Mortlock Ltd.	8-9-10 North Audley St., London W1.
Osler, F & C.	100 Oxford St., London.
Payne & Sons Ltd.	148 High St., Southampton.
Pearce & Co., Alfred B.	59 Ludgate Hill, London E.C.
Soane & Smith.	462 Oxford St., London W.
Stephenson Ltd., H.C.	Manchester.
Stonier & Co. Ltd.	78 Lord St., Liverpool.
Townsend & Co.	Newcastle on Tyne.
Waring & Gillow Ltd.	Oxford St., London W.
Waring & Gillow Ltd.	Deansgate, Manchester.
Wheaton & Bennett.	104 to 108 Oxford St., London.
India	
Dewan Chand & Sons.	Bombay.
Ireland.	
Callinan & James	Mansion House, 47 Grafton St., Dublin.
Whyte & Sons Ltd.	Dublin.
N. Ireland.	
Hogg & Co. Ltd. Rolf.	Belfast.
Scotland.	
Baker, J.W.	Aberdeen.
Scotland	
Baker, J.W.	Aberdeen.
Caulfield & Co.	Crystal Palace, 21 James St., Glasgow.
Frains	Dundee.
Wales	
Gross Bros. Ltd.	Cardiff.

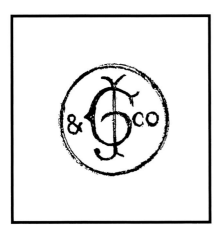

Impressed mark ca. 1862-1865.

Impressed mark ca. 1878+

Impressed mark ca. 1865-1877.

Printed mark ca. 1864.

Impressed mark ca. 1865-1877

Blue pad ca. 1865-1878.

Printed mark 'Brighton', ca. 1875.

Printed mark ca. 1885-1890.

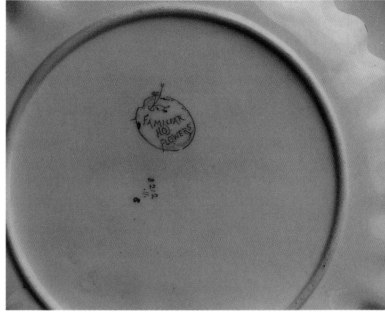

Printed mark ca. 1885.

Printed mark ca. 1885.

Printed mark ca. 1891-1900.

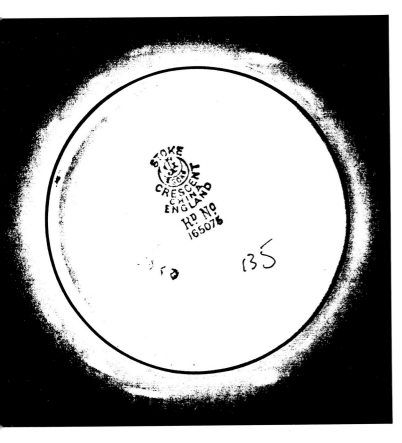

Printed mark ca. 1891-1900.

Printed mark 'Madras' ware, ca. 1895.

Printed mark 'Crescentine' ware, ca. 1895.

Printed mark 'Pastoral 1790', ca. 1898.

Printed mark 'Lasso', ca. 1900-1910.

Printed mark ca. 1900-1920.

Printed mark ca. 1900-1920.

Printed mark ca. 1895+

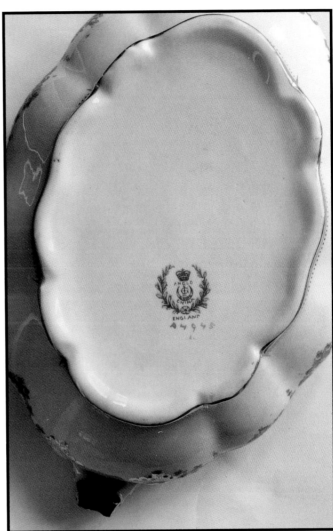

Printed mark ca. 1900-1920.

Printed mark ca. 1920-1951.

Printed mark ca. 1934+

Printed mark ca. 1948-1951

Printed mark ca. 1934+

Printed mark 'Woodland', ca. 1935. Old William Adams backstamp with
G. Jones substituted for W. Adams.

Printed mark 'Abbey', ca. 1915-1930.

Printed mark 'Genoa', ca. 1930. Old William Adams backstamp.

Printed mark 'Abbey', ca. 1900-1915.

Printed mark 'Abbey', ca. 1920-1930. Note rare Unicorn backstamp.

Illustrations of backmarks from the pre-1904 George Jones crest book.
Courtesy of Trustees of the Wedgwood Museum.

Illustrations of backmarks from the pre-1904 George Jones crest book.
Courtesy of Trustees of the Wedgwood Museum.

Bibliography

Bergesen, Victoria. *Majolica: British, Continental and American Wares, 1851-1915* London, Barrie & Jenkins Ltd., 1989.

Cameron, Elizabeth. *Encyclopaedia of Pottery & Porcelain: The 19th & 20th Centuries*: London, Faber & Faber, 1986.

Cushion, J. P. *Pocket Book of British Ceramic Marks including Index to Registered Designs 1842-83*: London, Faber & Faber, 1983

Dawes, Nicholas M. *Majolica:* New York, Crown Publishers, Inc. 1990.

Godden, Geoffrey A. *An Illustrated Encyclopaedia of British Pottery and Porcelain*: London, Barrie & Jenkins Ltd., 1980.

Godden, Geoffrey A. (ed.), *Staffordshire Porcelain*: London, Granda Publishing, 1983.

Hannah, Frances. *Ceramics:* London, Bell & Hyman, 1986.

Hepburn, James, ed., *Letters of Arnold Bennett:* London, Oxford University Press, 1968.

Hollowood, Bernard. *The Story of J. and G. Meakin:* Derby and London, Bemrose Publicity Co. Ltd., 1951.

Jervis, W. P. *The Encyclopaedia of Ceramics:* New York, Blanchard, 1902.

Jervis, W. P. *Rough Notes on Pottery:* Newark, New Jersey, W. P. Jervis, 1896.

Jervis, W. P. 'A Dictionary of Pottery Terms', *Pottery, Glass & Brass Salesman,* (USA), 15 February 1917 - 19 December 1918

Jervis, W. P. *A Pottery Primer*: New York, The O'Gorman Publishing Co., 1911.

Jewitt, Llewellynn. *The Ceramic Art of Great Britain*: London, Virtue & Co., 1878.

Jewitt, Llewellynn. *The Ceramic Art of Great Britain*: New York, R. Worthington, 1883.

Karmason, M. G. & Stacke, J. B.. *Majolica: A Complete History and Illustrated Survey,* New York, Harry N. Abrams, Inc., 1989.

Liveing, Edward. 'The Story of Royal Cauldon': typescript, in Hanley Reference Library, Stoke-on-Trent, 1975.

Mackenzie, Compton. *The House of Coalport 1750-1950*: London, Collins, 1951.

Scarratt, William. *Old Times in the Potteries*: Stoke-on-Trent, William Scarratt, 1906.

Stuart Denis, ed., *People of the Potteries*: University of Keele, 1985.

Williams, P. & Weber, M. R. *Staffordshire II Romantic Transfer Patterns*: Kentucky, Fountain House East, 1986.

Index

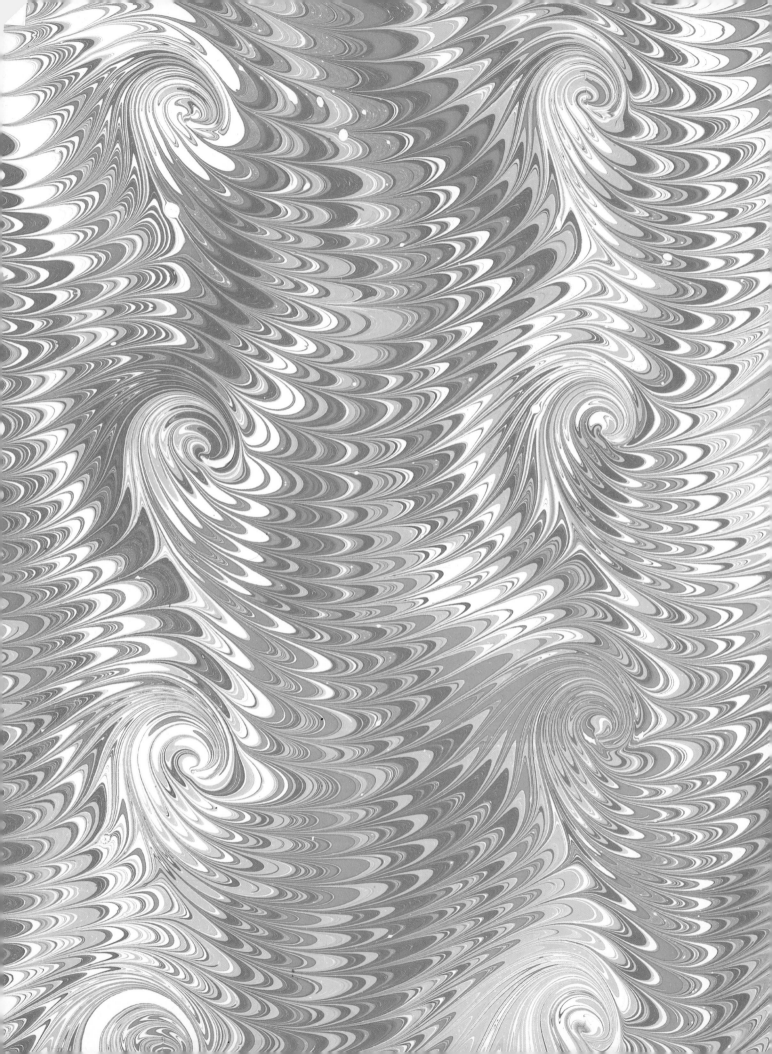